THE OLD NORTHWEST
as the
KEYSTONE OF THE ARCH
of
AMERICAN FEDERAL UNION

A Study in Commerce and Politics

By

A. L. KOHLMEIER

Professor of History, Indiana University

THE PRINCIPIA PRESS, Inc.
BLOOMINGTON, INDIANA
1938

Copyright 1938
By A. L. Kohlmeier

PREFACE

UNION is undoubtedly the greatest single fact in American history. There is little more reason, geographically, climatically, or economically why Massachusetts and Louisiana should be a part of the same country than why Norway and Italy should be under one central government. The advantages of the American union over the European system will not here be pointed out, but an examination of one of the most important causes of its continuance is the subject of this book.

While it is admitted that our country got off to a better start in the matter of union than did the countries of western Europe and while it is agreed that the article in the Federal Constitution providing for interstate free trade was basic to the preservation of the Union, the conclusion here reached is that the peculiar natural location and economic value of the eastern half of the upper Mississippi valley was the decisive factor in permanently tying our country together. The heart of that region was the section lying east of the Mississippi and north of the Ohio, now usually known as the Old Northwest and first organized as a territory under the Ordinance of 1787. Sectional lines can, of course, not be sharply drawn. At times adjacent regions, such as western Pennsylvania, Kentucky, northern Missouri, and just before the Civil War, eastern Iowa constituted parts of the section here under consideration.

At the time of the formation of the American union, because of the potential value of the western interior, the seaboard states were loath to lose their undivided interest in it. Later, as the region became populated and productive, the northeastern states and southeastern states were usually anxious to secure the support and the votes of that region in the decision of national issues.

The Northwest, with only a few natural gateways through which to send its increasing surplus products to the open sea and to the world markets, soon held the balance of power in the National government between the Northeast and the Southeast and inclined now to one side and now to the other in order to get improvement of its transportation facilities. The growth of this agricultural surplus in the Old Northwest, the perfecting of the transportation lines leading through the natural gateways to the seaports, the development of transportation lines in the interior of the Northwest leading to these gateways, and the continuing efforts of the Northwest to secure advantages by alternately log-rolling with the other two sections or threatening to do so, is the substance of this book. It is the hope of the author that by pointing another clue or key, he may have helped to make some of the movements of the first half of our national history more intelligible.

It is customary in a preface to make acknowledgement of indebtedness. Since the material for this work was so scattered, I had to search in many places. As a result I am under obligations to so many officials and attendants of libraries large and small that I cannot name them all. I will perhaps therefore be more fair if I don't name any. I do, however, wish to thank these people from whom I met with nothing but intelligent helpfulness and unfailing courtesy. I wish also to express my appreciation to the historical organizations, particularly the Illinois State Library, for permission to use in this book material that I had previously used in short articles on some aspects of this subject.

A. L. Kohlmeier

Bloomington, April 21, 1938

CONTENTS

		Pages
I.	Early Contacts of the Old Northwest with the Outside World, 1818-1835	1– 21
II.	The Attempt of the Southeast to Secure the Commerce of the Northwest, 1835-1839	22– 38
III.	Some Attempts to Bring About a Closer Alliance Between the Old Northwest and the Northeast, 1840-1844	39– 58
IV.	The Old Northwest and the Expansion and Low-Tariff Movements, 1845-1849	59– 96
V.	The Old Northwest and the Old Southwest Unite to Secure a Trunkline Railroad from the Lakes to the Gulf, 1850-1853	97–128
VI.	The West Engages in the Wrangle over Building a Railroad to the Pacific, 1854-1857	129–166
VII.	The Old Northwest During the Lean Years of 1857-1860	167–208
VIII.	The Two Extremes Against the Middle, 1860-1861	209–247

CHAPTER I

Early Contact of the Old Northwest with the Outside World, 1818-1835

VARIOUS STATES and sections of the country have at times claimed the distinction of serving as the keystone in the arch of the American Federal Union. There is evidence that for more than the first half century of the Union the Old Northwest can make the best claim to such a distinction. Even before the formation of the Federal Union the presence of the over-mountain country with its resources, its promise of affording future homes for settlers from the old states, and its supposed value for defraying the Revolutionary war debt tended to hold together the seaboard states in the expectancy of sharing and enjoying this common possession. There were those who would have been willing to make it possible for that region ultimately to have sufficient representation in the central government to dominate it. While this advantage was not granted, it did develop that the Old Northwest in the course of time had sufficient voting strength to hold the balance of power as between the Northeast and the Southeast, sections that had great difficulty in reconciling the clash of their economic interests and alternately sought to protect their interests now by threatening to nullify unfavorable acts of the Federal government or to withdraw altogether from the Union and now by bidding for the votes of the Northwest to unite with them in checking the undesirable tendencies. The support of the Old Northwest was now thrown on one side and now on the other but on most difficult occasions it was exerted for compromise.

The remote interiors of continents have in material development and civilization generally lagged behind the regions having access to the open sea. Whenever such interiors have been separated from the sea by foreign countries, such delay in development has frequently been protracted for centuries. The struggle of some of these interior regions like Russia or Poland to gain access to the sea makes up an important part of the history of such countries. The great interior of the North American continent has not been entirely an exception to the rule. The fact that the interior and the seaboard were parts of the same great political division only in part concealed the struggle by submerging it to a subordinate place in the domestic history of the country as a whole and by changing it from the character of an international conflict to that of a domestic problem. The ability of the settlers of the United States ultimately to rise above the primitive conditions of pioneers depended upon their ability to produce a surplus of something for which there was a market and their ability to get that surplus to the market and receive in return the things that they needed at a cost of transportation that would not be prohibitive. Such transportation from and to the Old Northwest of necessity passed through a few natural avenues and gateways. One of these, the northeastern gateway, was located at the eastern end of Lake Erie, and the avenue or outlet extended from there either by way of the St. Lawrence or the Mohawk and Hudson river valleys. Another outlet or avenue, the southern, extended by way of the Mississippi river to the Gulf of Mexico. A third outlet, the eastern, extended from the upper Ohio river across the mountains to the nearest arms of the Atlantic. The latter route was of course the shortest but had perhaps the greatest physical difficulties. The story of the increased production of the Old Northwest and of the development of its three avenues of communication with the outside world, at the instigation of the interior, by the exertions of the sections through which these avenues passed, and with the varying support of the Federal government constitutes a fundamental part of the history of the United States. The needs and demands of the interior have continued to the present day with slight variations. The extent of the settled interior has enormously increased and with it its influence in the Federal government. With it also have come differences of interest between parts of the great interior, but in one respect the problem is still unchanged. The transportation lines to the seaboard have increased in number but the problem of developing those having the most fundamental natural advantages and thus reducing still further the cost of transportation is still a problem of national concern. That development was in danger of being forever crippled when the Civil War threatened to break the country into fragments and to interpose between the interior and the seaboard one or more foreign countries, thus converting the problem into an everlasting international dispute. The Old Northwest, comprising the five states between the upper Mississippi, the Ohio, and the Great Lakes, constituted in certain respects the interior section of the settled country in the period before the Civil War.

Almost from the time that the Americans occupied the region west of the Alleghanies, the question of their trade with the outside world became for them a problem. As the simple pioneers of a community would give way to the farmers, there would develop a surplus of products in that community. For a few years, as new regions were being occupied farther west, a part of the surplus of the older settlements of the Old Northwest found a market in the newer settlements. However, a part of the surplus was from the beginning exported to pay for commodities that could not be produced in the interior. The difficult roads and trails leading through the eastern gateway from the over-mountain interior to the seaboard were used a little during the first two decades of the nineteenth century for the importation of goods but less for the export of commodities. The Mississippi river with its confluent streams was the one great natural outlet for the surplus production until the end of the first quarter of the nineteenth century. The obstructions that this traffic met at the hands of the foreign possessors of the mouth of the Mississippi from the time of the recognition of independence by England in 1783 to the cession of Louisiana in 1803 and the subsequent negotiations and international complications down to 1819 that were entailed in securing American control over the northern Gulf coast indelibly impressed the settlers of the Mississippi valley with the life and death importance of this natural outlet to the south.

By 1825 there was forwarded, among other things annually from the Old Northwest and from the other settled parts of the Mississippi valley to New Orleans no less than a hundred forty thousand barrels of flour, half that amount of corn, sixteen thousand barrels of pork, thirty thousand barrels of whiskey, and eighteen thousand hogsheads of tobacco.[1] This represented a surplus of about three quarters of a million bushels each of wheat and corn.

However, immediately after the United States had signed the definitive treaty recognizing her independence

1. James Hall, *Statistics of the West* (Cincinnati, 1837), 276-79.

in 1783, Virginia and Pennsylvania had taken steps to improve transportation lines from the Atlantic seaboard to the Ohio river. Virginia in 1784 incorporated the Potomac company to connect by canal the headwaters of the Potomac with some tributary of the Ohio. George Washington was a stockholder in this concern and was a moving spirit in the Virginia activities. He was anxious that Virginia should be the first to complete her canals connecting the Potomac with the upper Ohio and the James river with the Great Kanawha, in order to make the Chesapeake the outlet for the Great Lakes region as well as for the region drained by the tributaries of the Mississippi.[2] The Pennsylvania assembly began the surveying and building, 1785-1791, of the Pennsylvania state road to Pittsburgh, following in general the route of the old Forbes road.[3] During the first decade of the nineteenth century both the National government and some of the Middle Atlantic states were considering plans and projects for opening up avenues of trade to the interior. In one year, 1806, Congress passed an act to build the road from Cumberland, Maryland, to the Ohio river and the Pennsylvania assembly passed acts to build two turnpikes from Harrisburg to Pittsburgh.[4] Two years thereafter the Secretary of the Treasury, Albert Gallatin, made his elaborate and exhaustive report which included proposals for a number of roads and canals connecting the West with the

2. George Washington to Benjamin Harrison, October 10, 1784, in *Writings of Washington,* Worthington C. Ford, ed. (New York, 1891), X, 410.
3. *Minutes of the Supreme Executive Council,* in *Pennsylvania Colonial Records* (Harrisburg, 1852-1853), XV, 13, 599; XVI, 466-70.
4. 9 Cong., 1 sess., ch. 19, in *Public Statutes at Large of United States* (Boston, 1850), II, 358; *The Statutes at Large of Pennsylvania,* J. T. Mitchell et al., compilers (Harrisburg, 1915), XVIII, 73, 373.

seaboard.[5] The report did not result in any further action by the national government at that time, but the states continued their rivalry in planning and building down to the days of the Civil War.

Of the rival seaboard states New York and Pennsylvania both touched with their western boundaries the shore of Lake Erie, which in turn was in water communication with the entire Great Lakes region. New York had the advantage of having within her borders the only complete break in the Appalachian mountains, since the route from Albany to Buffalo passed over a region rising by gradual ascent from near sea-level to about 578 feet. Pennsylvania had the advantage of having on her western frontier the headwaters of the Ohio river as well as Lake Erie, but any route across that state from the Atlantic to the Western waters had to cross the Alleghany mountains. The route that was finally selected by Pennsylvania crossed the mountains at an elevation of a little less than twenty-three hundred feet above sea-level. Almost fourteen hundred feet of this ascent had to be made in a distance of ten miles.[6] Virginia and Maryland had the advantages of rivers like the Potomac and the James that penetrated far to the northwest, but the mountainous elevations separating their headwaters from the Ohio were even more formidable than those in Pennsylvania.

The old National road was completed by the National government from Cumberland, Maryland, to the Ohio river at Wheeling by 1818; but aside from serving for

5. *Report on Roads and Canals to Senate*, April 4, 1808, in *American State Papers, Miscellaneous* (Washington, 1834), I, 728.

6. H. S. Tanner, *A Description of the Canals and Railroads of the United States* (New York, 1840), 126, graphs opposite 144 and 222; A. L. Bishop, *State Works of Pennsylvania* (New Haven, 1907), 197 (In volume XIII of *Transactions of Connecticut Academy of Arts and Sciences*).

local traffic it was useful chiefly for the incoming of settlers with their household goods and a few farming implements and for the marketing of livestock driven eastward from the eastern parts of the interior.[7] Relatively small quantities of manufactured articles could stand the cost of transportation over this route into the interior and smaller quantities of the surplus products proceeded outward by this route. Only about ten thousand tons of merchandise were carried westward annually to Wheeling over the National road in the years immediately preceding 1825.[8] The Pennsylvania turnpike was completed to the Ohio at Pittsburgh in 1818 by the state of Pennsylvania.[9] It had a history very similar to the National road. Only about thirty thousand tons were carried across the Alleghanies by way of the Pennsylvania turnpike annually between 1818 and 1824 and most of this went westward.[10] About forty thousand head of horses passed over this road annually in the period between its completion and 1825. Most of these were drawing vehicles. Of the number of cattle, sheep, and hogs driven over it, only estimates can now be made.[11] The Erie canal was completed by New York state in 1825.[12] It connected the head of ocean navi-

7. Thomas B. Searight, *Old Pike* (Uniontown, Pa., 1894), 16, 107, 108; Archer Butler Hulbert, *The Cumberland Road* (Cleveland, 1904), 54, 70 (Volume X of *Historic Highways of America*).
8. Speech of Representative T. M. McKennan of Pa., Jan. 6, 1832, in *Register of Debates*, VIII, pt. 2, p. 2728.
9. *Year Book of Pittsburg Board of Trade* (1909), 14-16; A. B. Hulbert, *Old Glade Road* (Cleveland, 1903), 195 (Volume V of *Historic Highways of America*).
10. *Journal of House of Representatives of Pennsylvania, 1824-25* (Harrisburg, 1825), II, 280.
11. J. S. Ritenour, "Over the Old Roads to Pittsburgh," in *Western Pennsylvania Historical Magazine*, IV, 79.
12. *Buffalo Journal*, Nov. 29, 1825, quoted in *Buffalo Harbor Papers* (Buffalo, 1910), 387 (Volume XIV in *Buffalo Historical Publications*).

gation at Albany on the Hudson with Buffalo on Lake Erie. This route at that time, however, benefited no overmountain people except the transplanted Yankees of western New York and or northeastern Ohio. In northeastern Ohio the two tiers of counties that lay immediately south of Lake Erie and that in 1820 had a population of only about 40,000 were the only ones in the Old Northwest that in 1825 were transporting a part of their surplus over the new Erie canal.[13] The Mahoning, Muskingum, Scioto and other large tributaries of the Ohio river had their headwaters far up in northeastern Ohio and carried commodities southward. In northeastern Ohio the populous counties of Trumbull and Portage lying within 35 miles of Lake Erie were about as close to the Ohio river as to Lake Erie and could ship by southward flowing streams much more easily. The fourteen counties comprising the northwestern fourth of Ohio had just been created in 1820 out of the "New Purchase" and had a population in that year of only about 1500.[14] The Erie Canal in 1825 could and did help to bring the settlers and their household goods to this region but did not for some years to come have to transport much of their surplus products. Practically no products of the Ohio valley found their way out in 1825 by the northeastern gateway.

From 1822 to 1826 certain ports in the British West Indies and in Canada were open to American products of the farm except to salt meats in either British or American ships. Wheat and corn could be carried into those British possessions duty free, while flour paid a duty of only five shillings a barrel. This legislation on the part of

13. *Census for 1820* (Washington, 1821), see under Division of Ohio.
14. John Kilborn, *The Ohio Gazateer* (Columbus, 1821), see map in front and under names of counties.

the British government gave the farmer in the Ohio valley in the years immediately preceding 1826 a better market at New Orleans, because grain, flour, and whiskey could be carried from there to the British West Indies, while the settler in the Western Reserve before the completion of the Erie canal because of favorable British legislation probably found his best market in Canada.[15]

Throughout the decade, 1825-35, the agricultural surplus of the southern part of the Old Northwest continued to be almost wholly dependent upon the southern outlet at New Orleans. Only a little was conveyed eastward over the Cumberland road and over the Pennsylvania turnpike. The cost of transporting to the market was so great that prices in the Ohio valley were usually so low that there was little incentive to produce a surplus beyond that which could be sold to the newer settlements in the Old Northwest. And yet settlers had somehow to pay for their farms and for the little that they imported into the interior.

The western men looked to their own state governments for help in the way of financial relief and of building transportation lines, but they also looked to the Federal government and to other states for co-operation and help. This situation led to interesting political activities within the several western states and it also influenced the endeavors of the politicians and statesmen of other sections. Politicians of the Southeast and of the Northeast, anxious to further their own political ambitions and to benefit their own sections and states, took cognizance of the demands

15. 17 Cong., 1 sess., ch. 56, and 17 Cong., 2 sess., ch. 22, in *The Public Statutes at Large of the United States* (Boston, 1850), III, 681, 740; J. D. Richardson, *A Compilation of the Messages and Papers of the Presidents* (Washington, 1896), II, 184; 3 Geo. IV., C. 44, in *The Statutes of the United Kingdom* (London, 1822), VIII, 704, 709, 710; *American State Papers, For. Rel.* (Washington, 1832-59), V, 231 and VI, 246.

of the westerners. DeWitt Clinton of New York state in 1825 made a public procession through Ohio with the view of influencing the people of that state to build feeders to the Erie canal and of winning support for himself in national politics as the builder of a transportation system to the Northeast.[16] No doubt he succeeded in doing both. Andrew Jackson was both a southern and a western man. His views on the tariff were supposed to be acceptable to the Southeast and his views on the Indian question and public lands were acceptable to the Old Northwest. John Quincy Adams had views on the tariff and public lands acceptable to many in the Northeast, and his support of internal improvements should have appealed to the Old Northwest. Adams did not succeed in combining the electoral votes of the Northeast and Northwest in 1824 but did occupy the president's chair from 1825 to 1829 because of the support given to him in the election in the House by a leader of the Ohio valley, Henry Clay. However, Jackson, the old Indian fighter and defender of New Orleans, the southern gateway of the West, was given the largest electoral vote in 1824 and was elected to the presidency in 1828. Robert Y. Hayne, a leading statesman of the Southeast, made it clear in the great debate of 1830 that he was willing to stand by the West against a selfish policy of the national government in holding the government lands for higher prices if the Northwest would stand by the Southeast against a consolidated federal government such as Hayne said would result from a policy of piling up the funds from the sale of government lands. Daniel Webster, interpreting consolidation as synonymous with union, made a bid for the Northwest to align itself

16. Caleb Atwater, *A History of the State of Ohio* (Cincinnati, 1838), 266, 272.

with the Northeast in defense of a strong union and a strong central government that could help the interior gain access to the world markets. Henry Clay would try to get the Northwest to stand by the Northeast on a protective tariff if the Northeast would support internal improvements for the West and would distribute to the states the receipts from the sale of the public lands for that purpose. John C. Calhoun would try to induce the Southeast to accept the distribution of the public lands by the Federal government among the western states within whose boundaries the lands lay if the Northwest and the Southwest would support the Southeast in a low tariff. No wonder that the voters and the Congressmen from many parts of the Old Northwest had difficulty in deciding with whom they should align themselves.

Of these statesmen and politicians Adams occupied the president's chair during the larger part of the first half of the decade under consideration in this chapter and Jackson during the second half. Adams began his administration with high hopes for the realization of an extensive and comprehensive scheme of internal improvements which would have given the West additional lines of communication with the outside world.[17] Opposing politicians, arguing the absence of constitutional authority, blocked his efforts. He contented himself in his later messages with calling attention to the surveys of routes by the Government Board of Engineers and with securing the approval by the Federal Congress of such joint state enterprises as the Chesapeake and Ohio canal.[18]

As the result of an act of Parliament and an order in Council passed during the first part of Adams' adminis-

---

17. Richardson, *Messages*, II, 307, 311, 316, 877, 882.
18. Richardson, *Messages*, II, 388.

tration the British West Indies and Canada were again closed to American ocean-going ships. All that Adams seemed able to do was to retaliate by closing in 1827 American ports to British ships coming from a port closed to American ships. This had the effect of practically prohibiting direct trade between the United States and the British West Indies.[19] Under the terms of this British act American wheat could still be shipped to Canada in any lake vessels or to the British West Indies in English ships on payment of a duty of a shilling a bushel; and flour, on payment of five shillings a barrel, but American pork was still entirely excluded.[20] A little of the surplus wheat produced in northern Ohio found its way into Canada in 1825. There was stored in the warehouses of Canada at that time a surplus of nearly a million bushels of wheat supposedly produced in Canada, but replaced by imports from the United States, which were now to be admitted into England.[21] The closing of the British West Indies to American ships and the raising of the duty affected adversely the export by way of New Orleans, but most of the export from the West by way of New Orleans was destined for eastern states. The trade with French and Spanish West Indies remained fairly open.

Jackson soon made it clear by his veto of the Maysville road bill that the West could not look for much financial assistance from the Federal government for building transportation lines except those of a distinctly national char-

19. 6 Geo. IV., C. 114, sec. 4, in *Statutes of United Kingdom* (London, 1826), X, 491; *American State Papers, For. Rel.*, VI, 307, 333; Richardson, *Messages*, II, 376.
20. 6 Geo. IV., C. 114, sec. 7, 9, in *Statutes of United Kingdom*, X, 492, 493.
21. *Parliamentary Debates,* New Series (London, 1826), XIII, 1118; 6 Geo. IV., C. 64, in *Statutes of United Kingdom*, X, 162.

acter. He did, however, have the satisfaction of announcing in 1830 that the British West Indies were again open to American ships.[22] This had been brought about partly by his own peculiar type of diplomacy and partly by a realization on the part of the British that exclusion of American shipping was no longer of advantage to British interests. Whatever advantage the reopening of the British West Indies may have brought to the Old Northwest was naturally reflected in increased exports through the New Orleans gateway. In 1831, however, the British also saw fit to remove the duty on the importation of American grain, flour, meats, and livestock into Canada. This same grain, flour, and meat could then be retransported duty free to the British West Indies.[23] This was of course a boon to that part of the Old Northwest that was near enough to the Great Lakes to forward its surplus through the northeastern outlet. American wheat also replaced Canadian wheat exported to England where Canadian wheat could be imported at a much lower rate of duty than was imposed upon the importation of foreign wheat. American wheat could be ground into flour in Canada and then could enter England under the preferential treatment given to Canadian flour over flour imported from foreign countries.[24] This act of 1831 which continued in effect till 1842 gave the farmers in the northern part of the Old Northwest choice between the northeastern market of the United States and, through Canada, the English market.

By the end of the decade, 1825-35, however, several

22. 21 Cong., 1 sess., ch. 207, in *Public Statutes at Large of United States* (Boston, 1848), IV, 419, 817.
23. I. W. IV., C. 24, in *Statutes of the United Kingdom* (London, 1832), XII, 346.
24. 9 Geo. IV., C. 60, in *Statutes of United Kingdom* (London, 1829), XI, 490, 491; Richardson, *Messages*, II, 546.

new developments had occurred in the possible routing of the commodities of the interior. The state of Pennsylvania after much discussion of possible routes had in 1834 opened a line of transportation consisting of alternate links of canal and railway from the head of the Ohio river at Pittsburgh to the Delaware at Philadelphia. A canal extended eastward from Pittsburgh to Johnstown, a distance of a little more than a hundred miles; the Portage railroad extended from this place eastward over the mountain, a distance of nearly thirty-seven miles, to Hollidaysburg; a canal connected the latter place with Columbia, a distance of one hundred seventy-two miles; and a railroad some eighty miles in length connected the latter place with Philadelphia.[25] The same year that marked the completion of this enterprise saw also the linking of the upper Ohio river with Lake Erie by the Ohio canal, which ran through central Ohio from Portsmouth on the Ohio river to Cleveland on Lake Erie. That same year saw also the opening of the Miami canal from Cincinnati northward as far as Dayton.[26] The Miami canal furnished an improved outlet for the products of a fertile region in Ohio and Indiana to Cincinnati, where the raw products could be converted and then transported either to New Orleans or to Pittsburgh. Already in 1833 the Welland ship canal, which connected Lake Erie with Lake Ontario, had been

---

25. Tanner, *Description of Canals and Railroads*, 97, 98, 113, 126; *Report of Canal Commissioners*, in *Journal of House of Representatives of Pennsylvania, 1834-35* (Harrisburg, 1835), II, Appendix, p. 3; H. V. Poor, *Sketch of Rise and Progress of Internal Improvements* (New York, 1881), p. xviii (In *Manual of the Railroads of the United States* for 1881).

26. *Report of Canal Commissioners*, in *Journal of the Senate of the State of Ohio*, 33 General Assembly, 1 sess. (Columbus, 1834), 394. The Ohio canal and Miami canal were opened for navigation in 1833 except the locks at Portsmouth and Cincinnati, which were completed in 1834.

completed and opened for traffic,[27] and in 1830 the Louisville and Portland canal had been opened around the falls of the Ohio.[28]

Theoretically, then, it was possible by 1835 for a barrel of pork or whiskey to go from the vicinity of Chillicothe, Ohio, to the outside market by three different routes. It could go southeast by canal boat or flat boat down the Ohio canal to the Ohio river at Portsmouth and then by steamboat or flatboat down the Ohio and the Mississippi to New Orleans. It could after reaching the Ohio go by steamboat to Pittsburgh and thence by the main line of alternating canals and railroads to Philadelphia. It could go by canal boat northward over the Ohio canal to Cleveland, thence by lake vessel to Buffalo, thence by Erie canal to Albany, and by Hudson river packets or canal boats to New York City. Finally instead of going by lake vessel from Cleveland merely to Buffalo, it could go on the same lake vessel through the Welland canal to Oswego on Lake Ontario, where the cargo could be put upon the canal for Albany and New York City.[29] In 1835 the exports and imports of Chillicothe passed over all three of these routes.

27. Thomas C. Keefer, *The Canals of Canada* (Toronto, 1850), 16; N. E. Whitford, *History of the Canal System of the State of New York* (Albany, 1906), II, 1445, 1454. In 1829 boats began to pass from Lake Erie to Lake Ontario by using the canal part way and the Niagara river part way.

28. *U. S. House Ex. Docs.*, 34 Cong., 1 sess., vol. IX, no. 74 [serial 853], pp. 1, 84; *U. S. House Misc. Docs.*, 40 Cong., 2 sess., vol. I, no. 83 [serial 1349], pp. 34, 45. This document enumerates most of the official reports bearing on the history of the canal. See also *Report of Committee on the Best Mode of Improving Navigation at the Falls of the Ohio* (Cincinnati, 1859), 12.

29. *N. Y. Sen. Docs., 1836* (Albany, 1836), vol. II, no. 70, statement F, pp. 4, 5. Navigation between Lake Ontario and Montreal was made rather hazardous by a number of rapids. The series of canals between Lake Ontario and Montreal, the head of ocean navigation, were not entirely completed till 1856. Whitford, *Hist. of N. Y. Canals*, II, 1441-44.

Chillicothe was the dividing point on the Ohio canal for the shipment of pork and whiskey. Practically all surplus commodities produced north of that place went northward to Cleveland and thence through to the northeastern gateway at Buffalo, while all commodities produced south of that point went southward to the Ohio and thence either to the southern gateway at New Orleans or to the eastern gateway at Pittsburgh or Wheeling, chiefly to the former. All the wheat, flour, and corn cleared over the Ohio canal anywhere went northward, but none was transferred from the Ohio river to the canal at Portsmouth. Hardware and dry goods came by steamboat from Pittsburgh to Portsmouth and passed northward over the Ohio canal, some going as far north as Cleveland; furniture and salt came over the Erie canal and over the Welland canal and cleared southward at Cleveland and passed down as far as Chillicothe. Sugar and molasses came by steamboat from New Orleans and cleared northward over the canal from Portsmouth.[30]

While every producer and consumer in the Old Northwest theoretically had this same choice of three routes, he would find that the routes were not alike practicable or profitable for all purposes, and that under certain conditions they might all prove of little practical use to him. The farmer of the Ohio valley not located near the Ohio canal had to convey his corn, wheat, pork, or whiskey by flatboat downstream or by wagon over poor roads to the Ohio river or to one of its tributaries or to the Miami

---

30. *Ohio Legislative Docs., 1836* (Columbus, 1836), no. 19, pp. 22-24; *N. Y. Sen. Docs. 1836*, vol. II, no. 70, statement F, pp. 4, 5. These documents give arrivals and clearances of each article at every important place on the canals. From this the volume and direction of traffic can be ascertained.

canal. If he reached the Ohio by wagon or canal, the cargo had to be transferred to a steamboat before proceeding to New Orleans or to Pittsburgh. If he came by flatboat, he could drift with the current to New Orleans. If he lived near enough to a mill or distillery or porkhouse, he could convey his produce there and sell it. The buyer would convert the wheat to flour, the corn to whiskey, and the hogs to barrelled pork and then confront the problem of marketing the goods. If the buyer's mill or pork-house was in the interior, he had to resort to the same means of transportation by wagon, flatboat, or canal to reach the Ohio river. Once down to the Ohio with his larger quantity of goods, he would more often proceed by steamboat than would the small producer. By steamboat he could theoretically ship up stream to Portsmouth, the southern terminus of the Ohio canal, or to Pittsburgh, the western terminus of the Pennsylvania state works, or down stream to New Orleans. Either course was beset with difficulties. If he shipped to Pittsburgh, the goods had to be transferred at that point from steamboat to canal boat. Then after being conveyed about a hundred miles by canal, the goods had to be transferred to the Portage railroad and carried by means of it over the mountains for a distance of thirty-seven miles. It then had again to go by canal for a distance of one hundred and seventy miles, passing through more than a hundred locks. After being once more transferred to a railroad and carried some eighty miles, the goods reached Philadelphia,[31] an indifferent local market and a declining port for foreign trade. If he chose to use the northeastern route, his goods had to be transferred at Portsmouth from the Ohio river steam-

---

31. Tanner, *Description of the Canals and Railroads*, 97, 98, 113, 126, 227; Bishop, *The State Works of Pennsylvania*, 196-98; Poor, *Sketch*, xviii.

boat to canal boat; at Cleveland they had to be transferred to lake steamer; and at Buffalo, retransferred to canal boat. The length of the haul by lake could be lengthened and the length of the second haul by canal correspondingly shortened by passing with the lake steamer through the Welland canal and through Lake Ontario to Oswego, where it could be put upon the branch canal for Albany and New York City. Theoretically the products of the Lake region could be sent by canal to the Ohio river and thence by the Mississippi to New Orleans, but it was not profitable to do so.

The three outlets each had inherent characteristics that in a measure imposed limitations upon the kind of goods that could be carried. The northeastern outlet was frozen up three months in the year during the greater part of the pork-packing and pork-shipping season.[32] This obviously imposed a decisive handicap upon live stock production in the lake region for the time being. The eastern route from Pittsburgh to Philadelphia had the disadvantage of leading across the mountains. The Portage railroad with its system of inclined planes was not very satisfactory. The route was convenient for the passage of west-bound light-weight merchandise but was a poor competitor with the northeastern route for carrying outward-bound grain or with the southern route for carrying meats. The southern route was distinguished for steamboat disasters due to fires, snags, sandbars, and collisions.[33] These imposed upon

---

32. The annual Report of the Canal Commissioners always gave the dates of the opening and closing of the canal for the past year.

33. A. B. Chambers, *Statement,* in *Proceedings of the St. Louis Chamber of Commerce* in Relation to the Improvement of the Navigation of the Mississippi River (St. Louis, 1842), 33-35; *The Annual Review of the Commerce of St. Louis* published by the Missouri Republican (1849, 1860), gave lists of steamboat disasters on the Mississippi; James Hall, *Statistics of the West* (Cincinnati, 1836), 252-63, gives list for years preceding 1835.

the shipper the necessity of paying for insurance upon his cargo in addition to paying the freight rates. The rate of insurance during this earlier period varied from 12% to 18% of the value of the cargo.[34] New Orleans also remained deficient in warehousing facilities and this with the warm moist climate of that region sometimes resulted in the spoiling of grain shipped by way of the southern outlet.[35]

For the above reasons it happened that the exports of the settled parts of the Great Lakes region and of central Ohio as far south as Chillicothe in the year 1835 went by way of the northeastern outlet either by the Erie canal or by the Welland canal.[36] While the larger part of the exports of the Mississippi valley proper, including most of the Ohio valley, sought the southern outlet; a relatively small quantity of goods chiefly from the upper Ohio valley passed over the eastern route.[37] In 1835 the settled part of the Great Lakes region of the Old Northwest that had reached the stage of producing and exporting a surplus was practically limited to northern Ohio, the only exception being southwestern Michigan, which shipped something less than two thousand bushels of wheat, and northeastern Illinois, which shipped less than a thousand bar-

34. Keefer, *Canals of Canada*, 90; James Hall, *The West: Its Commerce and Navigation* (Cincinnati, 1848), 134.

35. W. J. McAlpine, *Report to the Harbor Commission* (Montreal, 1858), quoted in *Report of the Chief Engineer of the Public Works on the Navigation of the River St. Lawrence between Lake Ontario and Montreal* (Ottawa, 1875), 3.

36. *Documents, To the Thirty-Sixth General Assembly of the State of Ohio* (Columbus, 1837), no. 19, pp. 18-25. A few articles like pork and salt in 1837 came from the Ohio river at Portsmouth and moved northward over the canal.

37. *Journal of House of Representatives of Pennsylvania, 1835-36* (Harrisburg, 1835), vol. II, Appendix, p. 23.

rels of pork.[38] The Ohio valley, including the Wabash valley up to the central part of Indiana, and the lower half of the Illinois river valley were settled earlier and were exporting their surplus southward in 1835.

Of a total of less than a hundred and fifty thousand bushels of wheat exported from the Old Northwest in 1835, 83% went northeast and nearly all the remainder went south. Of a total of about four hundred thousand barrels of flour, the equivalent of approximately two million bushels of wheat, 25% went northeast by the Erie and the Welland canals, 70% went south to New Orleans, and 5% went east by way of Pittsburgh. Of a little less than a million bushels of corn exported, 98% went south and only trifling amounts went east and northeast. Of over two hundred thousand barrels of pork, 96% went south. Of forty thousand hogsheads of tobacco, 87% went south; and of less than forty thousand barrels of whiskey, 95% went south. Of some five hundred tons of wool all went east. Most of the hemp also went east.[39] In short, nearly all of the relatively small amount of unground wheat went northeast, while the wheat flour, corn, pork, tobacco, and whiskey went south. The first was the product of northern and north central Ohio, and the remainder, of the southern half of the Old Northwest.

These statistics not only indicate that the surplus of the region lying immediately south of the Great Lakes at first took the form of wheat almost exclusively but they also indicate how little the Ohio valley part of the Old Northwest profited by the canals connecting the Ohio river with Lake Erie, and Lake Erie with the Hudson.

38. *N. Y. Sen. Docs., 1836*, vol. II, no. 70, statement F, p. 5.
39. *Journal of the House of Representatives of Pennsylvania, 1835-36*, vol. II, Appendix, p. 23; *N. Y. Sen. Docs., 1836*, vol. II, no. 70, statement F; *U. S. House Ex. Docs.*, 50 Cong., 1 sess., vol. XX, no. 6, pt. 2 [serial 2552], pp. 200-02.

There were imported into the Northwest some one hundred fifty thousand tons of commodities. Of this, 33% came over the northeastern canals, 23% by the eastern gateway, and 44% by the southern. One-half of this total of imports, or seventy-five thousand tons, was salt. A little more than half of the salt was Liverpool and Turks island salt that came up through New Orleans, while somewhat less than half came by way of the Erie or Welland canals and comprised both New York and foreign production. Only a few thousand tons of salt came over the eastern route.

Of the more than twenty thousand tons of sugar and ten thousand tons of coffee, the next important items, New Orleans supplied practically the entire amount.[40] From the eastern gateway came more than ten thousand tons of iron for the western manufacturers.[41] The other thirty thousand tons of imports consisted of merchandise, furniture, and miscellaneous commodities that entered through the eastern and northeastern gateways. Of the imports through the northeastern gateway 80% went to northern and north central Ohio and most of the remainder to northern Indiana and Illinois.[42] Very little found its way by the Ohio canal into the Ohio valley.

In short, the northern part of the Old Northwest and the southern part each had its own commercial outlet or gateway. In fact, the southern part had two, the eastern and the southern. While the two parts of the Old Northwest were now connected by a canal that ran from the Ohio river to Lake Erie, neither part was making any considerable use of the outlet of the other part.

40. J. D. B. DeBow, *DeBow's Review* (New Orleans and Washington, 1846-67), I, 49; XXIX, 524.
41. *Journal of the House of Representatives of Pennsylvania, 1835-36*, vol. II, Appendix, p. 23.
42. *N. Y. Sen. Docs., 1836*, vol. II, no. 70, statement F, pp. 4, 5.

CHAPTER II

The Attempt of the Southeast to Secure the Commerce of the Northwest, 1835-1839

THE DEBATES in the early thirties over the tariff, the public lands, strict construction, and nullification had left different impressions upon such South Carolina leaders as Robert Y. Hayne, John C. Calhoun, James Gadsden, and Abraham Blanding. Hayne, by no means convinced by Webster's arguments, had yet been precipitated into the nullification movement and was chagrined at its outcome in spite of what Clay of the Ohio valley had done to make South Carolina's submission easier. He sincerely loved the Union and while he undoubtedly believed in the legality of nullification, he set resolutely and patriotically to work to make the application of that method by South Carolina unnecessary in the future. In 1835 he threw himself energetically into the task of trying to tie the Ohio valley and the Old Northwest permanently to the Southeast both economically and politically by sponsoring the building of a railroad that should connect Cincinnati with Charleston by way of the French Broad river valley. The idea may have originated with Hayne or with some other South Carolinian. Several men of the Southeast had advocated projects of reaching the West and the Northwest by railroad, and several conventions had been held to consider such projects during the first five years of the thirties.[1] The new impetus was given in 1835 by some citizens of Cin-

---

1. *Proceedings of the citizens of Charleston embracing the Report of the committee and the Address and Resolutions* (Charleston, 1835), 6, 7, 25; *Journal of the Senate of Ohio*, Thirty-fourth General Assembly (Columbus, 1835), 34.

cinnati and neighboring towns who held a series of meetings in August of that year at the Commercial Exchange in Cincinnati.[2] They adopted a report and some supporting resolutions and appointed a committee to draft an appeal to the interested states and to conduct a vigorous correspondence with state governors. This committee was an interesting combination of scholars, politicians, professional men, and business men. George H. Dunn, one of the members, was soon to be one of the prominent Whig orators in behalf of Harrison in the campaign of 1836 and the president of the Lawrenceburg and Indianapolis railroad. He was no doubt interested in promoting a through rail route from Lake Michigan to Charleston, South Carolina, of which his own road would be an important link. Dr. Daniel Drake and E. D. Mansfield were public spirited men and were interested in all kinds of things. Judge James Hall, the editor of the *Western Monthly Magazine* and author of many books on the resources of the West, was a great champion of western development and undoubtedly was sincerely interested in a southeastern outlet for the Old Northwest. He was, however, also interested in pushing William Henry Harrison of the Old Northwest for the presidency.[3] As early as February of 1835 he had begun the publication of a life of General Harrison, in which he stated that the general was entitled to the highest civic reward.[4] William Henry Harrison, himself a member of the committee and signer of its ap-

2. Edward Derring Mansfield, *Personal Memories* (Cincinnati, 1879), 298.
3. S. P. Chase to S. F. Venton, February 8, 1835, in Robert B. Warden, *An Account of the Private Life and Public Services of Salmon Portland Chase* (Cincinnati, 1874), 246.
4. *The Western Monthly Magazine* (Cincinnati, 1833-36), IV, 82, 231.

peal, had already been at least four times nominated for the presidency in that year before the occurence of the Cincinnati meeting[5] and was in a receptive mood. His hunger for the presidency perceptably grew as nominations followed one another. Whether Harrison was brought into the Charleston railroad boom to help the railroad or to help his candidacy or both would now be difficult to say. Apparently the two things were to help each other. Mr. Harrison's Ohio friends were making it clear to the South Carolinians that his attitude on the U. S. bank, on the tariff, on slavery, and on abolitionism was all that the South could ask for. Some of the South Carolinians understood the gesture perfectly and responded equally to the suggestion of a Charleston and Ohio river railroad and of a "Harrison for president" boom. The *Charleston Courier* at once began quoting passages from the speeches of Harrison and from his carefully prepared letters to J. M. Berrien of Georgia and other influential southerners that proved Harrison astonishingly in harmony with southern principles and interests.

At the same time the citizens of Charleston, including Hayne, promptly held several enthusiastic meetings, appointed committees to get charters from the states through which the railroad would run, and appropriated money for a preliminary survey.[6] In 1836 some three hundred and eighty delegates from nine states met in convention at Knoxville, Tennessee. Besides southern states, Ohio, Indiana, and Illinois were represented. The conven-

5. *Niles' Register*, XLVII, 331; Warden, *Chase*, 246, 247; D. B. Gobel, *William Henry Harrison* (Indianapolis, 1926), 306, 307 (Volume XIV in *Ind. Hist. Soc. Collections*).

6. *Report of South Carolina Commissioners to the Knoxville Convention* (Knoxville, 1836), 3; *Journal of the Senate of Ohio,* Thirty-fourth General Assembly, 24, 25, 31, 32.

tion unanimously elected Hayne president of the convention, accepted the charters granted by the four southern states through which the road was to run, and drew up a statement of the advantages of such a connection between the Northwest and Southeast.[7] In 1837 the Louisville, Cincinnati, and Charleston railroad company was organized, steps were taken to purchase the Charleston and Augusta road as an initial part of their through line, the valley of the French Broad was definitely chosen as the route, and Hayne was elected president of the road.[8]

The promoters of the project stated many times that their motives were commercial, social, and political. Hayne argued that the agricultural products of the Northwest would come to Charleston at greatly reduced transportation cost, would supply the Southeast, and would leave a surplus to be transported from the southern ports to Europe. From this he not only hoped to see the planters of the southeastern states left more free to devote themselves wholly to cotton production but also hoped to see a revival of the importance of the southern ports in the European trade. In return the Northwest would take the cotton of the Southeast and would become the manufacturer for that section. He even expected to see built up in the Northwest a manufacturing region that would not need the protection of a tariff and thus in time that section would be caused to take the southern view on protection against the Northeast. He expected the Northwest to profit by the slave economy of the South, become

---

7. *Proceedings of the Knoxville Convention in Relation to the proposed Louisville, Cincinnati, and Charleston Railroad* (Knoxville, 1836), 3, 11.

8. *First Annual Report of the President and Directors of the Louisville, Cincinnati, and Charleston Railroad Company* [signed by Hayne, Flat Rock, N. C., Oct. 16, 1837], 1, 5, 12.

reconciled to it, and then become a defender of it.' The Knoxville convention was of the opinion that such a railroad would exert a "controlling and permanent influence on the peace and perpetuity of the Union, by practically increasing the reciprocal dependence of the North and South, by establishing prejudices, creating greater uniformity in political opinions and blending the feelings of distant portions into a union of hearts."[10] Colonel Blanding of Charleston had the same idea. He said: "I regard a connection in a political point of view, with Cincinnati, as more important than with Louisville. It detaches from the East a powerful confederate in our political struggles as far as commercial and social intercourse can produce that effect, and may have a tendency to keep Ohio our friend on the slave question. She will receive the benefits of our slave labor indirectly without any of what she regards its evils."[11]

The project was entirely practicable. The length of road to be constructed was no greater than that of some of the other eastern trunk lines. The elevation to be crossed and the distance through the mountains was less than that to be overcome by the Pennsylvania or the Baltimore and Ohio railroads.[12] Since 1878 a railroad has been in operation through the very gap advocated by Hayne.[13] But Hayne met with many obstacles. First, the people of the Northwest did not continue to live up to their expected

---

9. *Proceedings of the Citizens of Charleston*, 13-17; *First Annual Report of Pres. and Dir. of the L. C. and C.*, 7.

10. *Proceedings of the Knoxville Convention*, 11.

11. Col. A. Blanding, *Address to the Citizens of Charleston on the Louisville, Cincinnati, and Charleston Railroad* (Columbia, S. C., 1836), 7.

12. *First Annual Report of the Pres. and Dir. of the L. C. and C.*, 3.

13. T. D. Jervey, *Robert Y. Hayne and his Times* (New York, 1909), 531.

performance. In his message of December, 1835, Noah Noble, Whig governor of Indiana and champion of internal improvements, called the attention of the General Assembly to the meetings at Cincinnati and Charleston and urged co-operation.[14] Joint resolutions were passed by the Assembly expressing warm approval of the projected railroad, pointing out the many economic, political, and social blessings that such a road would confer upon everybody concerned, and calling upon the Federal government for aid in making the surveys.[15]. The Indiana legislature was lavish in voting money for a vast system of transportation lines within the state but gave no financial aid to the Charleston road. It placed the credit of the state to the extent of a half million at the disposal of the Lawrenceburg and Indianapolis railroad, which was to serve as part of an extension of the Charleston road from Cincinnati to Lake Michigan, but subscribed to no stock in the Charleston road.[16] The governor of Ohio, too, continued to approve the building of the outlet to the Southeast in his messages to the state legislature,[17] but the people of that state spent their money in buying stock in the roads and canals radiating from Cincinnati northward instead of buying the stock of the trunk line that was to connect

14. *Journal of the Senate of the State of Indiana,* Twentieth session (Indianapolis, 1835), 21.
15. *Journal of the Senate of Indiana,* Twentieth session, 302, 607, 621 675; *Journal of the House of Representatives of Indiana,* Twentieth session (Indianapolis, 1836), 122, 389, 438, 468; *Laws of Local Nature of Indiana,* Twentieth session (Indianapolis, 1836), 385, 386, joint resolutions numbered 57 and 288.
16. *Laws of a General Nature, of Indiana,* Twentieth session (Indianapolis, 1836), 16, 17.
17. *Journal of the Senate of Ohio,* Thirty-fourth General Assembly, 9; *Journal of the House of Representatives of Ohio,* Thirty-fifth General Assembly (Columbus, 1836), 63.

Cincinnati with Charleston. The people of the Old Northwest seemed more concerned about building the local feeder lines to the trunk line than in building the trunk line itself. Laborers upon the public works in Ohio and Indiana consumed some of the agricultural products of the Northwest. New settlers occupied lands along the newly constructed roads and canals. These new settlers during the first year of their residence absorbed more of the surplus products. The pressure for a market seemed for a brief time relieved. Then came the panic of 1837 leaving the people of the Old Northwest no longer able to give financial encouragement to anything.

Hayne, therefore, in 1837 got the legislatures of three of the states through which the road would pass to grant banking privileges to the railroad company in order to furnish the circulating medium for building the road and for caring for the new business that would be created by the road.[18] He had a further political motive in advocating a Southwestern Bank with the mother bank in Charleston and branches in other states. It would stand in the way of another United States bank, an institution fairly popular in the Northeast, but not so popular in the South and in the West.[19] Another obstacle to the completion of the Charleston and Cincinnati railroad grew out of the local interests of the people in different parts of Kentucky and out of the opposition of some who were afraid that the project might advance the political hopes of Harrison and his friends.[20] Before the company was able to get a

18. *Exposition of the Claims of the Louisville, Cincinnati, and Charleston to the support of the Legislature and people of Kentucky* (n. d. [late in 1837]), 2-4.

19. *Second Annual Report of the L. C. & C.* (Charleston, 1838), 14.

20. The persistent effort of James Guthrie and others to bring about

charter from that state, it had to agree to build branch lines to Louisville and Maysville.[21] Blanding consoled himself with the hope that by extending the road to Louisville, it would reach the Ohio at the falls, the head of navigation for the larger steamboats, and would also give the road the exports and the support of those people of southern Indiana who found their most convenient market at the Falls Cities.[22] These branches would, however, increase the initial expenditure out of all proportion to the small proportion of stock subscribed in Kentucky.

Finally Hayne had both the covert and the open opposition of Calhoun. The sectional struggles of the early thirties seem, as has already been stated, to have had a different effect upon him than upon Hayne. Calhoun professed to be satisfied with the outcome of nullification, but he ever after at times betrayed a suspicion that his desire to maintain the Union might be hopeless. He still labored to enlarge the country and tried at times to become its president, but just as frequently he gave evidence of the determination that if separation should become inevitable, his own South should be found already consolidated and linked together. So in the period from 1835 to 1837 he busied himself with writing letters to some of the Georgia and South Carolina leaders with the hope of getting an extension of the Charleston and Augusta railroad through northern Georgia to Muscle Shoals on the Tennessee and to Nashville on the Cumberland. He argued that the Mis-

---

the failure of the project and his opposition to Blanding, the friend of Harrison, when he visited the Kentucky legislature in the interest of the road, were partially for political reasons. See *Journal of the Senate of the Commonwealth of Kentucky* (Frankfort, 1835), 75, 347.

21. *Ibid.*, 353, 355, 364, 452.
22. Blanding, *Address to the Citizens of Charleston*, 3.

sissippi system could be reached more easily by having the western terminals of the railroad on these two navigable rivers. If later the railroad was to be extended, it was to be extended past the mouth of the Cumberland to St. Louis.[23]. In either case Calhoun's Charleston Railroad inclined far more to the west and south and would touch the Old Northwest at its southwestern extremity instead of at its front door. He would waste no effort on trying to hold Ohio or Indiana to the Southeast, but would try to hold Missouri and possibly Illinois. Incidentally, Calhoun would bring South Carolina and Georgia into closer economic interdependence and political co-operation. His stand may have been in part due to his unwillingness to allow Hayne or Harrison to win popularity through the success of a project that he did not originate. But, often as Calhoun was driven to change the details of his plan, he always advocated a more southerly and westerly route than did Hayne.[24] The Old Northwest was still without a satisfactory southeastern outlet when Hayne and Blanding died in 1839 and it was still so when the Civil War began. It is said that in 1861 no less a person than Abraham Lincoln admitted that if the railroad from Charleston to Cincinnati had been built in the years immediately following 1835, the Civil War could not have come.[25]

The production, exportation, and importation that obtained in the Old Northwest in 1835 continued essentially the same to the end of the thirties except that there was a

---

23. J. C. Calhoun to J. S. Williams, Oct. 17, 1835, in *Correspondence of John C. Calhoun*, J. Franklin Jameson, ed., 346 (Annual Report of the American Historical Association, 1899, II); Calhoun to W. C. Dawson, Nov. 24, 1835, in *Ibid.*, 350.
24. Calhoun to J. E. Calhoun, in *Correspondence of J. C. Calhoun*, 431.
25. H. C. Carey, *To the Friends of the Union throughout the Union* (Philadelphia, 1876), 4.

A Southeastern Trunkline, 1835-39

gradual but rapid settling of the lands in parts of northern Indiana, northern Illinois, and southern Michigan with the consequent production of a surplus in those regions. The Erie canal, the Welland canal,[26] and the lake vessels facilitated both the process of settlement and of transportation of the surplus products.[27] The greater part of these newcomers were New Englanders or of New England extraction. During the settling process new settlements always consumed practically all that they produced and had to import not only merchandise from the Atlantic seaboard but such commodities as flour and meat from the older neighboring communities within the Old Northwest.[28] The period of beginnings in the lake region was, however, brief, and before the end of the thirties these newly settled regions began to show a steadily increasing surplus. Chicago had exported a little beef as early as 1833 and had followed this each year with consignments of the same article and of pork.[29] She began the export of wheat about 1838 or 1839.[30] Michigan had begun to export a little wheat as early as 1835.[31] Although areas in the western

26. The act of 1831 permitting the importation of wheat and flour from the U. S. to Canada duty free resulted in as much wheat from the U. S. going over the Welland canal by 1839 as went over the Erie canal. See *N. Y. Sen. Docs., 1840* (Albany, 1840), vol. III, no. 63, statements 8 and 27.

27. L. K. Mathew, *Erie Canal and Settlement of the West* (Buffalo, 1910), 194, 196, 197 (Buffalo Historical Society *Publications*, vol. XIV); *N. Y. Assembly Docs., 1853*, no. 77, p. 3; N. E. Whitford, *History*, I, 212.

28. [*First*] *Annual Review of the Business of Chicago for the year 1852 by Democratic Press*, 1; *Address delivered by Thomas Whitney*, 12; *Eighth Census, 1860*, Agriculture, p. cxlvi.

29. [*First*] *Annual Review of the Business of Chicago*, 2; *N. Y. Sen. Docs., 1836*, vol. II, no. 70, statement F, no. 5.

30. *First Annual Review*, p. 2, gives 1839 as first date; *U. S. Census, 1860*, Agriculture, p. cxlvii, gives 1838.

31. *N. Y. Sen. Docs., 1836*, vol. II, no. 70, statement F, no. 5, shows export in 1835.

part of central Ohio were still sparsely settled, partly because there was no convenient outlet for potential products of that region, the citizens of Ohio wanted this region occupied and developed. To meet this situation, the Miami Extension canal was being pushed northward from the terminus of the Miami canal at Dayton.[32] During this period, too, the Whitewater canal was constructed from the Ohio river near Cincinnati to the vicinity of Brookville, Indiana, to take care of the products of the Whitewater valley. Steamboats were being built at various points on the Ohio and on the Mississippi five times as fast as they were burnt or snagged. As a result of these developments the total exports of the Old Northwest through each of the three outlets had increased by 1839.

Comparing the exports of the Old Northwest in 1839 with those in 1835, one finds that the striking increases in the total quantity of items occurred in the cases of wheat, flour, and pork. The quantity of wheat was fourteen times as large, that of flour twice as large, and that of pork one and one-half times as large as in 1835. If the flour be considered as wheat, when a barrel of the former is estimated as the equivalent of five bushels of the latter, the total surplus of wheat exported will mount to six million bushels or three times the export of wheat and wheat products in 1835. Again if the pork and whiskey be counted as corn at the rate of fifteen and eight bushels of each to the barrel respectively, it will be found that the total surplus of corn exported will stand a little below six million bushels or somewhat less than one and one-half times the export of 1835.[33] It will thus be seen that the

32. *Ohio Legislative Documents, 1837-38* (Columbus, 1838), no. 19, p. 10.

33. Whether a hog that had been partially fattened upon the mast pro-

total exports in 1839 showed an increase of approximately 100% over those of 1835 in the quantity of wheat and corn and their derivatives taken together.

The small increase in the quantity of pork was carried almost equally through the eastern and the northeastern gateways. While the southern outlet took 50% more flour than formerly, the bulk of the increase in flour export and practically all the increase in wheat export passed through the northeastern gateway, through Canada and New York state. The British and Canadian laws stimulated the export of wheat and flour to Canada at this time as will be indicated later. The two together represented a surplus of wheat and wheat products exported through the northeastern outlet, increasing from an equivalent of one-half million bushels of wheat to a surplus of three and one-half millions in the four years. But in the export of wheat itself through the northeastern gateway the increase was even more striking. In that case it had mounted from one hundred and fifty thousand bushels to two million bushels.

Of more than eight hundred thousand barrels of flour exported from the interior in 1839, 53% went south, 40% northeast, and 7% east; of more than two million bushels of wheat nearly 97% went northeast; of more than a million bushels of corn 98% went south; of a little more than three hundred thousand barrels of pork and bacon 69% went south, 19% east, and 12% northeast; of over thirty thousand hogsheads of tobacco 90% went south and 9% went east; of thirty thousand barrels of whiskey 96% went south and 3% east; of the five hundred tons of wool

duced in the hardwood forests of the Ohio valley would consume as much as fifteen bushels of corn before being slaughtered would of course vary with the season and other conditions.

practically all went east.[34] The general direction of the export of each of the commodities in 1839 with one exception was the same as in 1835. Wheat still went northeast, wool east, and other commodities for the most part went south as formerly. The one exception was flour. The greater quantity of flour was still going south as in 1835, but in 1839 the northeastern route was about to overtake the southern outlet. Wheat and wheat flour, now being produced in larger and larger quantities in the northern parts of the Old Northwest as those parts were being settled, found their outlet through the northeastern gateway. The Erie canal and the Welland canal as well as the British law of 1831 admitting wheat and flour into Canada duty free facilitated the movement. The fact that there was less mast in the northern parts of the Old Northwest and the fact that the canals were frozen over in the pork packing and shipping season made the production of hogs for the time being unprofitable. Added to the shortage of mast was the presence of grassy prairies or oak openings in many localities which were with difficulty put and kept under proper cultivation for corn and were thus for some time not well adapted to the production of corn, so necessary in the fattening of hogs. In some localities the non-frost season was frequently too short for the maturing of the kinds of corn then produced.

Of the wheat exported northeastward, 82% went from Ohio alone, 12% from Michigan, 6% from northern Indiana, and 1% from northern Illinois; of the flour, 80%

34. Table of statistics compiled from: *N. Y. Sen. Docs., 1840*, vol. III, no. 63, statement 8; *Western Journal and Civilian* (St. Louis, 1848-56), I, 106; *U. S. House Ex. Docs.*, 50 Cong., 1 sess., vol. XX, no. 6, pt. 2 [serial 2552], pp. 200-18; *Journal of House of Rep. of Pennsylvania*, Session of 1840 (Harrisburg, 1840), vol. II, Appendix, p. 56, statement 3; Freeman Hunt, *Merchants' Magazine* (New York, 1839-70), V, 215.

went from Ohio, 17% from Michigan, and 2% from northern Indiana; of beef and pork, 79% went from Ohio, 8% each from Michigan and northern Illinois.[35] That is, northern Ohio in 1839 still supplied four-fifths of each and every important article exported through the northeastern gateway. All exports from Michigan, of course, sought the northeastern outlet but they were still small in quantity. From Illinois only those exports from the northeastern part, from Indiana only those from the northern third, from Ohio only those from the northern and from the central part as far south as Chillicothe were exported northeastward. The exports from the southern halves of those three states were exported east and south, but chiefly south. That is, increased export through the northeastern gateway was due to increased production in the lake region of the Old Northwest and not to the fact that parts of the Ohio valley that had once exported southward were now exporting northeastward. Not only did commodities not go from the Ohio river over the Ohio canal northward but also commodities placed upon the southern part of the Ohio canal went southward to the Ohio river.[36] The freight charges for more than three hundred miles on the Ohio canal, more than two hundred fifty miles over Lake Erie, more than three hundred fifty miles over the Erie canal, and nearly one hundred fifty miles over the Hudson river with transfer charges between each was more than the traffic would bear.

The total imports into the Old Northwest in 1839 from

35. *Report of the Engineer to the Directors of the Lockport and Niagara Falls Railroad Co.* (Boston, 1841), passim.
36. Tables of arrivals and clearances of each commodity at each station on the Ohio canals, in *Third Annual Report of the Board of Public Works of Ohio*, in *Documents to the 38th General Assembly of the State of Ohio for 1839-40* (Columbus, 1840), vol. II, pt. 3, no. 45.

all sources amounted to about two hundred thousand tons, an increase of 33% over the imports of 1835. The commodities entering through the northeastern gateway and through New Orleans had each risen from fifty thousand to more than sixty thousand tons, and those through the eastern gateway from thirty-six thousand to fifty thousand. Salt from western Virginia made up the remainder of the total. Salt imported to the extent of one hundred thousand tons still made up the largest single item of import and still comprised about one-half the total tonnage of imports. The salt came in nearly equal quantities through the Kanawha valley from western Virginia, through the northeastern gateway from New York, and through New Orleans from Turks island and Liverpool. Only some seven thousand tons came through the eastern gateway. The western meat packers had been for a number of years seriously discontented over the salt question. They charged that the import duties tended to keep out the better foreign salt or raise the price of it, that the Kanawha salt was unsuitable for meat packing because of the impurities that it contained, and that its price was kept up through a monopolistic organization.[37] Thomas H. Benton made himself the spokesman of this discontent, sent out questionnaires, prepared and presented the case of the westerners in an elaborate report to Congress, and tried to get remedial legislation but without much result. The sugar and the coffee were still supplied by New Orleans. Through this gateway there came into the Old Northwest in 1839 some fifteen thousand tons of coffee and twenty-five thousand tons of sugar, an increase of

37. *U. S. Sen. Docs.*, 26 Cong., 1 sess., vol. IV, no. 196 [serial 357], pp. 45, 86, 90, 93, 111; *N. Y. Sen. Docs., 1840,* vol. III, no. 63, pp. 13, 14, statement 5.

33% and 25% respectively.[38] Coffee and sugar entering the Old Northwest through the southern gateway was distributed throughout the interior of that region.

From the eastern gateway there came more than fifteen thousand tons of iron, a 50% increase over 1835. From each the eastern and the northeastern gateway there came some thirty thousand tons of merchandise such as drygoods, hardware, furniture, drugs, and chinaware.[39] Of the merchandise coming through the northeastern gateway in 1839, northern and central Ohio took 50%; Michigan, 24%; northern Illinois, 13%; northern Indiana, 8%; Wisconsin, Kentucky, Missouri, and Pennsylvania took trifling amounts. It will be noted that the percentage of the total of imports taken by the newer states in comparison with Ohio was much larger than their percentage of the total exports. A large part of this merchandise consisted of the household goods and other earthly belongings of settlers coming into the interior over the Erie canal. It is quite clear that it was the northern part of the Ohio valley and the region immediately to the south of the Great Lakes that had shown the most rapid increase in population, in production, and in export and import. The Erie, the Welland, and the Ohio canals had helped to make this possible. The Ohio valley proper had benefited scarcely at all by the Welland and the Erie canals, and by the Ohio canal only as a means of getting commodities down to the Ohio river. The export of wheat, including flour reduced to wheat, by the northern part through the northeastern gateway had increased by 1400% since 1835,

38. *DeBow's Review*, I, 49; XXIX, 524.
39. *Journal of House of Representatives of Pennsylvania, 1840*, vol. II, Appendix, p. 56, statement 2; *N. Y. Sen. Docs., 1840*, vol. III, no. 63, p. 13, 14, statement 5.

while the export of corn, including pork and whiskey reduced to corn, from the southern part of the Old Northwest through both the southern and eastern gateways had increased by only 17% in the same time. The export of flour from the southern part of the Old Northwest had increased by only 33%. It is clear that the southern part of the Old Northwest was not advancing economically in proportion to its population as fast in this period as the northern part. In the southern part settlement and production had already become stabilized on the basis of its market. Imports had increased in quantity for the Old Northwest between 1835 and 1839 by 33% while exports had increased by 100%. But the northern part and the southern part of the Old Northwest did not present the same picture in that respect. The northern part in spite of all the incoming of settlers with their goods and their increased consumption was increasing its exports many times faster than its imports, whereas the southern part was still increasing its imports a little more rapidly than its exports. The need and desire for a better outlet to the world market was about as great in the case of the Ohio valley in 1839 as it was in 1835 when Harrison and Hayne were trying to open up a railway to the southeast, but the panic had left the people financially prostrate and unable to co-operate in such an enterprise.

CHAPTER III

Some Attempts to Bring About a Closer Alliance Between the Old Northwest and the Northeast, 1840-1844

THE HARD TIMES inaugurated by the panic of 1837 still rested heavily upon the Old Northwest during the opening years of the forties. Ohio, Indiana, and Illinois were staggering under state debts that threatened to end in bankruptcy and repudiation. Prices of agricultural commodities were still low but getting a trifle better. This was especially true of the upper Ohio valley. Flour sold there at times in 1840 as low as $2.50 per barrel, wheat at 40 cents per bushel, pork at $2.00 per hundred, and corn at 25 cents per bushel.[1] The average price of the best wheat in Cincinnati during 1840 was only 54 cents, whereas the average price during each of the four following years was above 66 cents.[2] The New York and the Pennsylvania public works had brought no relief to the Ohio valley. Freight rates from Pittsburgh to New York City by way of New Orleans were still at times lower during 1840 than by way of Philadelphia or by way of the Ohio canal and the Erie canal.[3]

In the years 1840-44 at least three groups of activities that had for their object the partial relief of this situation were under way. First, some of the states within the Old Northwest continued or revived their projects of building transportation lines within that section. Before the

---

1. *Zanesville Gazette,* April 23, 1840, quoted in *Niles' Register,* LVIII, 144; *Niles' Register,* LVIII, 272, and LXVI, 272.
2. N. W. Aldrich, *Report on Wholesale Prices,* in *U. S. Sen. Reports,* 52 Cong., 2 sess., vol. III, pt. 2, no. 1394 [serial 3074, pt. 2], pp. 60-62.
3. *Pittsburgh Gazette,* quoted in *Niles' Register,* LVIII, 32.

close of 1843 the Wabash and Erie canal was open for navigation from Toledo through the Maumee valley of northwestern Ohio and through the Wabash valley of northern Indiana as far as Lafayette or Terre Haute.[4] The Miami Extension canal was building northward from Dayton but was not completed through to connect with the Wabash and Erie near Defiance until in 1845.[5] Before 1844 several short canals had been completed in Ohio which operated as feeders to the two trunk canals, the Ohio and the Miami.[6] These projects perhaps were no more for linking the Old Northwest with the Northeast than with the South.

A second group of activities comprised the building of a line of railroads through New York and New England, connecting the Northeastern gateway of the Old Northwest with the outside world. In 1841 an all rail route had been completed from Boston to Albany.[7] The following year witnessed the completion of the last link in an all rail route from Albany to Buffalo, thus giving to the Great Lakes a railroad connection with an Atlantic seaport.[8] This rail route was important, however, more in

---

4. L. Esarey, "Internal Improvements in Early Indiana," in Indiana Historical Society *Publications,* vol. V (Indianapolis, 1912), 130, C. P. McClelland and C. C. Huntington, *History of Ohio Canals* (Columbus, 1905), 37. Flicklin of Illinois, Jan. 10, 1844, in *Cong. Record,* 28 Cong., 1 sess., vol. XIII, pt. 2, p. 50 said southern terminus of canal at that time was Terre Haute.

5. *Documents to the 44th General Assembly of the State of Ohio, 1845-46,* vol. X, pt. 1, p. 293; *History of Ohio Canals,* 37; H. S. Knapp, *History of the Maumee Valley* (Toledo, 1872), 343.

6. McClelland and Huntington, *Ohio Canals,* 39-40.

7. *Annual Reports of the Railroad Corporations of Massachusetts for 1841,* in *Mass. Sen. Docs.,* no. 26 (Boston, 1842), 43.

8. *Seventeenth Annual Report of the New York Central and Hudson River Railroad Company,* 33-35; Henry V. Poor, *History of the Railroads*

the part that it was to play in the somewhat distant future rather than in its immediate bearing upon the commerce of the interior. In the first place, although there was now an all rail route from Buffalo to Albany, it was made up for almost a decade longer of seven end-for-end roads operated by different companies. The roads had different gauges and different types of rails.[9] As a consequence freight had to be loaded and unloaded many times in transit. To make things worse, the roads that comprised this route were obliged by their charters or by other legislation to pay into the state canal fund canal tolls on all through freight carried by them while the Erie canal was open for navigation.[10] One of the roads had to pay the canal tolls on all goods transported at any season.[11] The chain could be no stronger than the weakest link. This situation made it impossible for the

and Canals of the United States (New York, 1860), I, 231, 306, 311, 315, 322; F. W. Stevens, *The Beginnings of the New York Central Railroad* (New York, 1926), p. x.

9. Poor, *History of Railroads*, I, 232, 315, 322.

10. *Laws of N. Y., 1834* (Albany, 1835), ch. 228, the Auburn and Syracuse had to pay tolls on all goods same as if transported on canal; *Laws of N. Y., 1836*, ch. 349, the Auburn and Rochester might not transport goods so as to reduce tolls of canal; *Laws of N. Y., 1838*, ch. 241, the Buffalo and Batavia might not transport goods so as to reduce tolls of canal; *Laws of N. Y., 1838*, ch. 57, the Auburn and Syracuse had to pay canal tolls when Erie canal was open; *Laws of N. Y., 1844,* ch. 35, the Syracuse and Utica, the Auburn and Syracuse, the Auburn and Rochester, the Tonawanda, and the Attica and Buffalo might carry local freight west of Utica without paying tolls, but must make returns; *Laws of N. Y., 1847*, ch. 270, no goods passing from one road to another considered local; *Laws of N. Y., 1848*, ch. 140, all roads parallel or nearly so and within 30 miles of canal must pay canal tolls.

11. *Laws of N. Y., 1844*, ch. 335, the Utica and Schenectady might carry goods only when canal was not navigable and then must pay canal tolls; *Laws of N. Y., 1848*, ch. 270, Utica and Schenectady might transport freight at all times but must pay tolls on all freights.

railroads to carry through-freight except in entirely negligible quantities. Because of the necessity of frequent transfer of freight, the railroad route had but little advantage in speed of transportation over the canals in carrying fast freight.

The third group of activities had to do with the endeavors of the politicians and statesmen at Washington. Clay, who presumed to take complete charge of the Whig party after the election of 1840, again sponsored proposals for the distribution of the proceeds of the public land sales among the states and a higher tariff and a United States bank in the hope of combining the interests of the Northeast and the Northwest. The distribution project was supposed to commend itself particularly to some of the debt-ridden states of the West, who had about ruined themselves in building roads and canals, and the high tariff was intended to appeal to the manufactureres of the Northeast.[12] These two proposals would be in a way interdependent, inasmuch as the withdrawal of money from the United States Treasury through distribution of the proceeds might leave a shortage to be filled up by laying higher import duties. This was one of the very aspects of the proposal that President John Tyler and his followers from the Southeast did not like. While he was too much of a strict constructionist to approve of the indirect method of the Federal government assuming state debts for internal improvements through distribution of the proceeds of the land sales, yet he was willing to favor the West thus far if this was not made the means of boosting the tariff still

12. G. M. Stephenson, *The Political History of the Public Lands from 1840 to 1862* (Boston, 1917), 57.

higher. The Democrats in 1840 had made a bid for the vote of the West by creating the impression that they favored preemption, or the right of a settler who occupied and improved land owned by the Federal government to have the first chance of later buying it at the minimum government price. Their platform did not mention preemption specifically, but they introduced bills and resolutions in Congress favoring it, whereas the Whigs talked for preemption in one state and against it in another. In the election the Democrats had carried some of the more western states where preemption was most popular.[13] The westerners had always looked upon preemption as simple justice. After the election of 1840, Thomas H. Benton, from the West, introduced another preemption bill into the Senate, and Calhoun from the Southeast made a bid for the support of the West by not only accepting preemption but by offering to cede with certain restrictions the western lands to the states within which the lands lay. Consequently, Clay was forced to see grafted on to the distribution bill both a permanent preemption clause and a proviso that distribution of the proceeds of the public land sales should be suspended whenever it was necessary to raise the tariff rates above those contemplated by the compromise act of 1833. In this mutilated form his measure became a law in 1841. To get enough western votes for the measure, Clay had to make other concessions. Each of the western states in which the ungranted lands lay was to get in addition to its share of the net proceeds 10 per cent of the gross receipts of the lands sold in its borders and a gift of 500,000 acres. On

---

13. T. H. McKee, *The National Conventions and Platforms* (Baltimore, 1906), 42, 45; R. C. Wellington, *The Political and Sectional Influence of the Public Lands, 1828-40* (Riverside Press, 1914), 86.

demand of the westerners Clay had also to allow the passage of a temporary bankruptcy law. The next year when Clay tried to raise the tariff rates without suspending the distribution of the proceeds of the land sales he was twice blocked by a presidential veto, and the Clay forces had to content themselves with a higher tariff but with distribution suspended and practically a dead letter.[14] The temporary bankruptcy law that had been passed in 1841 to bring relief to the westerner was also repealed soon thereafter.[15] However, the Northwest still had its preemption act while the Northeast had its tariff of '42 as a result of all the wrangling at the federal capital during the first three years of the forties. Pre-emption was generally approved in the West but could benefit for the most part only those in the newer settlements or those in the older settlements who were ready to sell out and start over farther west. Little or nothing had been done by Congress that would assist in the substantial development and the prosperity of the Northwest. The two bank bills of 1841 introduced in accordance with Clay's program and intended to give greater uniformity and stability to the currency were both killed by the president. Perhaps the best that could have happened to the westerner was for him to be left alone by Congress to work out his own salvation, but the westerner did not think so. He wanted help from his government.

The tariff of 1842 had apparently little effect upon the commerce of the southern part of the Old Northwest; and so far as it affected the northern part at all, it seems to

14. 27 Cong., 1 sess., ch. 16, sec. 6, and 27 Cong., 2 sess., ch. 270, sec. 30, in *Public Statutes at Large*, V, 454, 567.

15. 27 Cong., 1 sess., ch. 9, and 27 Cong., 3 sess., ch. 82, in *Public Statutes at Large*, V, 441, 614.

have been adversely. This region had been permitted under the British act of Parliament of 1831 to export its wheat, corn, live stock, flour, pork, and beef into Canada duty free. From Canada these same commodities except the first three could under the same act be reexported to the British West India possessions without paying duty. The flour made in Canada out of the American wheat as well as the beef and pork made of American live stock could be sent to the British West Indies duty free.[16] Canadian wheat released and replaced by American wheat as well as flour made in Canada from American wheat could be exported to England and admitted there between 1828 and 1842 at a much lower duty than could wheat and flour coming directly from non-British ports. In fact when the price of wheat was 67 shillings per quarter in England, wheat from Canada was admitted at a duty of only 5 shillings per quarter, while wheat from foreign countries, including the United States, had to pay a duty of 18 shillings 8 pence per quarter. As the wheat rose in price in England above 67 shillings, the duty on wheat from Canada dropped at once to 6 pence per quarter, while the duty on wheat from foreign countries was only gradually reduced. As the price fell below 67 shillings, the duty on wheat from non-British ports increased in the exact amount of the fall in price so that when the price of wheat in England dropped to 50 shillings, the duty on wheat from non-British ports was 36 shillings, whereas the duty on wheat from Canada never rose above 5 shillings per quarter. Flour manufactured in Canada from American wheat and exported to England

16. 1W. IV., C. 24, in *Statutes of the United Kingdom*, XII, 346; Keefer, *Canals of Canada*, 24.

received exactly similar preferential treatment.[17] A considerable quantity of the commodities of the upper Northwest had therefore during the thirties and early forties gone into Canada for consumption, for reexportation, and for replacing Canadian exports to England. By 1839 almost as much wheat had gone eastward from the Old Northwest over the Welland canal as had gone eastward from Buffalo over the Erie canal. Moreover, only a small part of the former exports had ever returned to the United States over the Oswego canal.[18] This indirect way of getting American wheat into England was not as satisfactory as if it could have been transported directly into England from America duty free, but it was much better than to export directly and submit to the duties and uncertainties then entailed by law. Even when the price of wheat rose in England, the Baltic countries could rush a supply into the market and bring the price of wheat down and the duty up before a cargo from America could reach there. American grain growers and merchants and shippers were making the same arguments for the repeal of the English corn laws that were being made in England.[19]

But now suddenly things were to be for a few years apparently worse. As the result of an act of the Canadian government in 1842 and an act of the British Parliament in 1843 American wheat exported to Canada was to pay a duty there of three shillings per quarter and flour two shillings per barrel. The Canadian wheat released by this

17. 9 Geo. IV., C. 60, in *Statutes of the United Kingdom*, XI, 490, 491; *Niles' Register*, LVIII, 290.
18. *N. Y. Sen. Docs., 1840*, vol. III, no. 63, statements 8 and 27; Hunt, *Merchants' Magazine*, IV, 734 and V, 215.
19. James H. Lanman, "American Agricultural Commerce," in Hunt, *Merchants' Magazine*, V, 217; *Niles' Register*, LVIII, 72.

importation of American wheat and exported to England would be admitted there at one shilling per quarter,[20] whereas the American wheat transported directly to England still paid from one shilling to one pound duty as the price of wheat varied from 73 shillings or more to 51 shillings or less according to the terms of a statute passed in 1842.[21] By the act of 1843 the duty on American flour entering the British West Indies was reduced from five shillings per barrel to two shillings. This was a decided encouragement to the exportation of wheat and flour from the Old Northwest by way of the southern gateway at New Orleans instead of the northeastern gateway. The effect of the Canadian and West Indian duties on the importation of American wheat and flour was to immediately slow up the movement of grain northward over the Ohio canal during the latter part of 1843. John Brough, the able Democratic auditor of Ohio, called attention to this fact and argued that the British act was one of retaliation against the American tariff of '42 and that, while the wheat then already produced would ultimately go forward, eventually the British act would slow up production in the Northwest.[22] In the latter prophecy he was probably, however, mistaken. As long as settlers continued to pour into the Northwest and to take up new land, they had to produce a surplus and to export it regardless of bad prices and of bad humor. Then, too, it must be noted that even though American wheat trans-

20. 6 and 7 Vict., C. 29, in *Statutes of the United Kingdom* (London, 1843), LXXXIII, 173.
21. 5 and 6 Vict., C. 14, in *Statutes of the United Kingdom* (London, 1842), LXXXII, 71.
22. John Brough, "Annual Report of Auditor of State," in *Documents to Forty-Second General Assembly of Ohio* (Columbus, 1844), no. 6, pp. 40-41.

ported to Canada now paid a duty of three shillings per quarter instead of going duty free as formerly, the same wheat when reshipped to England now never paid more than one shilling duty, whereas before 1843 it had paid five shillings when the price was below sixty-seven. After 1843 as soon as the price of wheat dropped below 70 shillings in England, it was more profitable to send American wheat by way of Canada, pay the 3 shillings Canadian duty and the one shilling English duty than to ship the same directly from the United States to England. If the price of wheat in England dropped as low as 60 shillings, American wheat shipped by way of Canada entered England at 6 shillings less duty than if shipped directly from the United States.[23] However, when the price of wheat rose above seventy shillings in England after 1843, the duty on wheat sent directly from the United States gradually declined from four shillings to one shilling, thus making it unprofitable to export through Canada paying the three shillings there and an additional shilling when the wheat entered England. Thus the British act facilitated direct export of wheat from the United States when the price in England was high, but the Northwestern wheat grower was perhaps better off before when he could ship through Canada into England at a duty of six pence as soon as the price of wheat rose there to 67 shillings.

President Tyler no doubt was making a bid for the vote of the West in support of his presidential candidacy when in December of 1843 he urged Congress to make such appropriations for the improvement of the western rivers and lakes as would be constitutionally permissible.[24] Con-

23. Keefer, *Canals of Canada*, 26.
24. Richardson, *Messages and Papers of the Presidents*, IV, 270.

gress proceeded instead to pass two rivers and harbors bills, one for the East and one for the West. The western bill carried large appropriations for the improvement of the Ohio river and the Mississippi river with smaller sums for various lake ports.[25] The usual charges that there was an attempt at alliance between the Northeast and the Northwest were hurled back and forth. Many of the members from the Old Northwest seemed reluctant to enter such an alliance and accused the members from New York and Pennsylvania of attempting to secure the passage of the eastern measure as the price of voting for the western bill.[26] While the heaviest vote for the measure came from these sections, congressmen voted usually according to party dictates or because of local interests or factional fights. Ohio, New York, and Pennsylvania, the states most benefited, gave the measures most support. President Tyler vetoed the eastern bill and signed the western bill. He explained that he did so because the eastern measure was not national in character, whereas the improvement of the great Mississippi system was one that no single state could undertake and that the Great Lakes really constituted great inland seas.[27] The hand that had drafted the veto message may have been that of Tyler, but the reasoning was very much like that of Calhoun on a later occasion. Both had presidential aspirations. With Calhoun the hope was recurrent if not perennial. Tyler had a few days previous to the writing of the veto message been renominated by a special convention.[28] The handling of the rivers and harbors bill was

25. 28 Cong., 1 sess., ch. 44, in *Public Statutes at Large*, V, 661.
26. *Congressional Globe*, 28 Cong., 1 sess., vol. XIII, pt. 2, Appendix, pp. 38, 651, 776.
27. Richardson, *Messages and Papers of the Presidents*, IV, 332.
28. *Niles' Register*, LXVI, 200, 218, 259.

thus rather definitely in the nature of a bid of the Southeast for the support of the Northwest. But shrewder politicians than Tyler or Calhoun were to try their hands at building a political alliance of sections in the election of 1844. Conditions at the time were such in the Old Northwest that some of the farmers of the Ohio valley had been looking toward Texas as a future market for some of their surplus products ever since the Texan revolution.[29] Farmers both in the Ohio valley and in the Lake region had been for some time looking toward Oregon as a place to which they might wish to move if conditions did not grow better in the Old Northwest. Many of the planters of the Southwest wanted Texas annexed as a region to which they might wish to go with their slaves and in which they might wish to establish cotton plantations. Some of the southern politicians possibly wanted Texas for her vote in the Senate. President Tyler and Calhoun, his secretary of state, had for some time been conducting negotiations for Texan annexation and had allowed just enough of the evidence of British intentions of standing in the way of American expansion to become public to arouse the westerners to nationalistic fervor. The energy and restlessness of the western men was achieving much, but as so often happens in such a case, it was impatient at inevitable limitations and wanted to achieve more. If because of the low prices it was not to have its full reward for producing wheat and corn and pork, it could at least be consumed in a good fight against England or Mexico or both.[30] The men who drew up the platform for the democratic party in 1844 combined the demand for the reannexation of Texas

29. Atwater, *History of Ohio*, 312.
30. *Proceedings of the Oregon Convention held in Cincinnati, July 3-5, 1843*, in Appendix to the *Ohio Senate Journal, 1843-44* (Columbus, 1844), 43.

with the demand for the reoccupation of Oregon with the hope of securing an alliance of the Northwest with the South in the oncoming presidential election.

In 1844 the Old Northwest was still increasing in population, extending its occupied area as far toward the northwest as Wisconsin and producing and exporting an ever larger surplus to pay for the newly purchased lands of the settlers and for improvements by individuals and states. In 1840 Wisconsin territory had sent over the Erie canal 166 barrels of flour, which was probably her first consignment.[31] In 1841 Milwaukee in the same territory had sent her first shipment of wheat, consisting of some 4,000 bushels.[32] After that, the increasing size of the export of wheat and of other commodities each year from that territory or state bore evidence of its increasing surplus. If prices were low in the Old Northwest, the farmers were not often in a position to go back to the state or country from which they had migrated. They had to stay and make the best of it or move on. They would have to produce more in order to make up in quantity for the shortage in price. This they did and grumbled, even though prices in the northern part of the Old Northwest were getting better by the first of 1844.

The total export of flour and wheat from the Old Northwest in 1844 had in each case almost exactly doubled; that of pork, whiskey, and tobacco had in each case about trebled; while that of beef had increased eight fold since 1839. But the export of the bulkier commodity, corn, had increased by only about 20% since that time.

31. *Report of the Engineer to the Directors of the Lockport and Niagara Falls Railroad Co.*, 2.
32. *Address of Thomas Whitney at opening of Milwaukee Chamber of Commerce Rooms* (Milwaukee, 1863), 20; *U. S. Census,* 1860, Agriculture, p. cxlvii.

The export, however, of nearly eight hundred thousand barrels of pork probably represented something like twelve million bushels of corn, even after making due allowance for mast feeding. If the pork and whiskey both be counted as corn, the total export of corn surplus then amounted in 1844 to more than fourteen million bushels. This meant that the total surplus of corn and corn products as well as wheat and wheat products exported had in each case about doubled since 1839.

The export of flour, pork, whiskey, wool, and hemp east by way of Pittsburgh in 1844 was in each case about double that of 1839. In the case of tobacco the quantity had risen to five times the former amount. On the other hand, the export through the northeastern outlet of pork, whiskey, and tobacco was practically the same in 1844 as in 1839. The quantity of flour, however, exported by the northeastern outlet in 1844 was almost three times as large, that of wheat more than twice, and that of beef thirty times as large as in 1839. The export through New Orleans of beef, pork, whiskey, and tobacco had in each case about trebled; the export of corn had remained the same; that of flour had declined to almost half the former amount; and that of wheat had fallen to one fifth of the former. The outstanding features, then, were the large increases in the shipment of wheat, flour, and beef northeastward; beef, pork, whiskey, and tobacco southward; the less bulky freight like flour, pork, wool, and tobacco eastward; and the decrease in the shipment of wheat and flour southward.

Of the more than four million bushels of wheat exported in 1844 from the Old Northwest, 96% went through the northeastern outlet and the remainder went south. Of more than a million and a half barrels of flour exported, 63% went northeast, 31% went south, and 6%

went east. If the flour be considered as wheat, it will be seen that more than 76% of the twelve million bushels of wheat surplus of the Old Northwest found its outlet through the northeastern gateway. Of nearly a million and a half bushels of corn exported as corn, 90% went south and the remainder northeast. Of nearly eight hundred thousand barrels of pork and bacon 81% went south, 12% went east, and 7% went northeast. Of a hundred thousand barrels of whiskey 95% went south, 3% east, and 1% northeast. Of a hundred thousand hogsheads of tobacco 82% went south and 17% east. If the pork and whiskey be considered as corn, more than 82% of the total of fourteen million bushels of corn surplus found its outlet through the southern gateway. Of five million pounds of wool 60% went east and 40% northeast.[33] As in 1835 and in 1839 so in 1844 nearly all the wheat went northeastward and the pork, corn, and whiskey went south. But the northeastern outlet had now passed the southern outlet in the conveyance of flour and was rivaling the eastern outlet in the handling of wool.

Of the half million barrels of flour exported to New Orleans in 1844, Cincinnati forwarded about 25% and St. Louis 20%. Of the six hundred thousand barrels of pork and bacon 25% came from Cincinnati and 25% from St. Louis. St. Louis supplied nearly all the wheat.[34] It will be seen that about half the total of each commodity was forwarded by the two ports of Cincinnati and St. Louis

---

33. Statistical Tables compiled from: *U. S. House Ex. Docs.*, 50 Cong., 1 sess., vol. 20, no. 6, pt. 2 [serial 2552], pp. 200-18; *Western Journal and Civilian* (St. Louis, 1848-56), I, 106; J. L. Barton, *Brief Sketch of the Commerce of the Lakes* (Buffalo, 1847), 40; J. L. Barton, *Lake Commerce* (Buffalo, 1846), 32, 40; Hunt, *Merchants' Magazine*, XII, 98 and XIV, 194.

34. *Western Journal*, I, 103, 106; Hunt, *Merchants' Magazine*, XXI, 444; *Proceedings of the St. Louis Chamber of Commerce*, etc., 40.

and that the other half was brought by steamboats from the smaller river towns and by flatboats that were launched on the countless tributaries of the Ohio and upper Mississippi. A small percentage of these came from regions outside of the Old Northwest. The commodities forwarded by Cincinnati had been brought there originally from a region extending toward the north and toward the east for some hundred and fifty miles and toward the south and west for some fifty miles. The goods came by canal, rivers, and roads. Her contributions thus included a small but appreciable quantity from outside the Old Northwest. The commodities forwarded from St. Louis came originally from the Illinois river valley, from the settled parts of the Mississippi river valley lying in western Illinois and Wisconsin, and from the Missouri valley. Thus again a small quantity of goods forwarded was produced outside of the Old Northwest.

Of the four million bushels and more of wheat exported northeastward through the Welland canal and the Erie canal, Cleveland forwarded about 25%, Sandusky and Milan together contributed another 25%, Chicago forwarded 25%, while Michigan City, Toledo, Detroit, and Milwaukee with some assistance from smaller ports contributed the final 25%.[35] It is thus apparent that even though most of the wheat forwarded from Toledo was originally exported from northern Indiana, a little over 50% of the total quantity of wheat forwarded through the northeastern gateway was produced in Northern Ohio. Of the more than a million barrels of flour shipped northeastward in 1844, 50% went from northern Ohio and 40%

35. Barton, *Brief Sketch*, 28, 31, 33, 35; *First Annual Review of Chicago, her commerce, 1852*, 4; *Eighth Annual Report of the Board of Public Works of Ohio, 1844*, in *Documents to Forty-Third General Assembly of Ohio*, no. 22, p. 38.

went from Michigan. Of the pork shipped northeast in 1844, 75% went from northern Ohio and 20% from northern Indiana.[36] Ohio's share of the export of the Northeast had thus in general declined from 80% of the total to 50% since 1839. Ohio was, of course, increasing her exports but not as rapidly as Michigan and northern Indiana.

The line dividing the region that was commercially attached to the lakes from the region commercially attached to the Mississippi river system had by 1844 shifted slightly in south central Ohio and in north central Indiana. In south central Ohio on the Ohio canal the dividing line for some of the articles was farther north in 1844 than in 1839. All the wheat cleared over the Ohio canal still went northward as formerly, but corn and flour cleared over the canal at Chillicothe now went south. Both had gone northward in 1839. Pork and beef cleared over the canal at Chillicothe went south as in the earlier period, but whiskey and tobacco were now going south from as far up as Newark in east central Ohio.[37] It should be noted here that while all the wheat put upon the Ohio canal went northward, 90% of all the wheat put upon the canal was put upon the northern half of the canal and was evidently produced in northern Ohio; and while the two-thirds of the whiskey, pork, and beef put upon the canal moved southward, 75% of the entire quantity of each of these articles carried upon the canal was put upon the southern half of the canal and was apparently produced in southern Ohio.[38] The northern end of the Muskingum canal, which extended from Zanesville to Marietta or

36. Barton, *Sketch*, 40, 80.
37. Calculations based upon tables given in *Eighth Annual Report of the Board of Public Works of Ohio*, 38-58.
38. *Eighth Annual Report of the Board of Public Works of Ohio*, 38-58.

Harmar, was never connected with the Ohio canal. Goods of southeastern Ohio put upon that canal had to go southward as formerly to the Ohio river and thence east or south. The Miami extension not being completed through to the Wabash and Erie canal during this period, all goods from the Miami valley had still to go southward over the Miami canal to Cincinnati. The quantity of goods produced north of Dayton and placed upon the canal was still almost negligible.[39] The Wabash and Erie canal was, however, bringing from north central Indiana to Toledo some goods, which in the thirties would have gone southward by way of the Wabash river if there had then been any appreciable quantity of goods in those regions to export.[40] Before 1840 very little had been exported from that part of Indiana, but what had been exported had gone southward by way of the Wabash river. The products of southern Illinois and of the lower part of the Illinois river valley found their outlet through the Mississippi and went south to New Orleans.

The total imports into the Old Northwest in 1844 stood at two hundred and fifteen thousand tons, having and estimated value of $120,000,000[41] and showing only the very small increase of not more than 13% over that of 1839. The total tonnage entering over the canals and the railroads of the northeastern gateway had risen from a little below seventy thousand in 1839 to about seventy-seven thousand in 1844. As formerly salt made up a little less than half of this tonnage and different kinds of merchandise made up the remainder.[42] The total tonnage en-

39. *Eighth Annual Report of the Board of Public Works of Ohio*, 74-75.
40. Barton, *Sketch*, 30.
41. *Cong. Globe*, 28 Cong., 1 sess., vol. XIII, pt. 2, p. 110.
42. Barton, *Brief Sketch*, 40; *N. Y. Assembly Docs., 1844*, no. 145, p. 192.

tering through the eastern gateway had risen from about fifty thousand in 1839 to about fifty-two thousand in 1844 and was composed of the same proportions of salt, iron, and merchandise as formerly.[43] The imports from the south showed a little larger increase, advancing from fifty-five thousand to eighty-six thousand. The import of coffee by way of New Orleans had increased from about fifteen thousand tons to seventeen thousand, that of sugar had increased from sixteen thousand to twenty-five thousand, and that of salt from twenty-five thousand to forty-three thousand tons.[44]

The fact that exports exceeded imports in tonnage needs no comment. The agricultural commodities that were exported always weighed about four times as much as did the imports.[45] The fact, however, that imports had increased in tonnage by only thirteen per cent, while the export of the important agricultural products had increased by over a hundred per cent over those of 1839 is significant. The value of exports had mounted to a total estimated value of $115,000,000 and thus for the first time almost equaled the value of the imports.[46] If it be assumed that a considerable proportion of the imports consisted of household and farm accessories belonging to and accompanying new immigrants to the west, it must be concluded that the settlers of the West were now paying for what they were importing and were actually paying in some cases debts incurred in the past. There can be only one explanation. The western states and their citizens had just about exhausted their credit with the East during the

43. Hunt, *Merchants' Magazine*, XII, 98 and XIV, 195.
44. *DeBow's Review*, I, 49 and XXIX, 524.
45. W. J. McAlpine, *Address to the Chamber of Commerce at Cooper Union* (New York, 1873), 17.
46. *Cong. Globe*, 28 Cong., 1 sess., vol. XIII, pt. 2, p. 110.

late thirties in their state improvements and land purchases and were now facing the necessity of paying the interest through taxation and retrenchment. While a number of states ultimately virtually repudiated their obligations in whole or in part, the settlers of the Old Northwest were now trying to pay for their farms and for their state works by their exports and were importing only such things as they absolutely needed and as could not be produced by household industry or by the manufacturers of Cincinnati, Louisville, St. Louis, and other rising centers of industry in their midst. The southern half of the Old Northwest was, however, during this period advancing in prosperity more rapidly than the northern part. In the period between 1835 and 1839 the northern part had doubled her exports, while the southern part merely held her own. Between 1839 and 1844, however, while the northern section again doubled her exports, the southern part trebled hers. While the average price of winter wheat in Chicago declined from 68 cents per bushel in 1840 to 64 cents in 1844, the average price had risen in Cincinnati from 54 cents in 1840 to 69 cents in 1844.[47] In other words, conditions in the southern half of the Old Northwest had not only improved but were now better than in the northern part. It is usually admitted that a people who have suffered economic hardships and whose lot is slowly growing better are more prone to be restless and dissatisfied with the speed of the improvement than a people who are sinking into depression. This was true of the people in the Ohio valley. While in general the Whigs were willing to admit that conditions had improved, the Democrats were urging that conditions were worse or at best not so good as they should be.[48]

47. Aldrich, *Report*, pt. 2 [serial 3074, p. 2], pp. 60-62.
48. *Cong. Globe*, 28 Cong., 1 sess., vol. XIII, pt. 2, p. 94.

CHAPTER IV

The Old Northwest and the Expansion and Low-Tariff Movements, 1845-1849

THE VOTE for Polk in 1844 seemed to indicate that the campaign cry for the reannexation of Texas and the reoccupation of Oregon had struck a responsive chord in the South and in the West. By the passage, even before Polk's inauguration, of the resolution admitting Texas, the South had practically received her part of the political bargain of 1844. The Democratic administration now seemed honor bound to deliver Oregon. There now followed two or three lines of activity with respect to England and the Oregon question, one public and bold, another devious and half concealed, and another apparently unrelated. In fact, however, the lines of activity were intertwined and may have been one. Polk in his inaugural address asserted such an "unquestionable" claim to the country of the Oregon that it seemed that he would not hesitate at the cost of war.[1] To many westerners far removed from the reach of the British navy, this note in the address was welcome. To many of the commercial and manufacturing men of the northeast, now less interested than formerly in the trade between Oregon and the Far East, the address was disquieting. After allowing James Buchanan, the secretary of state, in July of 1845 to once more make the offer of the forty-ninth parallel on the ground that it had been so often made by preceding administrations that he should give the British an opportunity to accept this before resorting to extreme measures, and after this offer

---

1. Richardson, *Messages and Papers*, IV, 381.

had been offensively rejected in July by Richard Pakenham, the British minister to the United States, Polk caused Buchanan to formally withdraw the offer on August 30.[2] Now, in his first annual message of December, 1845, Polk reviewed the history of the negotiations, brought into bold relief the curt rejection of Buchanan's offer by the British and the equally curt withdrawal of the offer by the Americans, stated that he would now maintain our right to the whole of Oregon, and abruptly asked Congress to authorize him to serve notice upon the British government to terminate the treaty of joint occupancy of that region.[3] To many people both in America and in England this sounded warlike. If Polk had ever departed from the Democratic platform of 1844, he certainly seemed to be back on it now. Congress hesitated for a month before seriously taking up the matter and did not pass the resolution authorizing the President to serve notice on Great Britain until late in April of 1846.[4] Polk had sometime previous made it known to hesitating southern congressmen that he desired them to vote[5] with the western congressmen for the resolution. After the resolution had been passed in April of 1846, Buchanan apparently hesitated to draft the note to England but Polk urged him and helped him to do so.[6] All this looked as if Polk were deter-

2. J. K. Polk, *Diary of,* Milo M. Quaife, ed. (Chicago, 1910), I, 2, 11 (vol. VI in the *Chicago Historical Society Collections*); *U. S. House Ex. Docs.*, 29 Cong., 1 sess., vol. I, no. 2 [serial 480], pp. 169, 176, 192; John Quincy Adams, *Memoirs of* Charles Francis Adams, ed. (Philadelphia, 1877), XII, 248.
3. Richardson, *Messages and Papers,* IV, 395.
4. *The Statutes at Large and Treaties of the United States* (Boston, 1851), IX, 109.
5. Polk, *Diary,* I, 154, 155, 159.
6. Polk, *Diary,* I, 360, 363.

mined not to yield an inch to England without a fight. During the entire three or four months that the resolution was before Congress, many people in the United States believed that they were on the brink of war with England. In fear, people in increasing numbers clamored for the President to relent and accept a compromise. He continued to reassert his position. Only in the West did any considerable number of the people contemplate the approach of a war for Oregon with enthusiasm. They were accused by the other sections of the country of wanting war as a means of putting off their debt payment.

There had, however, been a second and entirely different line of activity paralleling this line. Soon after Polk's inaugural address Senator Thomas H. Benton had a conference with Buchanan and tried to convince him that America was not entitled to the northern part of Oregon as the Presidential address had implied. Polk apparently soon learned of Benton's views on the subject. It was soon after this that Polk on July 12, 1845, instructed Buchanan to renew the offer of the forty-ninth parallel which met with a curt rejection. It was not very long after Pakenham's rejection of the offer that Polk had knowledge of the fact that Lord Aberdeen, the British Secretary of Foreign Affairs, felt that the British minister had made a mistake in his curt rejection of the offer, and that if the offer of the forty-ninth parallel were renewed by the American government, the British government would give it consideration.[7] Many in America wanted Polk to renew the negotiations on this basis. Polk himself kept outwardly aloof from this and in his annual message of De-

---

7. Polk, *Diary*, I, 62, Oct. 21, 1845; Buchanan to McLane, Nov. 5, 1845, in *U. S. Sen. Docs.*, 29 Cong., 1 sess., vol. IX, no. 489 [serial 478], p. 33.

cember, 1845, and ever thereafter strenuously urged that he was ready to maintain the American right to all of Oregon. Things were not so bad as they seemed, however. A few days after the delivery of the message Polk had assurances from England that the British government was at the point of taking steps to renew the negotiations.[8] From earlier communications already referred to he was fairly sure that the British government would now be willing to negotiate on the basis of his former offer.[9] In view of this President Polk made it known to the British government that if the latter made a proposal he would submit it to the Senate for its advice.[10] This assurance was thoughtfully sent in the same dispatch that carried his belicose message to England. He must have felt convinced from the expressions in America of opposition to war that had followed his vigorous December message that the Senate would never assume the responsibility of advising the President to reject a British offer of compromise on the forty-ninth parallel. The American public of course knew little or nothing about this gesture for compromise now coming from the British side or of Polk's offer to submit a British proposal to the Senate. Throughout January and February of 1846, while Polk was urging Congress to authorize him to serve notice on the British government and Congress was still sweltering in a fever of excitement, his secretary of state, Mr. Buchanan, was sending one dispatch after another interspersed with private letters from himself and from the president to McLane, the American minister in England, emphasiz-

---

8. McLane to Buchanan, Dec. 1, 1845, in *U. S. Sen. Docs.*, 29 Cong., 1 sess., vol. IX, no. 489 [serial 478], p. 35.
9. Buchanan to McLane, Nov. 5, 1845, in *Ibid.*, p. 33.
10. Buchanan to McLane, Dec. 13, 1845, in *Ibid.*, p. 36.

ing the fact that Polk could make no offer but would submit to the Senate any respectable offer that the British government would care to make and that without the shadow of a doubt the Senate would advise acceptance of a proposition to compromise on the 49th parallel.[11] Two full months before Congress had finally been driven in April of 1846 into authorizing the notice, McLane had reported that without committing the president, he was certain that he could get the British government to make the offer of the forty-ninth parallel, and Buchanan had again assured him that the offer would be submitted to the Senate and that the Senate would undoubtedly advise acceptance.[12] When the notice to terminate the treaty was finally handed by McLane to Aberdeen, the latter had virtually agreed with McLane to submit through Pakenham a proposal which Buchanan had virtually agreed would be accepted.

There had yet been a third and a quite different line of activity paralleling this. To facilitate the movement of compromise on the Oregon question, the administration was ready to play with a gentleman's agreement for mutual tariff reduction in the two countries. Back in 1843 before Polk was a recognized candidate for the presidency, Duff Green was in England trying to feel out the Tory government and the Whig opposition on the possibility of a mutual reduction of the tariff both in England and in the United States as a means of making England more tolerant toward the anti-protectionist cotton producing slavery system in

11. Buchanan to McLane, in *Ibid.*, p. 37.
12. McLane to Buchanan, Feb. 3, 1846, in *Ibid.*, p. 39; Buchanan to McLane, Feb. 26, 1846, in *Ibid.*, p. 40; Buchanan to McLane, Feb. 26, 1846 (Private), in J. B. Moore, *Works of James Buchanan* (Philadelphia, 1909), II, 385.

America and more favorable toward a compromise on the Oregon question.[13] Lord John Russell assured Green that if the Whigs were returned to power, they would go for free trade.[14] The Tory ministry continued in power instead and reduced or removed the duties on a few American commodities chiefly from the South between 1842 and 1845. Sir Robert Peel had, of course, been inclining toward free trade in cabinet meetings at about this time, but Green apparently did not discover this and accomplished nothing officially.[15] He did, however, succeed at the time in arranging for press correspondence between the free trade papers of the two countries and this in a way helped to keep the idea of a tariff and Oregon agreement alive.[16] Moreover, Lord John Russell remained an outspoken champion of binding the two English speaking nations by such ties of friendship and commerce as would enable England to clothe America and be fed in turn by her. He maintained this attitude even while he was in nominal opposition to Peel.[17]

The day after Polk delivered his December message in 1846, his secretary of the treasury, Robert J. Walker, sub-

13. Calhoun to Duff Green, June 7, 1843, in *The Calhoun Correspondence*, II, 537; *Ibid.*, Sept. 8, 1843, II, 546; T. P. Martin, "Free Trade and the Oregon Questions," in *Facts and Factors in Economic History* (Cambridge, 1932), 479; Samuel Bonham, *The Oregon Treaty—A free-trade Deal* (Unpublished Masters Thesis at Indiana University, 1924), pp. 11-12.

14. Green to Calhoun, August 2, 1843, in *Calhoun Correspondence*, II, 847.

15. John Morley, *The Life of William Ewart Gladstone* (New York, 1911), I, 263.

16. Duff Green to Calhoun, September 29, 1843, in *The Calhoun Correspondence*, II, 884.

17. *Niles' Register*, LXIX, 401, quoting Speech at Glasgow, Jan. 12, 1846.

mitted a most interesting report on the tariff to Congress. In this report he enlarged upon the desirability of lowering the American customs duties, arguing that such a step would undoubtedly help the party in England that favored the repeal of the corn laws to succeed in its purpose.[18] An advance copy of this report probably given by Walker to Pakenham was forwarded by the latter in an official dispatch and reached England about the same time as did Polk's bellicose December message and as did Secretary Buchanan's instructions to the American minister in England that any proposal that the British government cared to make would be given careful consideration by the President.[19] As a result at the same time that Polk's threatening December message began to be discussed in England, the report of his secretary of the treasury began to be quoted and lauded by John Bright and others at the monster free trade gatherings in England. Bright urged that it be printed in every paper in the country and stated that it was America holding out the hand of friendship and that it would make war impossible.[20] Sir Robert Peel, the Prime Minister, liked Walker's report so well that in the latter part of January in his great speech introducing his motion for the repeal of the corn laws, he quoted approvingly and at length the American secretary's argument that the way to get your neighbors to take down their tariff barriers is to take down your own and not

18. *U. S. House Journal,* 29 Cong., 1 sess. [serial 479], p. 42; *Report from the Secretary of the Treasury,* Dec. 3, 1845, in *U. S. House Ex. Docs.,* 29 Cong., 1 sess., vol. II, no. 6 [serial 481], pp. 11, 13.

19. Hansard, *Parliamentary Debates,* 3rd Series, vol. LXXXIII, p. 422, 423; Buchanan to McLane, Dec. 13, 1845, in *U. S. Sen. Docs.,* 29 Cong., 1 sess., vol. IX, no. 489 [serial 478], p. 36; *Niles' Register,* LXIX, 416 and LXX, p. 1.

20. *Morning Chronicle,* Jan. 10, 1846, pp. 5, 6.

depend upon formal negotiations.[21] Aberdeen laid it before the House of Lords where it was ordered printed among the British documents.[22] No wonder, then, that Peel and Aberdeen were not unduly frightened at Polk's message. They no doubt believed that if England admitted American wheat into England duty free, as they now intended, it would go far toward appeasing the wheat producers of the West and cotton producers of the South even if the United States got a little less of the Oregon country than they had expected.[23] The British cabinet leaders could see further that the promise of reducing the American duties on British manufactured goods would help the ministry to carry the repeal of British duties on the American wheat which would have to pay for those British manufactured goods, which they expected to export in increased quantities to America, and would lessen the opposition of the manufacturers and freetraders in England to a peaceable adjustment on the Oregon question. In fact it later leaked out that Aberdeen during December and January had been discussing with McLane, Polk's minister to England, an understanding or agreement for the mutual reduction of the tariff in England and in America and for an accompanying compromise on the Oregon question.[24]

It had already leaked out that in the British cabinet

21. Hansard, *Parliamentary Debates*, 3rd Series, vol. LXXXIII, p. 278.
22. *Journal of House of Lords, 1846*, pp. 25, 47; *Session Papers of House of Lords, 1846*, XVIII, 107; Adams *Memoirs*, XII, 248; *Niles' Register*, LXIX, 400.
23. Charles C. F. Greville, *The Greville Memoirs, A Journal of the Reign of Queen Victoria*, Henry Reeve, ed., 2 vols. (New York, 1885), II, 72.
24. *Niles' Register*, Jan. 24, 1846, LXIX, 321.

meetings in early December of 1845 there had been much discussion of Oregon and of tariff, and that Peel and Aberdeen had then practically decided for a repeal of the corn laws. Moreover, the leak seems to have been intentional in order that the American government might keep pace in its own tariff reduction propaganda. Aberdeen seems to have deliberately and in violation of the tradition of cabinet secrecy allowed the editor of the *London Times* to publish some of these cabinet secrets in order that the interesting news might be wafted across to America and encourage developments there.[25] A month later the *London Times* gave a detailed account of how the American West should be won over from its belligerent support of Polk's unreasonable demands for the whole of Oregon by giving them a free entrance into English ports for their surplus grain and meat. From the confidential relationship existing between Aberdeen and the editor of the *Times,* one is safe in assuming that the paper in this case expressed the hopes and plans of the British Secretary of Foreign Affairs.[26] Viscount Morpeth on being elected to the House of Commons early in 1846 made a speech to his constituency in which he outlined the whole scheme of the arrangement and gave a glowing description of the beneficent and quieting effects that tariff reform would have upon the two peoples. He made light of the war cloud threatening England from the American West and believed that it would speedily disappear if the discontented people would be given a market in England for their surplus wheat.[27] Late in January of 1846 when many American Congressmen were still apparently afraid that Polk's

25. Greville, *Memoirs,* II, 46-48.
26. *London Times,* Jan. 3, 1846; *Niles Register,* LXIX, 339.
27. *Morning Chronicle,* Feb. 5, p. 5; *Niles' Register,* LXX, 17.

attitude would bring the United States into war with England, the speech from the throne in that country calmly assured members of Parliament that there was reason to believe that the Oregon question would soon be amicably adjusted. When members in Parliament asked Peel to explain the difference of tone in the Queen's speech and the president's message, he merely assured them that while Britain was ready to defend her rights, he did not believe this would be necessary.[28]

During January and February of 1846 Congressmen and editors of newspapers in America gradually began to see through the whole scheme and to call attention to it. Caleb B. Smith of Indiana as early as the first part of January expressed his misgivings about Polk's willingness to live up to his declarations on the Oregon question. A Congressman from New York during the same month referred to the efforts of Aberdeen and Peel to prepare through their newspapers the English people for compromise. A member of Congress from Tennessee expressed the belief that there had been far more diplomatic correspondence between the two governments with respect to Oregon than had as yet come to light and he proposed to know the correspondence before they authorized Polk to serve notice on the English government. A member of the House from New York expressed his disapproval of the effort to purchase access to the English market for our grain and breadstuffs.[29] A staunch advocate of the protective tariff referred to the advice of the Secretary of the Treasury to secure the repeal of the English tariff by repealing our own, to the favorable reception of this

28. Hansard, *Debates*, 3rd Series, vol. LXXXIII, pp. 3, 10, 15, 18.
29. *Congressional Globe*, 29 Cong., 1 sess., XV, 159, 261, 313, and Appendix, pp. 179, 343, 459, 753.

advice by the British ministry, and to the efforts on both sides of the Atlantic to change fundamentally the policy of the United States. The northeastern advocates of protection had several arguments against reduction of the tariff by which they attempted to win over the Congressmen from the Northwest. They argued that a reduction of the tariff would result in a reduction of the government's revenue. There would thus be less money to be used on improving the lines of transportation in and from the West. Without this the westerner might still be unable to get his surplus grain to the English market even after that market was made more favorable. They argued that the only change resulting from repeal of the corn laws in England would be that the western wheat would be exported through New York City instead of through Canada and that the westerner would lose in part the market in the northeastern industrial towns of the United States as they declined through industrial competition with England. Although these rumors and assertions concerning an impending compromise were filtering through in January, February, and March, not until the latter part of April did Congress pass the resolution to authorize the president to serve upon the English government the notice that was supposed to precipitate matters. It is difficult now to see how it could have been expected to precipitate anything but the compromise. The important newspapers both in England and in the United States by February treated the matter of securing the English market for American grain and cotton by repealing the tariff of '42 and yielding a part of the exaggerated claim to Oregon as little more than an open secret.[30]

30. *Niles' Register*, LXIX, 341, 370, 384, 385, 400, 412, 416, in some cases quoting other leading papers.

To what extent Polk was responsible for this second and third line of activity carried on by men appointed by him and responsible to him might be a matter for argument. Senator Benton was convinced that the president was anxious to compromise on the forty-ninth parallel, and that the president was underhandedly encouraging him and Senator W. H. Haywood of North Carolina to speak for a compromise which the Democratic administration openly could not encourage because of its campaign promises.[31] Haywood in the Senate one day stated that as a close friend of the president he was in a position to say that the president would compromise on the forty-ninth parallel but at a later day under fire of the western Democrats stated that he based this statement on Polk's messages.[32] No doubt Polk had in the meantime pointed out to Haywood that the messages did not preclude compromise. It is certainly true that when Polk was urging Congress to pass the resolution authorizing him to bring things to a crisis by serving notice upon England to terminate the treaty of 1827, he had assurances from McLane that the latter could get Aberdeen to offer the forty-ninth line without committing Polk.[33] He also had made it known to a number of senators that if such a proposal came from the British foreign office, it would be submitted to the Senate for preliminary advice before the president committed himself.[34] That Polk was anxious to have the tariff lowered and that he was ready to use this as a

31. T. H. Benton, *Thirty Years' View* (New York, 1856), II, 663, 666, 674.
32. *Cong. Globe*, 29 Cong., 1 sess., pp. 456, 458.
33. McLane to Buchanan, Feb. 3, 1846, and Buchanan to McLane, Feb. 26, 1846, in *U. S. Sen. Docs.*, 29 Cong., 1 sess., vol. IX, no. 489 [serial 478], pp. 39, 41.
34. Polk, *Diary*, I, 139, 249, 287.

means of getting the English to make concessions on the Oregon question is proved by his own words.[35] Whether or not he in turn was influenced to make concessions to the British on the Oregon question because they were willing to repeal their duties on American agricultural exports is not proved. That is, he was clearly in favor of a tariff-Oregon agreement, but whether or not he was in favor of the particular arrangement that was made is not clear. He seems to have had some hope that a reduction of the American tariff and the payment of a lump sum of money for the Hudson's Bay Company's interest would result both in the repeal of the English corn laws and in the English relinquishment of all of Oregon. Polk undoubtedly knew that due to the crop failures in Europe, the British government would be forced into a policy of reducing duties on American wheat at least temporarily anyway. He also knew that the reduction of American duties on British manufactured goods in turn would be greatly appreciated by British manufacturers and statesmen. He also knew that while the English were dependent upon the American West for food, they would be loath to engage in a war over Oregon. But whether Polk's policy of looking John Bull in the eye, even if the southern Democrats had supported him in that as firmly as did most of the western Democrats, could have won any more of Oregon than he got is improbable. The business-like Peel and the pacific Aberdeen knew perfectly well how far the Americans would force them to go and how far British political opposition would permit them to go.[36] Whatever may have been the president's part in the agreement—if

35. Polk, *Diary*, I, 191.
36. Frederick Merk, "British Party Politics and Oregon," in *American Historical Review*, XXXVII, 655-56.

what transpired may be called an agreement—he could not even with the consent of the Senate through his treaty-making power reduce the tariff rate. This part of the arrangement would have to be delivered by Congress. It was apparently believed that, if the Oregon boundary settlement, the mutual reduction of the tariff, and the measure for granting free land to the Oregon settlers were kept moving along together, each would secure more votes than would otherwise have been the case. Benton, a Democrat, had been given to understand that he was to line up as many of the western Whigs for the Oregon treaty as he could. He saw them all and was able to assure Polk on the night before the treaty came to a vote that the Whig senators would all be in their places and vote right.[37] The bill for the repeal of the English corn laws had passed the House of Commons on May 15.[38] The Senate advised the President to accept the treaty proposed by the British government in settlement of the Oregon question on June 12 and ratified the treaty on June 18.[39] The Walker tariff passed the Senate on July 28.[40] The news that the Senate had advised President Polk to accept the Oregon treaty reached England on the day that the repeal of the corn laws passed the House of Lords, June 25, and was announced to Parliament by Peel and his colleague in the dramatic speeches with which they retired from office four days later. The bill for free lands to the Oregon settlers failed to pass the Senate.[41] All the Democratic senators

37. Benton, *Thirty Years' View*, II, 675.
38. *Journal of the House of Commons*, vol. CI, pt. 1, p. 712.
39. *U. S. Senate Executive Journal* (Washington, 1887), VII, 89, 95.
40. *U. S. Senate Journal,* 29 Cong., 1 sess. [serial 469], p. 454, H. B. no. 384.
41. *U. S. Senate Journal,* 29 Cong., 1 sess. [serial 469], pp. 382, 693, S. B. no. 223.

of the West except Benton of Missouri and Turney of Tennessee voted against the Oregon treaty, some of them, no doubt, because they were still opposed and some because they, as possibly was the case with Polk, could not afford to go back upon their previous political promises. But, of course, it was known that the treaty could be ratified without their votes and it was. One may say that ratification was carried by the southern democracy with the support of two western Democrats and of the Whig senators including those from the West.[42] The tariff bill then long hung in the balance. Charges were made of attempts by British agents and by members of the president's cabinet to bribe and to influence Congressmen.[43] The measure for reducing the tariff was finally passed in the Senate by a majority of one vote. The two senators from Texas, who had been allowed to take their seats after the session had begun, voted for the measure. The antiprotectionist South thus speedily benefited by the admission of that state. The Democratic senators of the West also voted for the measure. The tariff measure was thus carried by the southern democracy with the support of all the Democrats from the West and of the few Democrats from the Northeast and of one western Whig.[44]

No doubt this was considered by some as a shrewd political adjustment. There was apparently something for each of the sections of the country. The grain growing

---

42. *U. S. Senate Executive Journal,* VII, 95; Senator Jarnagin, a Whig of Tennessee, did not vote. One northeastern Democrat voted for the treaty and one southern Democrat voted against it.

43. *Niles' Register,* LXX, 305.

44. *U. S. Senate Journal,* 29 Cong., 1 sess. [serial 469], p. 454; Jarnagin, a western Whig of Tennessee, voted for the tariff bill while Haywood, a North Carolina Democrat and personal friend of Polk's, resigned rather than vote for it.

West was to have as much of Oregon as it then needed and free access to the English markets for its surplus grain. If the people of the West could sell their grain to England at a good price, fewer would need to move to Oregon. The industrial and commercial Northeast was to escape the devastations of war with England and was to profit by the increased commerce but would have less opportunity to expand her manufactures. The South was to have an opportunity to send more cotton to England in return for taking more of England's manufactured articles under a reduced American tariff. But not all sections and parts of sections were alike enthusiastic in the reception of this compromise. The compromise got most of its support in the West and South, both in vote and in argument. But this was true only of the sections as a whole. Individuals refused to vote with their sections. Calhoun, although co-operating little with Polk, earnestly worked for all the different measures that constituted the compromise.[45] Adams of New England was very sure that the whole manipulation was of more injury to his section than of benefit.[46] Benton, the westerner, had worked consistently for the lowering of the tariff and for the ratification of the treaty. But not all the members from the West and the Northwest were satisfied. With some a continuation of opposition to some parts of the arrangement was probably mere playing of politics, but with others it was the sincere expression of what they considered their interest.

For instance, Senator Edward Hannegan of Indiana, although a freetrader, continued to denounce and to op-

45. Calhoun to T. G. Clemson, Dec. 26, 1845 and Jan. 23, 1846, in *The Calhoun Correspondence*, II, 674, 680.
46. Adams, *Memoirs*, XII, 248.

pose Polk for having deserted the West." He had some reasons for his discontent. He reflected the interests of the Ohio valley rather than of the Great Lakes region of the Old Northwest. The northern half of the Old Northwest was for some years to come in a better position to profit by the arrangement than was the southern half. It was naturally adapted to producing wheat more cheaply than the southern half, was nearer the lakes with their contact with the northeastern outlet, and was thus in a position to enjoy the effect on prices brought about by the permission to send its wheat to England practically duty free. The lower half of the Old Northwest was but little benefited. It could, generally speaking, not produce wheat as cheaply as the northern part. It would have to pay the additional freight charges from the vicinity of the Ohio river to the Lake region, a distance of some three hundred miles by rail or canal. The upper region kept increasing its production and thereby kept the price so low that the southern half could never profitably enter into the export northeastward to any considerable extent. As before, it continued to supply its own needs and to supply the needs of the South where the cheap river freight rate added very little to the price.

The great arrangement of 1846 for the country as a whole was immediately beneficial, more remotely harmful, and still more remotely beneficial. That is, the immediate result was to settle the Oregon question without war with England and leave America free to annex a part of Mexico. More remotely, however, the lowering of the tariff contributed still further to the economic separation of the northern grain growing region from the southern cotton growing

47. *Cong. Globe*, 29 Cong., 1 sess., XV, 460, 1198; *U. S. Senate Executive Journal*, VII, 94.

region and to the uniting of each of those two regions more closely to England commercially than to one another. With England taking cotton and wheat in return for her manufactured articles, the northern grain region continued to stretch farther and farther toward the northwest, and the southern cotton region continued to reach out ever farther to the southwest. It was weighting the two extremes. The *Charleston Mercury* stated that if the tariff of 1842 had remained in effect for ten years, the South would have ceased to export raw cotton. As it was, the cotton planters became more dependent upon slavery and tried to spread out through Texas and into Mexico. The northeastern men had to meet British competition in manufacturing or move to the northwest along with the incoming foreigners, or get into the business of transporting western and southern commodities. The economic divergence between the extreme North and the extreme South continued to increase until the Civil War. The southern part of the Old Northwest and the states of Kentucky and Tennessee and Missouri saw these currents pass them on either side with little effect.

Still more remotely, however, the arrangement of 1846 largely determined that when the Civil War did come the North and not the South would be victorious. The South thought cotton was king in England in 1861, whereas it was really wheat. When England repealed her corn laws, she deliberately made herself dependent upon the outside world for food. After the Civil War had begun, she found herself more in need of the wheat of the Northwest than of the cotton of the South. The freetrade humanitarian group in England were and remained in pretty close and sympathetic touch with the grain growers and adherents of free labor in the northern part of the United States.

The fact, too, that the southern part of the Old Northwest did not directly participate in the movement of the two extremes played its decisive part in the saving of the Union as will be later seen.

While these important arrangements were occupying the attention of the leaders at the national capital, one of those leaders was engaged in furthering a little arrangement between the South and the West on his own account. The leader was Calhoun and the occasion was the Memphis convention of 1845. The movement, at first a purely local affair, grew until it attracted considerable attention and then passed into history without any tangible results. As an evidence, however, of what men were trying to do, it is interesting. Nearly all the southern and the western states were represented at the convention. They appointed committees on connecting the Great Lakes with the Mississippi, on connecting by rail the southern Atlantic ports with the lower Mississippi, on building military roads from the lower Mississippi westward, on improving the western rivers, on sponsoring manufacturing in the South, and on furthering several other projects. Calhoun's journey to the convention and his address there were looked upon at the time as a preparation for his candidacy for the presidency in 1848 by combining the votes of the Northwest with the South. Calhoun was even able to reconcile this vast scheme of improving the western rivers with his strict constructionist views by arguing that the Mississippi system was like a great inland sea that could be improved only by the national government.[48] It should be noted,

---

48. St. George L. Sioussat, "Memphis as a Gateway to the West," in *Tennessee Historical Magazine*, III (Mar. and June, 1917), 96 passim; *Reports of Select and Spec. Com.* (Washington, 1887), III, 18, in *U. S. Senate Reports*, 29 Cong., 1 sess., no. 14 [serial 477], p. 1.

however, that the projects that were emphasized by the convention and by Calhoun were not to constitute altogether an equal bargain between the West and the South. Southern projects predominated. Ten years before when Hayne wanted to build a transportation line from Charleston to Cincinnati, Calhoun wanted to direct it toward the confluence of the Ohio and the Mississippi; but now the project was to build such a transportation line to a point as far south as Memphis and then to continue it westward. The South was to be linked together by a sectional east and west line and the Northwest was then to be linked to the South if practicable. No wonder that Calhoun for a long time was slow about supporting Polk in his Oregon project until he was practically forced into line. He had a project of his own, in which the concession made to the Northwest by the South would have been less than even Polk gave. Calhoun was too late anyway. It should have been in the days of Hayne. While Calhoun was feebly laboring to restore Charleston and other southeastern ports to their former relative importance in the foreign trade, New York City was fast becoming the one great outlet for all American exports except cotton. As early as 1821 New York had passed all of her rivals in the total amount of foreign trade, but in the later forties appeared the evidence that she was to completely dominate in that trade. New Orleans, due largely to her cotton, still exported a trifle more goods of American production than did New York, but New York imported nine times as much during that year as did New Orleans.[49] Many causes were operating to make it so.

49. *U. S. House Ex. Docs.*, 31 Cong., 1 sess., vol. VII, no. 15 [serial 576], p. 304.

In the forties was established the system of ocean steamship liners which sailed on schedule between definite ports on opposite sides of the Atlantic. Due to the application of steam and of the water thermometer the liners could cross the ocean in the path of the gulf stream, whereas the sailing vessels had formerly crossed in the path of the trade winds farther south. New York harbor, as the tidewater outlet for the Erie canal, had already outdistanced the other Atlantic ports. It was now selected as the terminal for the sea liners. The liners limited by their schedules could not delay their sailings and frequently cut freight rates to get a full cargo. These lower freight rates and the certainty and regularity of transportation facilities caused more and more of the products of the interior to seek the New York market.

Government subsidies to mail carriers helped the process. New York City in both the American and in the British government subsidy contracts entered into during the last half of the forties was given more attention than were all the other American ports combined.[50] In 1846-49 England repealed her corn laws and American wheat could be introduced into England by payment of only the revenue duty. From 1843 to 1846 American wheat and corn had been imported into Canada on paying a small duty and re-exported to Great Britain as Canadian wheat or corn, by paying a nominal duty. If the same wheat was shipped from New York to Great Britain during those years, it naturally had to pay the English import duty. This resulted in considerable quantities of American wheat going during those

50. 28 Cong., 2 sess., ch. 69, in *Public Statutes at Large*, V, 749; 29 Cong., 2 sess., ch. 62, in *U. S. Statutes at Large*, IX, 187; *U. S. House Ex. Docs.*, 30 Cong., 1 sess., vol. V, no. 51 [serial 518], pp. 6-11; *British Parliamentary Papers*, 1849, vol. XII, no. 571, pp. 132-33.

earlier years by way of the Welland canal and the St. Lawrence river. The St. Lawrence route now, by the repeal of the English corn laws, lost this advantage over New York and not only the American wheat went out from the American ports, 1846-49, but a considerable part of the Canadian wheat went that way also. The entire cost of sending a bushel of wheat from western Canada to Liverpool by way of New York was less than by Montreal.[51] Added to the change in the British tariff laws was the fact that the New York harbor was not troubled with the ice as was the St. Lawrence in the winter. Finally there always seems to be a tendency toward aggregation, so that after a city or port has reached a certain preponderance, everything is irresistibly swept into the vortex. New Orleans and Charleston along with other ports declined relatively as New York grew in importance.

During this period the transportation lines from the gateways of the West to the exterior markets saw no significant change or improvement, but several developments in transportation lines within the West that might have had an influence on the production and on the internal and external commerce of that region took place. In 1840 was opened the Pennsylvania and Ohio canal which connected the Ohio canal with the Pennsylvania and Erie canal. The Pennsylvania and Erie canal connected Lake Erie with the Ohio river at Beaver, Pennsylvania.[52] In 1845 the Miami Extension, connecting Dayton on the Miami canal with Defiance on the Wabash and Erie canal, was completed.[53] A canal route was thus opened north and south through

51. Keefer, *Canals of Canada*, 26.
52. McClelland and Huntington, *Ohio Canals*, 40.
53. *Documents to the 44th General Assembly of the State of Ohio, 1845-46*, vol. X, pt. 1, p. 293.

western Ohio connecting Cincinnati on the Ohio river with Toledo on Lake Erie, and completing the third of the connecting links between the Ohio river and Lake Erie. Another development was the opening in 1848 of the Illinois and Michigan canal, connecting Peru on the Illinois river, a tributary of the Mississippi, with Chicago on Lake Michigan.[54] A third new development was the completion during this period of several railroads in the Northwest. One in 1849 connected New Buffalo on the southeastern shore of Lake Michigan with Detroit on the river connecting Lake Huron with Lake Erie.[55] A second rail route by 1848 connected Cincinnati on the Ohio with Sandusky on Lake Erie.[56] Besides these two rail routes that had both their terminals on great waterways there had been constructed a number of railroads that ran from some port on a waterway back into the interior of the Old Northwest. One such road had been opened in 1847 from Madison on the Ohio river northwestward for nearly a hundred miles into central Indiana.[57] Another such road ran westward from Chicago for some ten miles,[58] a third ran northeastward into Michigan from Detroit,[59] a fourth ran westward from Monroe and Toledo on Lake Erie into southern Michigan

---

54. *Report of the Trustees of the Illinois and Michigan canal for the year ending Nov. 30, 1848*, in *Reports made to the Fifteenth [Sixteenth] General Assembly of the State of Illinois* (Springfield, 1849), House Reports, p. 374.

55. *Third Annual Report of the Directors of the Michigan Central Railroad to the Stockholders* (Boston, 1849), 14.

56. The Little Miami from Cincinnati to Springfield, and the Mad River and Erie from Springfield to Sandusky. *Sixth Annual Report of the Little Miami Railroad Co.* (Cincinnati, 1848), 2.

57. The Madison and Indianapolis.

58. The Galena and Chicago Union.

59. The Detroit and Milwaukee.

for some fifty miles,[60] while a fifth ran southward from Sandusky.[61] The Wabash and Erie Canal had also been extended farther into Indiana reaching Terre Haute in that state in 1849.[62] So many breaks continued to occur in the lower end of this canal, however, that it was not used for transportation south of Covington and not extensively south of Lafayette,[63] its terminus in 1844.

The total exports from the West in the period between 1844 and 1849 showed almost as rapid an increase as they had in the period between 1839 and 1844. The total exports in 1849 were again almost double those of 1844. The total export of flour had almost doubled and that of wheat had increased by nearly a third. But when the flour is counted as wheat at the rate of five bushels to the barrel, it is found that the total surplus of wheat and wheat products exported amounted to more than twenty-one million bushels and lacked only a little of being double that of the preceding period. The total export of corn as such more than quadrupled, while that of pork almost doubled and that of whiskey a little more than doubled. But if the pork and whiskey are counted as corn at the rate of fifteen bushels and eight bushels to the barrel, respectively, it is found that the total amount of corn produced for export in 1849 amounted to more than twenty-eight million bushels and was almost exactly double that of 1844. The total export of some minor commodities like wool also

60. The Michigan Southern.
61. The Sandusky and Mansfield.
62. *Annual Report of the Trustees of the Wabash and Erie canal for 1849*, in *Documents to the General Assembly of Indiana at the Thirty-Third session* (Indianapolis, 1850), pt. 2, no. 11, pp. 254, 259.
63. *Annual Report of Trustees of the Wabash and Erie canal for 1849*, pp. 251, 268, 273, 298-304, tables of commodities cleared from each toll station in 1849.

doubled. But the total export of beef lacked a considerable amount of again doubling, and the export of tobacco actually declined by about a third of its former quantity.

The three great gateways of the Old Northwest, with one or two exceptions, reflected this doubling of exports of individual commodities. Thus through the northeastern gateway the export of flour, pork, and beef had doubled; but the export of whiskey had increased fifty times, that of corn eighteen times, and that of wool four times, while that of wheat had increased only twenty-five per cent. Through the eastern outlet the export of pork and wool had doubled, that of whiskey had increased seven times, that of flour and tobacco both had declined, and that of wheat, never of much importance, had practically ceased. Through the southern gateway the export of wheat, flour, corn, and pork had doubled, but the export of whiskey had increased by only fifty per cent, and that of tobacco had declined by thirty-seven per cent.

The percentage of the total export of each commodity from the interior that went out through each of the three great outlets in 1849 in general was about the same as in 1844. In spite of the fact that the export of wheat from the interior to New Orleans had more than doubled during the period, of a total export of more than five and a half million bushels of wheat from the interior 92% still went northeast and the remainder south. In 1844 about 96% had gone northeast. The export of flour to the south as well as to the northeast had doubled since 1844, but the ratios between the ports had changed little. Of a total export of more than three million barrels of flour from the interior 63% went northeast, 31% south, and 5% east. These are almost the exact percentages of 1844. If the flour be reckoned as wheat, it will be found that 70% of the total of 21 million bushels of wheat surplus of the Old Northwest went northeastward in 1849 instead of 76% as in 1844. From the Census of 1850, giving the statistics for the wheat harvested in 1849, it appears that the western states with a population of nearly seven and a half millions produced about forty-seven and a half million bushels of wheat. It was assumed that ordinarily one person ate four to seven bushels of wheat per year. If, accordingly, twenty-nine and a half million bushels were consumed by the people of that region, the surplus for export would be only eighteen million bushels. The region as a whole, however, exported twenty-one million. Not all parts of the region, however, produced a surplus. Kentucky and Tennessee would each lack about two million bushels of having the required four bushels per person, Missouri had a paltry surplus of two hundred fifty thousand bushels, Illinois south of the National road would scarcely have enough to feed herself, Indiana south of the same line would have only a half million to spare, and Ohio south of the line would have only a million and a half. Northern Ohio had a surplus of five million; northern Indiana, nearly two; northern Illinois, six; Michigan, over three; Wisconsin, three; and Iowa, almost one, making for that northern area a total surplus of about twenty million bushels. Practically all of the surplus wheat and flour produced south of the National road, and in addition a few hundred thousand bushels from Missouri, about a million bushels each from Iowa, from the Illinois river and Rock river in northern Illinois, and from the middle Wabash river in northern Indiana found its way to the southern gateway. It is possible that quantities of the surplus produced in the northern part of the West went to make up the deficiency in Kentucky and Tennessee but not very probable. It is more probable that the consumption of wheat per capita in the northern section was considerably above four bushels, while the consumption in Kentucky and Tennessee, due to liking of cornbread, was considerably below.[64]

In 1849 twice as much corn went to New Orleans as in 1844, but to the northeast there went eighteen times as much in 1849 as in 1844. Of a total export of nearly six million bushels of corn in 1849, 60% now went northeast and 40% went south, whereas in 1844 almost 90% had gone south. But with this, the superior showing of the northeastern outlet was exhausted. Of the total export of tobacco 78% went south, 20% east, and 2% northeast. While the quantity of pork exported by the three outlets in 1849 was in each case about double that of 1844, of a total of nearly one and a half million barrels exported in 1849, 80% still went south, 11% went east, and 9% went northeast. These were practically the same ratios as in 1844.

From the census of 1850 it would appear that the million and a half barrels of pork exported annually from the West at that time represented the larger part of an annual surplus production of about three and a half million hogs in that region. After making due allowance for supplying the needs of their own people and for a relatively small number of hogs driven through the mountain roads from eastern Kentucky and Tennessee, the latter two states would each furnish a fourth of the swine for the pork export. Missouri and Illinois and Indiana would each pro-

64. I. D. Andrews estimated the per capita consumption at seven bushels and the St. Louis merchants estimated it at four bushels. *U. S. Sen. Ex. Docs.*, 32 Cong., 1 sess., no. 112 [serial 622], p. 709; Memorial of St. Louis Union Merchants' Exchange. There was probably that much difference in the average consumption for persons living in the Great Lakes region and those in the vicinity of the Ohio river.

duce a little more than an eighth. Ohio, Michigan, and Wisconsin would not produce enough to afford their own population the normal consumption of pork. Of a total of nearly two hundred thousand barrels of whiskey 67% went south, 25% went northeast, and 8% went east. The shipments of whiskey through the northeastern and eastern outlets, while still relatively small, represented practically a clear gain since 1844. If the pork and whiskey be considered as corn, it will be found that 70% of the total of twenty-eight million bushels of corn surplus went southward in 1849 in place of 82% as in 1844. It is interesting to note then that the northeastern outlet took almost exactly 70% of the total of the wheat-flour surplus while the southern outlet took 70% of the total of the corn-pork-whiskey surplus in 1849.[65]

Of the million barrels of flour received at New Orleans, St. Louis forwarded between a third and a half and Cincinnati about a sixth.[66] Cincinnati's absolute contribution had grown slightly, but the part contributed by her had declined relatively, as in 1844 she had contributed about a fourth of the total. Of the million barrels of pork and bacon received at New Orleans, Cincinnati still forwarded considerably over a fourth and St. Louis about a sixth.

---

65. Statistical tables based upon: *N. Y. Assembly Docs., 1850*, vol. VI, no. 140, pp. 113, 117; Barton, *Sketch*, 40, 80; *Census of 1860*, Agriculture, p. CXLVIII; *Monthly Summary of Commerce and Finance*, January, 1900, in *U. S. House Docs.*, 56 Cong., 1 sess., vol. LV, no. 15, pt. 7 [serial 3942], p. 1960; *Statistics of Foreign and Domestic Commerce*, in *U. S. Sen. Ex. Docs.*, 38 Cong., 1 sess., vol. I, no. 55 [serial 1176], p. 162; *U. S. House Ex. Docs.*, 50 Cong., 1 sess., vol. XX, no. 6, pt. 2 [serial 2552], pp. 200-18; *DeBow's Review*, VII, 420; Hunt, *Merchants' Magazine*, XXII, 204 and XIV, 194 and XL, 734.

66. *Western Journal*, II, 133 and V, 55; *DeBow's Review*, VII, 179; *A Review of the Commerce of St. Louis for 1849*, p. 16; Hunt, *Merchants' Magazine*, XXIII, 542.

Of five million bushels of wheat exported through the northeastern gateway, Chicago forwarded about 39%,[67] Milwaukee 20%,[68] Cleveland, Sandusky, and Toledo each 15%.[69] Of the two million barrels of flour exported northeastward, Cleveland sent 20%, Toledo and Milwaukee 7% each, Chicago and Sandusky 3% each. Of the three and a half million bushels of corn almost 60% went forward from Toledo, 18% from Chicago, and 15% from Cleveland. Of the one hundred and twenty thousand barrels of pork and bacon exported northeast, Toledo sent 30%, Cleveland 18%, and Chicago 15%. Of the seventy thousand barrels of beef exported northeastward Chicago sent 71%, Cleveland and Toledo each sent almost 15%. It is interesting to observe that Cleveland's share of the northeastern exports had now relatively declined to 20% of the total from 50% in 1844 and 80% in 1839. Chicago now sent twice as much wheat and Toledo twice the pork and four times as much corn as Cleveland. Speaking very generally, Chicago forwarded almost half the wheat and three-fourths of the beef, while Toledo forwarded almost two-thirds of the corn and one-third of the pork. This does not mean that the exports of Cleveland had declined in the absolute but that she had not gained as rapidly as the more western ports.

The new lines of transportation in the interior had conferred local benefits and stimulated settlement and pro-

67. I. D. Andrews, *Report on Trade and Commerce*, in *U. S. Sen. Ex. Docs.*, 32 Cong., 1 sess., vol. XI, no. 112 [serial 622], p. 218.
68. *Monthly Summary of Commerce and Finance*, Jan. 1900, p. 1960-62; *U. S. Census, 1860*, Agriculture, p. CL.
69. Andrews, *Report*, 168, 177; *Thirteenth Annual Report of the Board of Public Works of the State of Ohio for the year 1849*, in *Documents to the Forty-eighth General Assembly of Ohio* (Columbus, 1850), vol. XIV, pt. 2, no. 6, pp. 24, 78.

duction in certain localities. The Miami extension canal was literally built around and through Indian villages."[70] It was not long, however, before much of that part of northwestern Ohio was settled and under cultivation. The new routes of transportation, however, changed the general course or direction of the outflow of commodities very little. The completion of the Miami Extension canal opened another through route between the Ohio river and Lake Erie, but it was little used as a through route. The wheat, flour, and corn from Dayton and all places south of there, and the pork and beef from as far north as Piqua and beyond continued to go southward to Cincinnati just as they had done before the Miami Extension had connected the Miami canal with the Wabash and Erie.[71] The same was true of the rail route that paralleled this canal route. The Little Miami road made connection at Springfield with the Mad river and Sandusky road, but a large proportion of the exports put upon the Little Miami road went south to Cincinnati while those that were put upon the Mad river and Sandusky road were carried north to Sandusky. That such a condition applied to the Ohio canal between Portsmouth and Cleveland in 1844 has already been alluded to above. The condition was still about the same in 1849. The dividing point upon the Ohio canal for commodities going north and for those coming south had moved a little farther north by 1849. The situation with respect to wheat and flour remained unchanged, all the former going north and the latter going north from all places above Circleville about fifty miles from Ports-

70. Knapp, *History of the Maumee Valley*, 337.
71. *Thirteenth Annual Report of the Board of Public Works of Ohio for 1849*, in *Documents to Forty-eighth General Assembly of Ohio*, vol. XIV, pt. 2, no. 6, pp. 587, 62 et seq.

mouth on the Ohio river. The dividing point for corn and tobacco was in 1849 at Carrol, for pork at Newark, and for beef and whiskey at Columbus.[72] The three last-named places were a little south of central Ohio on or near the National pike. Taking Newark as a point dividing the canal into equal halves, one finds that of the total quantity of commodities put upon the canal, one-ninth of the wheat, one-seventh of the beef, three-eighths of the whiskey, one-half of the corn, two-thirds of the tobacco, and five-sixths of the pork was put upon the canal south of this midway point. That is, although in 1849 as in 1844 practically all the wheat cleared over the canal went northward, practically all was shipped from the northern half of the canal; while nearly all the pork cleared over the canal went southward, nearly all was shipped from points on the southern half of the canal. The extension of the Wabash and Erie canal southward from Lafayette to Terre Haute by 1849 had not materially changed the course of trade in that region. Products of the vicinity of Lafayette went northeastward as formerly by canal to Toledo,[73] while the products of the region between Lafayette and Terre Haute continued to pass down the Wabash river, because freight rates from that region to New York were still lower by way of New Orleans than by way of Buffalo.[74] The opening of the Madison and Indianapolis railroad did not materially affect the general direction of commerce in that region. When the road was built, a con-

72. *Thirteenth Annual Report of the Board of Public Works of Ohio for the year 1849*, p. 54 et seq.
73. *Annual Report of the trustees of the Wabash and Erie Canal, for 1849*, in *Documents of the General Assembly of Indiana at the Thirty-third session* (Indianapolis, 1850), pt. 2, no. 11, pp. 298-302.
74. *Annual Report of the Trustees of the Wabash and Erie Canal for 1849*, pp. 259-61; *Western Journal*, V, 256, quoting *Vincennes Gazette*.

siderable proportion of the arable land through which it ran had not been put under production,[75] but the surplus that had before 1847 been produced south of Indianapolis had always sought the Ohio river and after the building of the road continued to do so down to the days of the Civil War. The road, of course, stimulated settlement and production along its line.[76] The opening of the Illinois and Michigan canal in 1848 changed the general direction of commerce less than was anticipated. It conferred local benefit but never played any important part in through traffic between Lake Michigan and the Mississippi river.[77] The region through which the canal ran and which was near the lake had exported its commodities by wagon to Lake Michigan from the time of settlement and continued to do so. The region along the canal at some distance from the lake was just in the process of settlement while the canal was being constructed and the proposed opening of the canal speeded up the settlement.[78] This region began to produce a surplus by the time the canal was completed and began to export for the most part northward. Without the canal its products would probably have followed the Illinois river, the upper end of which the canal paralleled,

75. John Brough, *A Brief History of the Madison and Indianapolis Railroad* (New York, 1852), 12.

76. Brough, *Brief History of Madison and Indianapolis Railroad*, 10, for tables of quantity of freight carried each year, 1846-52.

77. James W. Putnam, *The Illinois and Michigan Canal* (Chicago, 1918), 120 (vol. X of Chicago Historical Society *Collections*). Gives somewhat different conclusion.

78. *Seventh Annual Report of the Commissioners of the Illinois and Michigan Canal to the General Assembly,* in *Reports made to the Senate and House of Representatives of the State of Illinois,* 13th General Assembly, vol. I, House Reports (Springfield, 1842), 65; *Report of the Illinois and Michigan Canal* (London, 1844), 146. See map opposite for evidence of small part of land sold by 1840.

INTERNATIONAL COMPLICATIONS, 1845-49   91

southward to the Mississippi. The region of the Illinois river below Peru or LaSalle, the southern terminus of the canal, had always exported its products southward and for the most part continued to do so. The quantities of wheat, flour, oats, and pork cleared northward over the canal at LaSalle, the southern terminus, was in every case almost exactly equal in amount to those cleared southward over the canal at Chicago, the northern terminus. But in the case of corn there was a lone exception. Nearly a half million bushels of corn from the Illinois river region around and below LaSalle cleared northward over the canal,[79] and constituted practically the whole of Chicago's relatively small export of corn through the northeastern outlet in 1849.[80] On urgent solicitations from the boards and trustees of the canals of Ohio, Indiana, and Illinois the New York canal commissioners had made a special effort to accommodate the export of corn to the northeastward by reducing the New York canal tolls on corn by one-third,[81] and thus preventing its going to New Orleans. The great corn belt at this time lay in Ohio, Indiana, and Illinois precisely in that region where the product could go either to the Northeast or to the South. While the receipts of corn at New Orleans during the last five years had doubled, the export through the northeastern outlet, due to the fact that the Wabash and Erie canal and the Illinois and Michigan canal had been opened almost at

79. *Report of the Board of Trustees of the Illinois and Michigan canal*, pp. 141-42, in *Reports to Sixteenth General Assembly of the State of Illinois* (Springfield, 1849), 513-14; *Annual Review of the Commerce and Railroads of Chicago* (Democratic Press, 1853), 4.

80. [*First*] *Annual Review of the Commerce and Railroads of Chicago*, 5.

81. *Annual Report of the Trustees of the Wabash and Erie canal*, in *Indiana Documents for 1849*, pt. II, doc. 11 (Indianapolis, 1850), 260.

the very same time that the regions through which those canals passed were being settled and put under cultivation, was eighteen times as large as in 1844 and now was nearly twice as large as that to New Orleans. The completion of the railroad from the southeastern shore of Lake Michigan to the head of Lake Erie could not and did not materially change the general direction of commerce, since it merely shortened an old route. The bulkier commodities for the most part continued to go around by lake for many years. In general, then, the upper Northwest was becoming commercially more firmly attached to the Northeast and the lower Northwest to the South.

The total imports of 1849 into the West had not doubled those of 1844 as in the case of the exports. They had risen from a little more than a total of two hundred fifteen thousand tons in 1844 to more than three hundred sixty thousand in 1849 valued at about two hundred million or an increase of about 68%. By 1844 exports had begun to just about pay for imports annually and were by 1849 exceeding them to a sufficient extent to pay off some of the sectional indebtedness incurred in the past. But the three gateways had not all alike shared in the increase. The imports through the northeastern gateway had leaped from less than eighty thousand to almost one hundred seventy-five thousand tons, thus considerably more than doubling. The imports through the southern gateway had risen from eighty-six thousand to one hundred twenty-five thousand, while the imports through the eastern entrance had risen from fifty-two thousand to only a little more than sixty-five thousand and were thus falling hopelessly behind. Of the imports through the northeastern entrance nearly a hundred thousand tons or a little more than half consisted of merchandise and furniture and the remainder consisted of salt. The quantity of furniture imported was decreasing both relatively and absolutely. Of the merchandise northern Ohio took 25%, Michigan 18%, Wisconsin and northern Illinois each 12%, northern Indiana 9%, and some western states outside the Old Northwest took amounts of less than 5% each.[82] Ohio's share of the total imports from the Northeast had quite naturally declined both because of increase of population of neighboring states and because of her own manufactures. The merchandise that went to Ohio, Indiana, and Illinois followed the canals and the railroads southward as far as Newark and Piqua in Ohio, Lafayette in Indiana, and LaSalle in Illinois. Some commodities like coffee went still farther south, while others like sugar and molasses did not go as far. Of the imports through the eastern gateway one-half, or about thirty-two thousand tons, consisted of merchandise; almost one-third, or eighteen thousand tons, consisted of bloom and bar iron; and one-fifth, or thirteen thousand tons, consisted of salt.[83] From the south came some fifty thousand tons of sugar, forty thousand tons of salt, twenty thousand tons of coffee, besides some molasses and other commodities.[84]

As a whole it was still true that the farmer in the northern half of the Old Northwest was getting on better than the farmer in the Ohio valley. Prices indicated this. Wheat sold at the same time in 1849 in some of the northern counties of Ohio at a dollar a bushel and in some of the southern counties at sixty-five cents. Corn in the northern counties sold at thirty-three to forty-four cents and in the southern counties at twenty to twenty-four cents a

82. *N. Y. Assembly Docs.* (Albany, 1850), VI, 125, 209.
83. Hunt, *Merchants' Magazine*, XXII, 204.
84. *DeBow's Review*, IX, 663 and XXIX, 524.

bushel.[85] The larger increase in the importations into the northern part of the Old Northwest also to a certain extent indicated its greater prosperity. This was in part due to the incoming of more settlers who in many cases brought merchandise and furniture with them and to the absence there of manufacturing cities such as were found along the Ohio river. It should be noted that the increased importation into the Northwest through the northeastern gateway was not due to the New York railroads terminating at the northeastern gateway as is sometimes stated. They contributed less than 5% of the total importation at that point.[86] The Erie and Welland canals continued to bring the bulk of the imports.

The census of 1850, which gave the statistics for 1849, indicated that that part of the Old Northwest lying south of the Old National road produced about nine million bushels of wheat and had a population of a million seven hundred sixty thousand. If each person had eaten the four to seven bushels of wheat that the statisticians expected him to eat, southern Ohio and southern Indiana would each have lacked more than a million bushels of supplying their own needs, and southern Illinois would have lacked a little less than a million. But instead they exported over half of this total product and no doubt ate cornbread and mush instead of light bread. The parts of Ohio, Indiana, and Illinois north of the Old National road with a population of over two million produced a total of twenty-one million bushels. They should have consumed fourteen million bushels, leaving northern Ohio less than two, In-

---

85. *Report of the Board of Agriculture*, in *Documents to the Forty-seventh General Assembly of Ohio* (Columbus, 1849), vol. XIII, pt. 1, no. 19, pp. 306, 308, 319, 322, 326, 329.

86. *N. Y. Assembly Docs.* (1850), vol. V, no. 92, pp. 13, 88, no. 140, p. 62.

diana less than one, and northern Illinois only four million bushels or a total of seven million to export. Instead they together exported thirteen millions of bushels. The census of 1850 would indicate that the part of Indiana and Illinois south of the Old National road had, after allowing one hog to be consumed by each individual, a surplus of nearly one and a half million of hogs, while the northern parts of those two states had a surplus of a million. Southern Ohio produced only a small surplus while northern Ohio was showing a shortage on this basis of calculation. The small export of pork northeastward left most of the pork produced in the valley of the Illinois river and of that part of the Wabash between Terre Haute and Lafayette to go southward.[87]

87.
POPULATION AND PRODUCTION STATISTICS—NORTHERN AND SOUTHERN PARTS OF THE OLD NORTHWEST IN 1840, 1850, AND 1860

(The following figures are given in thousands)

		Population	Swine Produced	Swine Surplus
Ohio	Southern part	740.9	1094.3	353.4
1840	Total	1519.4	2099.7	580.3
	Northern part	778.5	1005.4	226.9
1850	Southern part	976.2	1078.6	102.4
	Total	1980.3	1964.7	−15.6
	Northern part	1004.1	886.1	−100.
1860	Southern part	1150.6	1157.9	7.3
	Total	2339.5	2251.6	−87.9
	Northern part	1188.9	1093.7	−95.2
Indiana	Southern part	458.4	1063.2	604.8
1840	Total	685.8	1623.6	937.8
	Northern part	227.4	560.4	333.0
1850	Southern part	585.5	1528.2	942.7
	Total	988.4	2263.7	1475.3
	Northern part	402.9	735.5	532.6
1860	Southern part	741.6	1747.3	1005.7
	Total	1350.4	3099.1	1748.7
	Northern part	608.8	1351.8	743.0

		Population	Swine Produced	Swine Surplus
Illinois	Southern part	165.1	521.1	356.0
1840	Total	476.1	3335.3	2859.2
	Northern part	311.0	2814.2	2503.2
1850	Southern part	229.6	657.2	427.6
	Total	851.4	1915.9	1064.5
	Northern part	621.8	1258.7	636.9
1860	Southern part	391.2	719.6	328.4
	Total	1711.9	2502.3	790.4
	Northern part	1320.7	1782.7	462.0

		Wheat Produced	Wheat Consumed	Wheat Surplus
Ohio	Southern part	8733.7	5186.3	3547.4
1840	Total	16571.6	9635.8	6935.8
	Northern part	7837.9	4449.5	3388.4
1850	Southern part	5602.1	6833.4	−1131.5
	Total	14487.3	13862.1	625.3
	Northern part	8885.2	7028.7	1756.7
1860	Southern part	8416.8	8054.2	362.6
	Total	15119.0	16376.5	−1257.5
	Northern part	6702.2	8322.3	−1619.1
Indiana	Southern part	2351.7	3208.8	−857.1
1840	Total	4049.3	4800.6	−751.3
	Northern part	1697.6	1591.8	105.8
1850	Southern part	2705.0	4098.5	−1393.5
	Total	6214.4	6918.8	−704.4
	Northern part	3509.4	2820.3	689.1
1860	Southern part	8278.2	5191.2	3087.0
	Total	16848.2	9452.8	7395.4
	Northern part	8570.0	4261.6	4308.4
Illinois	Southern part	806.1	1155.7	−349.6
1840	Total	1495.2	3332.7	−1837.5
	Northern part	689.1	2177.0	−1487.9
1850	Southern part	734.9	1607.2	−872.3
	Total	9414.5	5959.8	3454.7
	Northern part	8679.6	4352.6	4327.0
1860	Southern part	4264.5	2738.4	1526.1
	Total	23837.0	11983.3	11853.7
	Northern part	19573.5	9244.9	10327.6

See also totals on page 204 of the present work and graphs on pages 248-249.

CHAPTER V

The Old Northwest and the Old Southwest Unite to Secure a Trunkline Railroad from the Lakes to the Gulf, 1850-1853

THE WEIGHTING of the northern and southern extremes of the country through the political arrangements during the first part of Polk's administration soon brought to a crisis the tendency of the country to break at the middle. The Northeast and the northern part of the Old Northwest were becoming economically and physically ever more closely knit together. The surplus grain produced in the Lake region was driving more of the northeastern farmers out of agriculture and forcing them into manufacturing or into commerce or into migrating westward to increase still further the grain production there.[1] Improvement of lines of transportation from the Lake ports to the North Atlantic ports facilitated the process. The New Englanders driven into the cities consumed ever larger quantities of the surplus produced in the region of the Great Lakes. Population in northern Ohio, northern Indiana, northern Illinois and in Michigan, Iowa, and Wisconsin was increasing rapidly. The increase in the last named state had been almost 900% between 1840 and 1850 and the absolute increase had been nearly three hundred thousand souls. While the percentage of increase in Ohio, Indiana, and Illinois was, of course, nothing like this, the increase in absolute numbers in each of these states was

---

1. J. B. DeBow, *Statistical View of the United States* (Washington, 1854), 170-74. The decline from 1840 to 1850 in the quantity of agricultural products and livestock produced in the New England states varied from one-fourth to one-half of the total in 1840.

even larger than it was in Wisconsin. More than two-thirds of this increase in Indiana and Illinois was, however, in the northern halves of those two states. The Southeast and the lower Southwest on the other hand were extending themselves westward into Texas and were anxious to occupy northern Mexico and southern California. The push toward the extreme southwest was thus about as pronounced as the movement toward the northwest. These movements were passing-by the great middle western zone, extending from the old National road to the southern boundary of Tennessee. This region, the Ohio valley with its tributaries, had been the first to fill up with people, but its rate of increase had now subsided until it was considerably below the average rate for the nation and below that for some of the old states like Pennsylvania and Massachusetts.[2]

But even before the northern part of Mexico had been acquired by the American government the divergence of interests of the two extremes of the country began to endanger the Union. In 1849 the Democratic party and the Whig party each showed indications of breaking into northern and southern factions. The members of each of these parties in Congress, whether from the North or South had in the past usually shown a disposition to vote together on important measures as a matter of preserving

2. Percentages of increase in population between 1840 and 1850 were as follows: Wisconsin 888%, Iowa 350%, Michigan 87%, Northern Ohio 30%, Northern Indiana 81%, Northern Illinois 100%, Southern Ohio (exclusive of Cincinnati) 22%, southern Indiana 26%, southern Illinois 39%, Kentucky (exclusive of Louisville) 22%, Tennessee 21%, the United States 36%. By northern Ohio, Indiana, and Illinois are meant the counties of those states lying wholly north of the national road. DeBow, *Statistical View*, 40, 98, 101, 218, 224, 230, 284, 290; *Sixth Census*, 1840, pp. 694, 748, 914.

party solidarity. But in 1849 many of the northern Democrats defiantly deserted their southern colleagues and voted with the northern Whigs.[3] Southern Whigs and southern Democrats were equally inclined to vote together. By 1850 some of the southern leaders went so far as to make the question of breaking up the Union the issue in a southern state election and the subject for consideration in a number of southern state conventions and in one southern interstate convention.[4] In Congress there were not only threats of disunion but there was already such absence of unity of purpose as made legislation on important questions for a long time seem impossible. The apparent seriousness of the situation finally helped in its own solution. A series of measures were carried through Congress which together constituted the great Compromise of 1850 and which deferred the day of attempting to break the country into northern and southern halves. In voting on the different measures that constituted the compromise, Representatives in Congress of the extreme northern states from New Hampshire to Wisconsin generally voted for the bills that were meant as concessions to the northern antislavery forces and against those parts of the compromise that were intended as favors to the South. Representatives of the lower South from the

3. *Cong. Globe*, 30 Cong., 2 sess., pp. 1, 83, vote on Gott resolution; 31 Cong., 1 sess., vol. XXI, pt. 1, pp. 91, 376, vote on Root resolution and on Doty resolution.

4. H. V. Ames, *State Documents on Federal Relations* (Philadelphia, 1906), 257, 266, 274; P. M. Hamer, *The Secession movement in South Carolina, 1847-1852* (Allentown, 1918), p. 23, 94; U. B. Phillips, "Georgia and State Rights," in *Annual Report of the American Historical Association*, 1901, vol. II, 164; Cleo Hearon, "Mississippi and the Compromise of 1850," in *Publications of Mississippi Historical Society*, vol. XIV, p. 67; D. T. Herndon, "Nashville Convention of 1850," in *Alabama Historical Soc. Trans.*, vol. V, p. 203.

Carolinas to Texas voted for the parts of the compromise that pleased them and against those that were to please the North. The nearer a state lay to the Mason and Dixon's line or to the Ohio river the larger the percentage of her representatives voting for all the parts of the compromise whether drawn in behalf of the North or South. It may furthermore be said that the farther west that one of these states in the middle zone lay, the larger the proportion of her representatives supporting both sides of the compromise. Thirty-six members of the House voted with the anti-slavery representatives from the North to abolish the slave trade in the District of Columbia and then united with the representatives of the South to provide that section with a more effective fugitive slave law. Twenty-two of these thirty-six representatives were from the West and seventeen of these twenty-two were from Ohio, southern Indiana, southern Illinois, and extreme western Virginia and Pennsylvania. If these representatives from the West or even those from the Ohio valley had refused to vote for the fugitive slave law, the measure would apparently have been defeated. In that case the efforts for compromise in 1850 would have surely failed, and the forcible attempt to break up the Union would have been made then instead of ten years later. Forty-eight representatives were able to reconcile their consciences to voting for the admission of California with her constitution prohibiting slavery and at the same time vote for a more drastic slave-catching law. Half of these lived either in the Ohio valley or within one hundred fifty miles of the Ohio river. Measures which contained within their own provisions the elements of compromise like the bill for organizing a territorial government in New Mexico without specifically protecting slavery therein or prohibiting it therefrom were supported by even larger numbers of representatives from this middle zone, while irreconcilable abolitionists of the North and fire-eating defenders of slavery in the South for once united and voted against the measure.[5] While some credit must be given to individuals representing states as far separated as Maine and Texas, it is very clear from the votes cast for the various measures that it was the Ohio valley that held the balance of power in the compromise of 1850 and deserves the credit or the blame for having deferred the great disunion conflict to another day. Representatives from this region expressed horror at the thought of the words of southern members who admitted that their people had been "calmly calculating the value of the Union." To the representatives of the Ohio valley such loose talk about disunion seemed almost sacreligious. The same representatives indulged in emotional oratorical flights in which they swore to fight for the rights of the South under the Constitution but to die for the Union.[6] Possibly these men of the borderland had not calculated as coldly the value of the Union as had some of the men in South Carolina and Massachusetts where nullification and secession had been periodically threatened. Possibly they had done some calculating but had come to a different conclusion as to the value of the Union for their own region. Senators and representatives from the Middle West asked where the line of separation would be drawn in the West. They vowed that the Mississippi could never be cut and they stoutly insisted that they would fight to maintain their free commercial ap-

---

5. *U. S. House Journal*, 31 Cong., 1 sess. [serial 566], pp. 1423, 1452, 1457; East of the Alleghanies the border state of Pennsylvania did most to pass the compromise.

6. *Speech of W. H. Bissell of Illinois in House of Representatives*, Feb. 21, 1850, p. 8.

proaches to the ocean both by way of the mouth of the Mississippi and by the outlets of the Great Lakes.[7] The language of one southern Hoosier is rather typical. He said, "But sir, in the contemplated dissolution where are we of Ohio, Indiana and Illinois to go? Are we to go north and be tied to the northern capitalists; and our farmers become tributary slaves to protect manufacturing capital? God forbid and save us from such a destiny! The life blood of my people depend upon their trade upon the great waters of the Mississippi; and sir, we as naturally go there with our produce as a child goes to its mother's breast for sustenance and support. We never will be cut off from it. . . . But if the South ask us of the North to give our consent to extend slavery one inch by law, we say no."[8]

During the next three years it was the practice among politicians and statesmen generally to try to prevent the rift between the North and the South from reappearing by refraining from speaking of it and by making believe that it was no longer existant. During these years reflection on the narrow escape of the country in 1850 seems to have made many men more sober and more determined to preserve the Union. It was during this period that at least one step was taken to tie the Northwest and the Southwest more closely together economically and commercially. This was done by making provision for the building with the aid of the Federal government of a grand north and

---

7. Speech of J. A. McClernand of Illinois, June 10, 1850, in *Cong. Globe*, 31, Cong., 1 sess., Appendix, vol. XXII, pt. 1, p. 701; Speech of H. Clay of Ky., Feb. 6, 1850, in *Ibid.*, p. 127; Speech of T. L. Harris of Ill., Mar. 25, in *Ibid.*, p. 413; Speech of S. A. Douglas of Ill., Mar. 14, in *Ibid.*, p. 365; Speech of T. S. Haymond of (Northwestern) Va., May 21, in *Ibid.*, p. 599.

8. Speech of W. A. Gorman of Indiana, Mar. 12, in *Ibid.*, p. 320.

south railroad connecting the Great Lakes with the Gulf of Mexico. This time the idea of linking the Old Northwest by a great transportation line to one of the other sections of the country not only originated in the northwest but the Federal legislation that made possible the project was secured by the political management of some of the leaders of that section. Different parts of this plan had been advocated and even undertaken by state enterprise before 1850.[9] But it was left for Stephen A. Douglas, who had done so much to get the Compromise measures of 1850 finally passed, and his colleagues of Illinois by a series of shrewd political bargains to bring these different parts into one grand scheme that would command enough votes of different sections interested to secure the aid of the Federal government. During the period of the internal improvement craze of the thirties in the Old Northwest, Illinois had taken steps to build a railroad which would connect the southern terminus of the proposed Illinois and Michigan canal with the mouth of the Ohio river.[10] The plan was for a time dropped after the panic of '37 but was revived with some modifications in the early forties.[11] In the later forties attempts were made to get the Federal government to aid the project through the giving of preemption rights in government lands to a railroad company or by ceding such lands outright to the state.[12] Congress seemed, however, unwilling at that time to aid what ap-

9. W. K. Ackerman, *Historical Sketch of the Illinois-Central Railroad* (Chicago, 1890), 5-9.

10. *Laws of Illinois*, 1835-36, p. 129 and *Ibid.*, 1836-37, p. 121.

11. *Laws of Illinois*, 1843-44, p. 199; *Cong. Globe*, 28 Cong., 1 sess., p. 72.

12. *Cong. Globe*, 29 Cong., 1 sess., p. 208, and 29 Cong., 2 sess., pp. 52, 473; *U. S. Senate Journal*, 29 Cong., 1 sess. [serial 469], pp. 106, 685, S. B. no. 52; *Ibid.*, 29 Cong., 2 sess. [serial 492], p. 217.

peared to be a local or state enterprise. In 1848 such a measure passed the Senate[13] but was defeated in the House.[14]

There were, however, under consideration other local projects which might be combined in such a way with the Illinois project as to make of the whole a national enterprise. In the late forties the citizens of Mobile had decided to build a railroad from their port northward to the mouth of the Ohio where it would connect with the Illinois project. The legislature of Alabama, Feb. 3, 1848, had granted a charter of incorporation, the legislatures of Mississippi, Tennessee, and Kentucky had granted right of way; and steps had been taken to build the Mobile and Ohio road as a semi-private enterprise.[15] The citizens of New Orleans had also been considering projects of building a road from their city northward. The citizens of Iowa at the same time were hoping to connect Dubuque on the Mississippi with the central part of their state by railroad. Then it was that Senator Stephen A. Douglas of Illinois in 1850 came forward and managed with the aid of his colleagues to secure the union of a number of these projects into one comprehensive scheme.[16]

The act as finally passed provided for two end-to-end railroads.[17] One part of this so-called central railroad, the

---

13. *U. S. Senate Journal*, 30 Cong., 1 sess. [serial 502], pp. 125, 314, S. B. no. 95.

14. *U. S. House Journal*, 30 Cong., 1 sess. [serial 513], p. 1270; *Cong. Globe*, 30 Cong., 1 sess., pp. 74, 214, 230, 723 and Appendix, pp. 535-37.

15. *Proceedings of First Annual Meeting of Stockholders of the Mobile and Ohio Railroad Company* (Mobile, 1849), p. 3 and Appendix A; *Laws of Miss., 1848*, p. 93.

16. *Cong. Globe*, 31 Cong., 1 sess., vol. XXI, pt. 1, pp. 102, 344, 900-04, and vol. XXI, pt. 2, pp. 1431, 1485, 1838.

17. 31 Cong., 1 sess., ch. 61, in *U. S. Statutes at Large*, vol. IX, p. 466.

Illinois Central, was to extend from the mouth of the Ohio to the southern terminus of the Illinois and Michigan canal with branches extending northward to Dubuque and to Chicago. The other part of this central railroad, the Mobile and Ohio, was to reach from the mouth of the Ohio river to the city of Mobile. Alternate sections of land for six miles on each side of the two roads were given by the Federal government to the states of Illinois, Mississippi, and Alabama for building the roads. By extending the branch to Dubuque, the support of the congressional members of Iowa was obtained; by extending a branch to Chicago, not only the support of the members from northeastern Illinois but also of some members and capitalists from the Northeast was enlisted; by uniting it with the project for the Mobile and Ohio, the votes of members from the Southwest were secured; and by making the scheme so comprehensive and national in scope, the objections of many strict constructionists were headed off.[18] The measure in its final passage in 1850 had supporters and opponents in every section but naturally received its heaviest support from the members of Congress representing the Northwest and Southwest.[19]

The legislature of Illinois at once took steps to make possible the construction of that part of the system lying north of the Ohio river.[20] Activities for the construction of the Mobile and Ohio were at once redoubled. At the

18. *Letters of Senator Douglas Defending himself and Colleagues against the Attacks of Judge Breese*, etc. (n. p., n. d.), p. 12, 13.

19. *U. S. House Journal*, 31 Cong., 1 sess. [serial 566], p. 1490; *U. S. Senate Journal* [serial 548], p. 321, S. B. no. 22; H. G. Brownson, "History of the Illinois Central Railroad to 1870," in vol. IV of *University of Ill. Studies in Social Science* (Urbana, 1909), pp. 29, 31.

20. *General Laws of Illinois, 1851*, p. 193; *Private Laws of Illinois, 1851*, p. 61.

same time steps were taken in Louisiana and Mississippi to build a road from some point on the Mobile and Ohio line to New Orleans.[21] Before the end of 1853 it appeared, then, that there was to be a great north and south system connecting Dubuque or Dunleith on the upper Mississippi and Chicago on the Great Lakes with both Mobile and New Orleans on or near the Gulf. This was, of course, not an attempt to provide a new outlet for the Old Northwest, but to improve one of the three great outlets that had always existed. There was already a water route by canal and river from Chicago to New Orleans, subsidized throughout by Federal aid; but it was now to be supplemented by a rail route in the same way that the water route by lakes, canals, and rivers from Chicago to New York was being supplemented by an all rail route. It was clearly and avowedly an attempt to improve the southern outlet as an alternative and rival to the northeastern outlet.[22] In the rivalry between the two outlets both Douglas and Breese, the two Illinois senators, undoubtedly expected and hoped that New Orleans would more than hold her own. At that time there was little to make such an attempt seem unreasonable. The experiences of the past seemed to favor New Orleans rather than New York. The distances from Chicago to New Orleans and to New York

21. The New Orleans, Jackson and Great Northern; the Mississippi Central; and the Tennessee Central were organized and incorporated for this purpose. Frequent changes were made and the connection as later completed was not made by the route as originally planned. *Second Annual Report of the President and Directors of the Mississippi Central Railroad Company* (Holly Springs, 1854), 1, 7, 8, 10; *Report of the New Orleans, Jackson and Great Northern* (New Orleans, 1852), 10; *Laws of Mississippi, 1850*, p. 70; *Ibid., 1852*, p. 78; *Ibid., 1854*, pp. 74, 132.

22. Brownson, "History of the Illinois Central Railroad to 1870," p. 76.

were about the same. The distances from the southwestern part of the Old Northwest to New Orleans was still smaller. This project inaugurated in the early fifties was, however, to be carried to completion in the future. Other projects affecting the Old Northwest were already being brought to completion during these years.

From 1849 to the close of 1853 there was also other rapid development in the lines of transportation leading from the interior to the external markets. In 1851 the New York and Erie railroad was opened through to Dunkirk, thus connecting Lake Erie with the harbor of New York City by a rail route composed of a single road.[23] That same year, too, Boston was connected by rail with Ogdensburg on Lake Ontario through the completion of the Northern New York railroad.[24] This latter route with the one by way of Albany gave Boston two almost independent rail connections with the Great Lakes. That same year, too, the Hudson River railroad was opened between Albany and New York City.[25] This railroad, with the end-for-end roads between Albany and Buffalo, made a second all rail route from New York City to Lake Erie. That same year also the railroads between Buffalo and Albany

23. Poor, *History of Railroads*, I, 280; Poor, *Sketch of Internal Improvements*, p. xxii. The eastern terminal of the New York and Erie railroad was at Pierpont fifteen miles north of Jersey City but by 1853 the road secured the right of terminal in the latter city. The Buffalo and New York City railroad completed in 1852 ran from Buffalo to Hornelsville on the New York and Erie. Hunt, *Merchants' Magazine*, XXX, 312.

24. C. Dinsmore, *American Railway Guide* (New York, 1850-60). Dinsmore's guides were issued monthly with time tables for sections of roads in operation and thus enable one to determine month by month what sections of roads had been completed and were open for business; H. V. Poor, *Railroad Manual, 1868-69*, p. 16.

25. *Seventeenth Annual Report of the N. Y. Central and Hudson River Railroad Company*, 35; Poor, *History of Railroads*, I, 259.

were exempted by the New York Assembly from paying the canal tolls, on the ground that their new competitor, the New York and Erie road, by its charter, was exempt from such payments.[26] Exemption from toll payment did not, however, at once materially increase the amount of freight traffic over these roads. Two years later, in 1853, the ten roads between Buffalo and Albany were permitted by the state assembly to consolidate into a single corporation and to operate as one continuous line, the New York Central.[27] This line with the Hudson River road now made a continuous rail route from Lake Erie to New York City, broken only by the river at Albany.

By the beginning of 1853 two railways also connected the eastern gateway with Atlantic ports. The Pennsylvania Railroad Company, by using the Allegheny Portage railroad over the mountains and by running over the state's railroad from Philadelphia to Columbia, had in January of 1853 opened an all-rail route between Pittsburgh on the Ohio river and Philadelphia.[28] The beginning of that same year also witnessed the completion of the Baltimore and Ohio road from Baltimore to Wheeling on the Ohio river.[29] By the completion of the Western and

26. *Laws of State of New York for 1851,* ch. 497, July 10, 1851.

27. *Seventeenth Annual Report of the N. Y. Central and Hudson River Railroad Company,* 33; *Laws of State of New York for 1853,* ch. 76, April 2, 1853. There were ten companies with ten roads completed, one under construction, and two proposed in this consolidation between Buffalo on the west and Albany and Troy on the east. Of the completed roads, seven were end to end, two parallel to parts and one linking road. See map opposite IX in F. W. Stevens, *The Beginnings of the New York Central Railroad.* The Schnectady and Troy division crossed the Hudson river over the bridge of the Rensselaer and Saratoga railroad. There was no bridge at Albany.

28. *Sixth Annual Report of the Pennsylvania Railroad Company* (Philadelphia, 1853), 9.

29. *Twenty-seventh Annual Report of the Baltimore and Ohio* (Balti-

Atlantic railroad in 1851 between Chattanooga and Atlanta where it connected with other roads already linking the latter place with Charleston and Savannah, the southeastern outlet had been improved.[30]

The railroad developments in certain parts of the interior of the West had been no less rapid. This was especially true in the Old Northwest. The same year, 1853, that saw the consolidation of the roads east of Buffalo into the New York Central witnessed the filling in of the last gaps in an all rail route from Buffalo and Dunkirk through Cleveland and Toledo to Chicago.[31] This line was, however, still made up of a half dozen end-for-end roads of different gauges and operated by different companies and not so connected that freight cars would always pass from one track to the other.[32] In the meantime two more rail routes had connected Lake Erie with the Ohio river. One

more, 1853), Engineers Report, 185, p. 26. The road was opened for trains, Jan. 1, 1853, for active business April 1, 1853.

30. *Western and Atlantic Railroad of the State of Georgia*, J. H. Johnston, compiler (Atlanta, 1931), 21, 39, 43; The Western and Atlantic connected with the Macon and Western railroad and with the Georgia railroad. The Macon and Western connected at Macon with the Central (Georgia) railroad and the latter road had its terminus at Savannah. The Georgia railroad connected at Augusta with the South Carolina railroad and the latter had its terminus at Charleston. See C. Dinsmore, *American Railway Guide, 1850* and *Ibid., Dec. 1853*.

31. *The Railroads, History and Commerce of Chicago*, Democratic Press (Chicago, 1854), 13.

32. The Michigan Southern and Northern Indiana, from Chicago to Adrian, Michigan; the Erie and Kalamazoo from Adrian to Toledo; the Toledo, Norwalk and Cleveland from Toledo to Cleveland; The Cleveland and Erie from Cleveland to Erie, Pa.; the Erie and Northeast from Erie to State Line; the Buffalo and State Line from State Line to Buffalo. See Dinsmore, *American Railway Guide* (New York, 1853) issued monthly with maps and time tables; see also F. L. Paxson, "Railroads of the Old Northwest," in *Wisconsin Academy of Sciences, Arts, and Letters Transactions*, vol. XVII, pt. 1, p. 259.

of these was completed in 1851 and connected Cleveland with Cincinnati;[33] the other was completed in 1852 and connected Cleveland with Pittsburgh and with Wellsville.[34] Lake Michigan had also been connected in 1853 with several points on the Ohio river by means of a line which ran from Michigan City to Indianapolis and there connected with lines that radiated to Cincinnati, to Lawrenceburg, to Madison, and to Jeffersonville.[35] Finally, there was completed before the close of 1853 an all rail route from Chicago on Lake Michigan to Alton on the Mississippi river, almost opposite St. Louis.[36] There were also all-rail routes from Pittsburgh to Cincinnati and to Indianapolis. The route from Pittsburgh to Cincinnati was, however, made up of four different roads, the one to Indianapolis of seven, and both routes were somewhat circuitous. Be-

33. The Little Miami, from Cincinnati to Xenia and to Springfield; the Xenia and Columbus from Xenia to Columbus; the Cincinnati, Cleveland and Columbus from Columbus to Cleveland. See American Railway Guides for time tables of sections of roads in operation.

34. The Cleveland and Pittsburgh, from Cleveland to Alliance and to Wellsville; the Ohio and Pennsylvania, from Alliance to Pittsburgh. See *Seventh Annual Report of the Directors of the Pennsylvania Railroad Company* (Philadelphia, 1854), 74.

35. The Salem and New Albany from Michigan City to Lafayette; the Indianapolis and Lafayette, from Lafayette to Indianapolis; the Indiana Central from Indianapolis to Richmond; the Eaton and Hamilton from Richmond to Hamilton; the Cincinnati, Hamilton and Dayton, from Hamilton to Cincinnati; the Indianapolis and Cincinnati, from Indianapolis to Lawrenceburg; the Madison and Indianapolis, from Indianapolis through Columbus to Madison; the Jeffersonville, from Columbus to Jeffersonville. See Dinsmore, *American Railway Guide*, issued monthly, 1853.

36. The Galena and Chicago Union, from Chicago to Aurora; the Chicago, Burlington and Quincy, from Aurora to Mendota; the Illinois Central, from Mendota to Bloomington; the Chicago, Alton and St. Louis, from Bloomington to Alton. Dinsmore, *American Railway Guide; The Railroads, History and Commerce of Chicago*, Democratic Press (1854), 14.

sides these routes that connected important river towns with lake ports, a number of short roads had been opened that ran from lake ports or river ports into the interior. The roads running westward into the interior from Milwaukee and from Chicago had been extended. Roads from Evansville and from New Albany, both on the Ohio, ran northward into the interior. In 1853 the southern end of the Wabash and Erie canal was opened, completing the canal between Evansville on the Ohio river, and Toledo on Lake Erie.[37]

South of the Ohio building of transportation lines still lagged. In 1851 a railroad was in operation from Louisville on the Ohio river into the interior of Kentucky for about a hundred miles through Frankfort to Lexington.[38] During 1853 the Nashville and Chattanooga railroad was opened up from the former place to a point on the Tennessee river about twenty-five miles above Chattanooga. This made possible the transfer of commodities from the Cumberland river to the Tennessee river at a point near the southeastern gateway.[39] Western products could now ascend the Cumberland river to Nashville and be transshipped by rail to the Tennessee, or they could ascend the Tennessee, going around the Muscle Shoals either by canal or railroad, and proceed to Chattanooga and from there be conveyed by the Western and Atlantic railroad to At-

37. *Annual Report of the Trustees of the Wabash and Erie canal for 1853*, 6.

38. *History of the Ohio Falls Cities* (Cleveland, 1882), 1, 58; The Lexington and Ohio railroad (after 1847 the Lexington and Frankfort) had been completed between Lexington and Frankfort in 1835. The Louisville and Frankfort was completed between those two places in 1851. *Fourth Annual Report of the President and Directors of the Louisville and Frankfort R. R. Co.*, (Louisville, 1852), 8.

39. C. Dinsmore, *American Railway Guide,* December 1853.

lanta whence railroads radiated to the South Atlantic ports.

The new lines of transportation connecting the West with the outside world—the Northern New York railroad, the New York Central and the Hudson River roads, the New York and Erie, the Pennsylvania, the Baltimore and Ohio, and the Western and Atlantic railroad—effected little change in the external trade of the interior down to the close of 1853. The new roads carried a share of the rapidly increasing export of the interior, but it is difficult to see that they materially affected either the quantity of production or of export or the general direction of that export. The New York Central and the New York and Erie carried eastward small quantities of commodities in comparison with that carried by the Erie, the Oswego, and the Welland canals. The Erie canal alone carried eastward from Buffalo in 1853 four times the salt meat, four times the flour, ten times the wool, ninety times the wheat, and two hundred forty-nine times the corn that the three railroads than ran eastward out of that place carried from there.[40] In addition almost as much goods passed through the Welland canal from Lake Erie into Lake Ontario as passed from Lake Erie over the Erie canal. The goods that went through the Welland canal went in large part to the Oswego canal to rejoin the Erie

40. *N. Y. Assembly Documents, 1854* (Albany, 1854), no. 145, pp. 112, 121; *Report of the New York Central Railroad Company to the State Engineer and Surveyor for the year ending Sept. 30, 1854* (Albany, 1854), 9; Hunt, *Merchants' Magazine*, XXX, 311, 312, 314. The three roads carrying goods eastward out of Buffalo in 1853 were the Buffalo and Rochester (a part of the N. Y. Central after June), the Buffalo and Niagara Falls (the Buffalo and Lockport, merged in the N. Y. Central, ran over its tracks to Tonawanda and joined the Rochester, Lockport and Niagara, a member of the N. Y. Central, near Lockport) and the Buffalo and New York City which connected with the New York and Erie at Hornelsville.

canal farther down; a relatively small part went to Ogdensburg to be borne by rail to Boston, and a small part also went by the St. Lawrence to Montreal and beyond. The New York and Erie railroad carried about the same quantities eastward from Dunkirk that the New York Central carried from Buffalo.[41] The canals of New York and Canada could easily have carried the additional tonnage that was carried by the northeastern railroads. The railroads contributed, however, two advantages. They operated when the canals were frozen up, a fact of some importance in the matter of marketing meat during the slaughtering and packing season. Then, too, the railroads could successfully carry livestock, which the slow going canal boats could not do. In comparison with the Ohio valley, the region immediately south of the Great Lakes had, however, not up until 1853 gone into the production of livestock for export purposes to any considerable extent. But after that date the increase in livestock production in that region was fairly rapid and the railroads may well be given some credit for having made the change profitable.[42]

What was true of the New York railroads was largely

41. The New York and Erie railroad carried eastward from Dunkirk in 1853 about 56,228 tons including a little less than 100,000 bbls. each of flour and of meats. *Report of the Directors of the New York and Erie R. R. Co.* (N. Y., 1853), 84, 102. The New York Central carried eastward from Buffalo between 50,000 and 75,000 tons including about 194,928 barrels of flour, 19,562 barrels of pork and bacon, 20,553 barrels of beef and 89,502 hogs. Hunt, *Merchants' Magazine*, XXX, 311.

42. Comparisons are based on tables compiled from: *Tables of Trade and Navagigation of the Provinces of Canada for the year 1853* (Quebec, 1854), 2-4; *N. Y. Assembly Documents, 1854*, no. 145, pp. 112, 115; Hunt, *Merchants' Magazine*, XXVIII, 304, *Ibid.*, XXX, 311-14; *Eighth Census, 1860,* Agriculture, p. cxlviii; *Report of the New York Central Railroad Company, to the State Engineer, for year ending Sept. 30, 1854*, p. 9; Andrews, *Report on Trade and Commerce*, 67; *Statistics of Foreign and Domestic Commerce*, 162.

114   THE OLD NORTHWEST

true of the Pennsylvania railroad and of the Baltimore
and Ohio. The Pennsylvania railroad in 1853 transported
eastward from Pittsburgh only 15% more of tonnage than
did the Pennsylvania canal from the same point in 1849.
It carried less tobacco, less meat, less whiskey, less wool,
and less hemp and only a trifle more of flour than the canal
had carried in 1849. The Pennsylvania railroad and the
Baltimore and Ohio together transported eastward from
their western terminals on the Ohio river in 1853 just
about twice the quantity of salt meat, of whiskey, and of
grain and a little less than half the quantity of wool and
of tobacco that was transported eastward from Pittsburgh
alone in 1849 over the canal.[43] In addition, however, these
two railroads carried about nine thousand tons of livestock, a commodity which the canal had carried only in
negligible quantities.[44] How many tons of live hogs, cattle,
and sheep were driven eastward on the hoof in 1849 from
Pittsburgh over the Old Glade road and from Wheeling
over the Old National road is not now ascertainable, but
it probably amounted to more than nine thousand tons.[45]
The export through the southeastern gateway over the
Western and Atlantic although of local importance was
not of sufficient size to play any appreciable part in the
total exports of the West.[46]

43. The canal by 1852 had ceased to carry any considerable quantity
of the agricultural products eastward from Pittsburgh. See Thomas Bald-
win and Joseph Thomas, *A New and Complete Gazateer* (Philadelphia,
1854), 930.
44. Comparative tables compiled from Statistics given in: *Seventh Annual Report of the Directors of the Pennsylvania Railroad Company*, 75;
*Twenty-eight Annual Report of the Baltimore and Ohio Railroad Com-
pany* (Baltimore, 1854), 29-30; Hunt, *Merchants' Magazine*, XXII, 204.
45. Searight's, *The Old Pike*, and Hulbert's, *Old Glade Road*, give only
general statements.
46. Export of western commodities from Chattanooga eastward

A SOUTHERN TRUNKLINE, 1850-53   115

The total exports from the Northwest in 1853 had increased by an average of only about 20% over that of 1849. While the export of wheat as such had doubled, that of flour had increased by only about 5%. If the flour be counted as wheat, the total surplus of wheat and wheat products exported in 1853 amounted to a little more than twenty-eight million bushels, which showed less than 33% increase since 1849. The export of corn as such had increased by only 25% since 1849, the export of pork had just held its own, while that of whiskey had increased by 28%. If the pork and whiskey be counted as corn, it is found that the total surplus of corn and corn products exported in 1853 amounted to thirty-one million bushels and was thus only about 10% larger than in 1849. This ignores the corn converted into beef and into the hogs exported on foot. The export of beef had increased by some 30%. How the two hundred fifty thousand live hogs exported in 1853 compared with those driven out in 1849 can not now be stated, but even if none had been driven out in the earlier year, the increase in the export of live hogs in 1853 would not have made good the decline in the export of barreled pork in the latter year. The total

amounted to probably little over 25,000 tons per year. Apparently no records were kept by the Western and Atlantic of quantity of different commodities carried. At this time the road earned about $3000 per mile on through freight. See *Report of Superintendent, 1854-55*, p. 8. Average freight rates on railroads varied in 1853 from 2½ to 6 cents per ton per mile. At this rate the Western and Atlantic would have carried a total tonnage of 50,000 to 100,000 tons both ways or about 25,000 to 50,000 tons eastward. As the rates on southern railroads were usually higher the correct estimate would probably be near the 25,000 tons. *U. S. Senate Reports*, 52 Cong., 2 sess., vol. III, pt. 1 [serial 3074, pt. 1], p. 616; Seventh *Annual Report of the Directors of the Pennsylvania Railroad Company*, 77.

quantity of agricultural exports had thus probably increased between 15% and 20%.

When one compares the character and proportion of exports from the interior by the three major outlets in 1853, the figures show only a little change from that in 1849. Of a total export of a little more than eleven million bushels of wheat over 99% went northeast. Between 92 and 96% of this commodity had been going out through the northeastern gateway during the preceding decade. Of a total export of a little more than three million barrels of flour, 62% went northeast, 28% south, and 10% east. The eastern gateway had thus gained 5% since 1849 at the expense largely of the southern outlet, which not only took a smaller proportion of the total quantity of flour produced in the West but had also decreased her actual receipts by 20% since 1849. Of a total export of nearly eight million bushels of corn, 62% went northeast and 37% went south—showing again a very small relative gain by the Northeast at the expense of the South, although the latter took a larger quantity in 1853 than in 1849. Of nearly one and a half million barrels of pork exported from the interior, 58% went south, 23% went east, and 18% northeast. The eastern and northeastern gateways had both doubled their relative percentages of the total at the expense of the southern gateway. New Orleans thus took 22% less of the total pork exported from the West in 1853 than in 1849 but also actually took 20% less pork in 1853 than in 1849. Three times as much beef went northeast as went south, but nearly five times as much pork still went south as northeast, and more pork went eastward over the Baltimore and Ohio railroad alone than over all the routes from the northeastern gateway. Of a total export of a little less than two hundred fifty thousand barrels of whiskey, 56% went south, 33% northeast, and 11% east. The proportion of the total quantity of whiskey produced in the West in 1853 that found its outlet through New Orleans was thus 11% less than in 1849 in spite of the fact that the actual receipts there had increased during that time. The total export of tobacco was larger in 1853 than in 1849 but not quite so large as in 1844. Of a total of nearly ninety thousand hogsheads, 83% went south, 11% went east, and 5% northeast. New Orleans thus took 50% more tobacco than in 1849 and took 5% more of the total tobacco produced in the West in 1853 than in the former year. Of nearly seventy-five thousand tons of wool exported, 78% went northeast and 22% went east. In 1849 slightly more had gone east than northeast. Of a total of over two hundred fifty thousand live hogs exported, 67% went northeast and 33% east. Of some thirty-seven thousand cattle over thirty-five thousand went through the northeastern gateway and the remainder went east, chiefly over the Baltimore and Ohio.[47]

Of the eight hundred thousand barrels of flour received at New Orleans in 1853, Cincinnati sent 25% and St. Louis 50%. Of the three million bushels of corn received at New Orleans, St. Louis sent about 30%, Evansville and the Wabash valley about 25%. About half the St. Louis flour came from the Illinois river valley or was manufactured at St. Louis out of wheat imported from the Illinois valley, and a third of the St. Louis corn came from there. Cincinnati's export was produced within a radius of one

---

47. *Seventh Annual Report of the Pennsylvania Railroad Company,* 75; *Twenty-eighth Annual Report of the Baltimore and Ohio,* 29-30; *Tables of Trade and Navigation of the Province of Canada for 1853,* pp. 2-4; *Eighth Census,* Agriculture, p. cxlviii; Hunt, *Merchants' Magazine,* XXVIII, 204, 304; *Ibid.,* XXX, 303, 313; *Ibid.,* XXXVIII, 693-97.

hundred fifty miles and came from southwestern Ohio, southeastern Indiana, and northern Kentucky. Of something less than eight hundred thousand barrels of pork received at New Orleans, Cincinnati contributed 25%, Louisville 20%, St. Louis 12%, and the remainder came from the Illinois, the Ohio, the Wabash, the Cumberland, and the Tennessee. Cincinnati sent about a hundred thousand barrels less of pork to New Orleans in 1853 than in 1849 and sent almost exactly that amount up the Ohio river to Wheeling and to Pittsburgh. In 1849 she had sent only half that amount up the river. Other towns on the upper Ohio were sending some of their pork through the eastern gateway.[48]

Of the eleven million bushels of wheat exported northeastward, 19% went from Cleveland and constituted the export of northern Ohio; 15% from Toledo and constituted for the most part the export of northern Indiana; 12% from Chicago, the export of northern Illinois; and 11% from Milwaukee, the export of Wisconsin. Of two million two hundred thousand barrels of flour exported through the northeastern gateway, 44% went forward from Cleveland, 14% from Toledo, 9% from Milwaukee, and 4% from Chicago. Of nearly five million bushels of corn exported northeastward, about 45% went from To-

48. Comparative tables compiled from: *Annual Review, History of St. Louis, Commercial Statistics,* Missouri Republican (St. Louis, 1854), 25-28; *Annual Review of the Trade and Commerce of Cincinnati for the year ending Aug. 3, 1853,* p. 17; *Western Journal,* IV, 256; *Annual Report of the Directors of the Evansville, Indianapolis, and Cleveland Straight Line Railroad Company* (Indianapolis, 1855), 22; *U. S. House Ex. Docs.,* 50 Cong., 1 sess., vol. XX, no. 6, pt. 2 [serial 2552], pp. 200-18; *Monthly Summary of Commerce and Finance,* Feb., 1900, in *U. S. House Docs.,* 56 Cong., 1 sess., vol. LV, no. 8 [serial 3942], p. 2287; *Ibid.,* Jan., 1900, pp. 1958-59.

ledo, 52% from Chicago, and 3% from Cleveland. Of nearly two hundred eighty thousand barrels of pork, 35% went from Toledo, 45% from Cleveland, 13% from Chicago, and 6% from Milwaukee. Of over ninety thousand barrels of beef, 70% went from Chicago, 18% from Cleveland, 10% from Toledo, 3% from Milwaukee. Of a hundred seventy thousand live hogs about 65% were forwarded through Cleveland.[49]

Of the exports from Cleveland about three-fourths of the wheat and flour and about one-sixth of the pork came over the Ohio canal and had been produced in north central Ohio. About a fourth of the wheat and five-sixths of the pork came over the Cleveland, Columbus and Cincinnati railroad. Nearly all the wheat and flour brought in by the railroad came from way stations north of Columbus, but the greater part of the relatively small quantity of pork came from stations south of that place. About an eighth of the flour exported was milled in and around Cleveland. Two-thirds of the live hogs exported through the northeastern gateway were forwarded by Cleveland and were brought there by the railroad for the most part from the region north of Columbus.[50] The exports of Toledo came almost entirely by the Wabash and Erie

---

49. *Annual Report of the Commerce, Manufacutring, Public Improvements and Railroad System of Milwaukee for the year 1855, by the Board of Trade* (Milwaukee, 1855), 4; *Railroads, History and Commerce of Chicago* (1854), 67; *Seventeenth Annual Report of the Board of Public Works to the fifty-first General Assembly of Ohio* (Columbus, 1854), 97-101; *Monthly Summary of Commerce and Finance*, Jan., 1900, pp. 1960, 1961; Hunt, *Merchants' Magazine*, XL, 303-04.

50. *Seventeenth Annual Report of the Board of Public Works*, 31-59; *Third Annual Report of the Directors of the Cleveland, Columbus and Cincinnati Railroad Company* (Cleveland, 1854), 18; Hunt, *Merchants' Magazine*, XL, 303-04.

canal from the valleys of the Maumee in northwestern Ohio and the upper Wabash in northern Indiana.[51] Of the exports of Chicago nearly all the corn came by way of the Illinois and Michigan canal from the region in northeastern Illinois through which the canal ran and from the upper valley of the Illinois river with which the canal was connected. Half the flour and three-fourths of the wheat exported by Chicago came over the Galena and Chicago Union railroad from the extreme northern part of Illinois including the fertile upper valley of the Rock river. Nearly all the remainder of the wheat came over the Chicago and Illinois canal and the remainder of the flour was milled in the city.[52]

Of the goods exported eastward over the Pennsylvania and the Baltimore and Ohio railroads in 1853, practically all had been brought to Pittsburgh and Wheeling, the western terminals of those roads, by Ohio river steamboats. The Baltimore and Ohio road at that time had no other connections than the river and the National road.[53] The Ohio and Pennsylvania railroad connected Allegheny opposite Pittsburgh, the western terminal of the Pennsylvania railroad, with the roads that radiated to Cleveland, Columbus, and Cincinnati, but very little commerce came to the Pennsylvania over those lines in 1853. One handicap was the absence of a railroad bridge at Pittsburgh.[54] Of more than three hundred thousand barrels of pork transported eastward over the two railroads, about 30%

51. *Seventeenth Annual Report of the Board of Public Works of Ohio*, 97-101.
52. *The Railroads, History and Commerce of Chicago* (1854), tables giving sources of imports and means of exports. Almost the entire export of Chicago came from the northern third or even fourth of Illinois.
53. *Twenty-seventh Annual Report of the Baltimore and Ohio*, 26.
54. *Seventh Annual Report of the Pennsylvania Railroad*, 16, 17.

came by steamboat from Cincinnati alone. Of the thirty thousand barrels of whiskey Cincinnati sent practically all. Of the three hundred thousand barrels of flour, however, Cincinnati sent less than 7%; while Harmar at the southern terminus of the Muskingum improvement in southeastern Ohio sent about 23%.[55] In general, the commodities passing out through the eastern gateway over the two railroads came from every port along the Ohio river and had been produced in the Ohio valley. The relatively small quantity of corn and pork carried from Chatanooga, now the southeastern gateway of the West, over the Western and Atlantic railroad was produced in south central Tennessee. Nearly all the commodities produced in the valleys of the Tennessee and the Cumberland still found their way by steamboat to New Orleans.[56]

The new routes of transportation in the interior of the Old Northwest had changed the general direction of the external trade only to some extent in the case of two important commodities which will be referred to later. The goods shipped through the northeastern gateway from Chicago, Toledo, and Cleveland came as formerly to those places by the railroads and canals from northern Illinois, northern Indiana, and northern Ohio. The commodities going east through Wheeling and Pittsburgh and south to New Orleans, came from the southern halves of the three above named states and from Iowa, Missouri, Kentucky, and Tennessee. The line dividing the region shipping northeastward from that shipping east and south was about where it was in 1849. In western Illinois it had

55. *A Review of the Trade and Commerce of Cincinnati for 1853*, 17; *First Biennial Report of the Board of Public Works to the Governor of Ohio* (Columbus, 1856), 171 et seq.

56. *U. S. House Ex. Docs.*, 50 Cong., 1 sess., vol. XX, no. 6, pt. 2 [serial 2552], pp. 214, 222.

swung somewhat farther north for most products. Goods produced in the Illinois river valley south of LaSalle usually went southward to St. Louis, while commodities produced north of that place were carried to Chicago by the canal.[57] On the railroad route connecting Chicago with St. Louis, the dividing line seems to have been near Bloomington, about midway between the two places. Commodities shipped from places south of that place went to Alton and St. Louis, while goods shipped from points north went to Chicago. Almost the whole of Chicago's receipts of agricultural commodities had been produced in the extreme northern third of the state.[58] Goods produced in Indiana at some distance north of Lafayette went to Lake Michigan by the newly completed Salem and New Albany railroad. This region as yet exported comparatively little, however.[59] Goods produced in the upper Wabash valley as far south as Lafayette went as formerly by the Wabash and Erie canal to Toledo, while that exported from the region lying south of Terre Haute, Indianapolis, and Richmond went by the rivers and railroads to the Ohio river. The dividing line still crossed the canals and railroads in the state of Ohio at Piqua, Springfield, Columbus, and Newark.[60] In general, then, the northeastern gateway con-

57. *Western Journal*, VI, 320.
58. *Annual Review, History of St. Louis* (1854), 25-28; *The Railroads, History and Commerce of Chicago* (1854), 57-66. Table indicate sources of imports for the two cities and the railroads, rivers and canals by which imports came.
59. Andrews, *Report*, 215.
60. *Annual Report of the Trustees of the Wabash and Erie Canal for 1853*, pp. 48-66; *Seventeenth Annual Report of the Board of Public Works of Ohio*, 26-101, give arrivals and clearances of each commodity at each toll station; *Third Annual Report of the Directors of the Cleveland, Columbus and Cincinnati Railroad Co.*, 18, gives quantity of each commodity transported from Columbus and south of Columbus to Cleveland. Only

tinued to be the outlet for the part of the Old Northwest north of the National road. Any increase in the export through that outlet reflected increased production in that region, while the southern and eastern gateways took the commodities produced west and south of that area. The southern gateway had, however, decreased its receipts of flour by about 20% and its pork by 27% constituting about 300,000 barrels of each since 1849. Its whole loss in receipt of flour and nearly all its loss in the receipt of pork had inured to the benefit of the eastern gateway. A little of the pork south of central Ohio had found its way through the northeastern gateway and a little in central and south central Tennessee through the southeastern gateway. Much of the flour and pork formerly exported through New Orleans had been for Baltimore and the Atlantic ports south of that city. The commodities were now beginning to go in part to those same ports by the shorter rail route.

The West was once more increasing her imports at a greater rate than her exports. While exports between 1849 and 1853 had increased by only about 15 or 20%, her imports had increased by more than 100%, rising from three hundred sixty thousand to nearly eight hundred thousand tons. Of the eight hundred thousand tons at

---

15,890 bushels of wheat went to Cleveland from Columbus and stations south of that place, while 468,217 bushels went there from stations north of Columbus. However, the equivalent of 90,000 barrels of pork went to Cleveland from stations south of Columbus, while only 40,000 bbls. went from stations north. Pork both on the canal and on the railroads was moving northward from Cincinnati in larger quantities than it was going to Cincinnati from the north. Live hogs were moving toward Cincinnati and toward Columbus in about equal numbers over the railroads connecting those two points. Of 119,521 live hogs shipped to Cleveland, 71,775 were shipped from stations north of Columbus. See also *Little Miami Railroad Co., Twelfth Annual Report of the Directors* (Cincinnati, 1854), 39.

least 20% consisted of railroad irons, 17% of salt, 15% of sugar, 6% of coffee, 10% of dry goods.[61] The northeastern gateway continued to increase that ascendancy over the other two gateways first shown in 1849 and advanced its receipts from one hundred seventy-five thousand to about four hundred seventy thousand tons, almost three times the former amount. The receipts through the eastern gateway had mounted meanwhile from sixty-five thousand to ninety thousand, and those through the southern from one hundred twenty-five thousand to two hundred twenty-five thousand tons. The receipts through the southeastern gateway were probably about twenty-five thousand. Of the imports through the northeastern gateway three hundred eighty thousand tons came through the Erie and Welland canals in almost exactly equal quantities. The commodities coming through the Welland canal had almost all originally come through New York over the Oswego canal, a branch of the Erie canal.[62] The railroads terminating at Buffalo and Dunkirk contributed the other ninety thousand tons arriving at the northeastern gateway.[63] The two largest items in the importations and

61. *N. Y. Assembly Documents, 1854,* p. 191; *Seventh Annual Report of the Pennsylvania R. R. Co.,* 9; *Twenty-Eighth Annual Report of the Baltimore and Ohio,* 38; *DeBow's Review,* XVII, 626 and XXIX, 524. Known quantities of goods imported included: railroad irons, 147,636 tons; salt, 131,671 tons; sugar, 117,455 tons; molasses, 50,000 tons; coffee, 44,813 tons; dry goods, 29,626 tons; groceries, 10,496 tons; furniture, 17,207 tons. The westward tonnage of the New York Railroads consisting of about 90,000 tons and of the Western and Atlantic consisting of about 25,000 tons was composed of unknown articles probably largely dry goods and hardware, but are not therefore included in the above.

62. *N. Y. Assembly Docs., 1854,* no. 145, pp. 121, 191; *Tables of Trade and Navigation of the Province of Canada,* 2-4.

63. Goods arriving from the East at Dunkirk and Buffalo in 1853 over the New York and Erie railroad amounted to 41,311 tons. *Report of the*

constituting together just half the total tonnage brought through the northeastern gateway were a hundred forty-five thousand tons of railroad iron and ninety thousand tons of salt brought almost altogether by canal. The other two hundred and thirty-five thousand tons consisted of merchandise including sugar and molasses, coffee, nails, hardware, drygoods, furniture, and drugs.[64] The greater part of the railroad iron went to Illinois and Ohio in almost equal quantities, although small amounts went to every state in the Northwest. Of the merchandise brought to the northeastern gateway by the canals, northern Ohio took 27%, northern Indiana 8%, northern Illinois 18%, Michigan 16%, and Wisconsin 12%. Very small quantities went to other western states and Canada. Of the ninety thousand tons of imports through the eastern gateway the Pennsylvania railroad brought to Pittsburgh fifty-two thousand tons, exactly the same amount as had been brought there by canal in 1849, and the Baltimore and Ohio brought to Wheeling something less than forty thousand tons. Of the arrivals at Pittsburgh over half the tonnage came through from Philadelphia and over half of that consisted of drygoods. The other commodities consisted of merchandise of all kinds.[65] The imports over the

Directors of New York and Erie (New York, 1853), 84. Arrivals from East at Buffalo over the New York Central roads in 1850 was probably about 49,000 tons. Hunt, *Merchants' Magazine*, XXX, 311.

64. In this 235,000 tons of merchandise brought to the northeastern gateway by the canals, there was included 14,211 tons of sugar, and 10,475 tons of coffee. *N. Y. Assembly Docs., 1854*, no. 145, p. 191. Since the canals brought no dry goods and since the Pennsylvania railroad and the Baltimore and Ohio carried to their western terminals over 30,000 tons of dry goods, it would probably follow that about this quantity of dry goods was contributed by the New York railroads and included in the 235,000 tons.

65. *Seventh Annual Report of the Pennsylvania Railroad Company*, 75, 77.

Baltimore and Ohio were similar except that coffee and groceries held a more prominent part.[66] From the south there came a little over a hundred thousand tons of sugar, fifty thousand tons of molasses, fifty thousand tons of salt, and twenty-five thousand tons of coffee. The southern gateway was still supplying 90% of all the sugar and molasses and 60% of the coffee entering the West.[67] Of more than a hundred thousand tons of sugar shipped up the Mississippi river, Cincinnati and St. Louis each took more than twenty-seven thousand tons, or nearly four times the total amount of sugar reaching the interior from the east and the northeast. Most of the sugar imported by Cincinnati was of course for redistribution in the Northwest.[68] Nearly five thousand tons of this sugar were cleared northward from Cincinnati on the Miami canal alone. From this source three thousand tons were distributed to the towns on the Miami canal and on the upper Wabash and Erie canal, and the remaining two thousand tons arrived by canal at Toledo for distribution by way of the Great Lakes.[69] The sugar arriving from New Orleans at Portsmouth, Ohio, supplied the towns along the Ohio canal as far north as Dover, or more than two-thirds the distance across the state of Ohio. Of eight thousand tons of coffee imported into Cincinnati, chiefly from the south, the larger part was re-exported. Cincinnati supplied

66. *Twenty-eighth Annual Report of the Baltimore and Ohio*, 38. Included were 5159 tons of coffee, 244 tons of sugar, 9549 tons of other groceries, and 13,091 tons of dry goods.

67. *DeBow's Review*, XVII, 626 and XXIX, 524.

68. *Annual Statement of Commerce of Cincinnati for the year ending Aug. 31, 1861*, p. 43; *Annual Review, History of St. Louis*, Missouri Republican (1854), 25-28.

69. *Seventeenth Annual Report of the Board of Public Works... of Ohio*, 31-59, 77-101.

the towns along the Miami canal and helped to supply the towns on the upper Wabash and Erie canal in northern Indiana.[70] Of the twenty-five thousand tons of coffee forwarded by New Orleans, eight thousand tons were imported by St. Louis. This was largely for re-export to Illinois, Missouri, and the upper Mississippi. The commerce of the interior had grown a trifle but not changed in character. Exports from the Old Northwest as a whole had not increased much during the last four years. Imports into the region as a whole had on the other hand doubled. The northern half and the southern half had, however, not shared equally in this. Exports from the northern part of the Old Northwest had increased a little and imports into that section had grown surprisingly, but the direction and the routes of trade remained unchanged. The production of a surplus in the southern part of the Old Northwest and in the Old Southwest had about come to a standstill. That region had increased its production sufficiently to take care of its own increase of population and to supply the needs of the South and that was about all. A considerable part of the pork and flour produced in the eastern end of the Ohio valley that had formerly been sent to the South Atlantic states by way of New Orleans now went through by rail.

In 1853 the people of the West were obviously enjoying better times and were hopeful of the future. It was the year in which Chicago and St. Louis had been linked to the Atlantic seaports with continuous railway communication. Many branch or feeder lines were being built and many more planned. Danger from the side of southern disunion-

70. *Seventeenth Annual Report of Board of Public Works . . . of Ohio*, 31-59, 77-101.

ists seemed over, and steps had been taken to strengthen the commercial lines between the Northwest and the Southwest. Since the discovery of gold in California fifty millions annually in gold had been added to the money to enlarge the basis of the circulating medium and credit. Commodity prices had been rising rather steadily in the West for a decade.[71] From 1839 to 1849 the people of the West had increased their exports much more rapidly than they did their imports. During that period in every five years they doubled or increased the quantity of their exports by one hundred per cent while increasing their imports by only half that much. Now the process was more than reversed. Between 1849 and 1853 they had doubled the quantity of their annual imports while increasing their exports by only about twenty-five per cent. While this reversal was much more pronounced in the region that was tributary to the Great Lakes[72] than in the Ohio valley, both sections were apparently entering upon a period of expansion.

71. The average price of prime wheat in Cincinnati was about 66 cents in 1843, 69 in 1844, 70 in 1845, 65 in 1846, 79 in 1847, 81 in 1848, 77 in 1849, 87 in 1850, 67 in 1851, 65 in 1852, 83 in 1853. Aldrich, *Report*, in *U. S. Sen. Reports*, 52 Cong., 2 sess., vol. III, pt. 2, no. 1394 [serial 3074, pt. 2], pp. 60-62.

72. On the basis of careful calculations exports of the West through the Buffalo gateway in 1853 were only worth forty million dollars whereas imports were worth eighty-five million or more than twice as much. Hunt, *Merchants' Magazine*, XXX, 304.

CHAPTER VI

The West Engages in the Wrangle Over Building a Railroad to the Pacific, 1854-1857

THE TRUCE between the North and the South during the period from 1850 to 1853, when projects for commercially linking more closely the Old Northwest and the Old Southwest were agreed upon, was largely supplanted in the period from 1854 to 1857 by a revival of the old tendency of the North and the South to reach out toward the west and to link up along east and west lines—the tendency so dominant in the period from 1845 to 1849. Consciously and subconsciously there was the desire on the part of sections to organize territory to the west of them for further settlement in order to secure the benefits of the resultant interstate and foreign trade and to secure for their sections the resultant additional weight in the Federal government. By 1854 the Northeast was well connected by railroad and waterway with the western limits of the Old Northwest and there now developed the desire to extend those railroad connections and settlements to the western limits of the Far Northwest. The Southeast had some good water connections through its coastal and river steamship lines with the Old Southwest and was about to complete a railroad line from Charleston to Memphis. The Southeast now developed the hope of extending its connections to the Far Southwest. The Old West naturally welcomed these projects and proposals as the means of giving it one more gateway to the outside world. To the northeastern, eastern, southeastern, and southern outlets there might now be added a western.

The project of a Pacific railroad had been advocated by

a few dreamers as far back as the early thirties.[1] But in the restless period of westward extension between 1845 and 1849 the project was brought to the attention of the public and kept there by the ceaseless activities of Asa Whitney, the New York merchant. His plan was to have Congress grant him a wide strip of land along both sides of the proposed railroad upon which he would plant foreigners and Americans, who in turn were to do the work in the building of the railroad and to provide it with business as soon as any part of it had been completed. He addressed meetings of business men and politicians in most of the important cities and in many cases secured resolutions approving his plan. He seems, however, to have been more successful with his meetings in the Ohio valley than in any other section. He addressed state legislatures in the North and in the South and secured instructions from the legislatures of some seventeen or more states to their senators and congressmen asking them to support his project.[2] He memorialized Congress again and again and succeeded in having bills introduced incorporating his ideas but never succeeded in getting any of them passed.[3] When he presented his first memorial in 1845, the United States claimed the Pacific coast from latitude 42° to 54° 40'. It was quite natural then that his project should assume a route from Lake Michigan to the mouth of the Columbia. This would have been at that time for the American West a fairly central route. But by 1849, as a result of the Ore-

1. J. P. Davis, *The Union Pacific Railway* (Chicago, 1894), 13 et seq.
2. Asa Whitney, *Address before the Legislature of Pennsylvania* (Harrisburg, 1848), 3, 9; A. Whitney, *Address before the Legislature of Alabama on the Project of a Railroad; U. S. House Reports*, 31 Cong., 1 sess., vol. I, no. 140 [serial 583], p. 21.
3. *Cong. Globe*, 29 Cong., 1 sess., p. 1171; *Ibid.*, 30 Cong., 1 sess., pp. 875, 1011; *Ibid.*, 30 Cong., 2 sess., pp. 381, 382, 388.

gon treaty on the one hand and of the treaty of Guadaloupe Hidalgo on the other, the western coast of the United States extended from latitude 31° 28' to 49°. The American Far West had in a sense shifted bodily southward down the coast. In the meantime the discovery of gold had attracted a considerable population to the southern half of this region and that part was now ready for admission into the Union as the state of California. In 1845 there would have been no possibility of a southern route except through Mexican territory. Even a route directly west from St. Louis would have soon fallen outside the southern boundaries of the United States, but by 1849 all was changed. The St. Louis route would by the latter date have been central in location. In that year Senator Benton introduced his bill for a central railroad from St. Louis to San Francisco. Senator Sam Houston of Texas introduced a bill for a railroad from Galveston to southern California, and Hartwell Carver and others petitioned Congress for charters to build a railroad west from some point on Lake Michigan or on the Mississippi or Missouri river. Senator Niles of Connecticut was still trying to get Congress to pass his bill for a grant of land to Whitney for the purpose of getting a road built.[4] Thus there were at one and at the same time projects for northern, southern, and central Pacific railroads. A large convention of delegates from fourteen middle and northern states met at St. Louis in the same year, condemned Whitney's project for a northern route, and indorsed St. Louis

---

4. *Cong. Globe,* 30 Cong., 2 sess., pp. 470-74, 551; *U. S. Senate Journal,* 30 Cong., 2 sess. [serial 528], pp. 192, 227, 283; *Senate Bills,* 30 Cong., 2 sess., no. 451, no. 472; Dr. Hartwell Carver, *A Memorial for a Private Charter, Asked for by Dr. Hartwell Carver and His Associates for Building a Railroad* (Washington, D. C., 1849), 3, 4.

as the proper eastern terminus. When it came to defining the remainder of the route, however, the divergence of views of the delegates to the St. Louis convention was reflected in the decision to cross the Rockies farther north than Benton had suggested. A few days later a convention of delegates of fifteen southern states met at Memphis and in their resolutions expressed a preference for a route with its eastern terminus between the mouths of the Ohio and the Red rivers.[5] A Pacific Railroad convention composed of northeastern and northwestern delegates met at Chicago the same year and advocated a road due west from Chicago. Clearly the sectional interests in Pacific railroad building were so sharply in conflict that it would have been difficult to agree upon any route. Each section wanted to use the railroad to extend its own settlements westward and to bring to its own doors the trade of the Orient. The Old West instead of uniting in an effort to secure at least one of these outlets, itself tended to divide into sections, each section hoping with the support of the section to the east of it to secure the route running directly west from it. The differences of opinion concerning the proper route for a Pacific railroad paralleled the differences of opinion on the proper method of disposing of the Mexican cessions and of settling various questions with regard to slavery. But when Clay of the Ohio valley urged Congress to settle the question concerning the Mexican cessions and slavery by compromise in 1850, he unfortunately did not include among his measures the plan of Benton for a central route for a Pacific railroad. Nor

5. *Official Proceedings of the Mississippi Valley Railroad Convention held in St. Louis, Nov., 1852* (St. Louis, 1852), 14; *U. S. House Reports*, 31 Cong., 1 sess., vol. III, no. 439 [serial 585], pp. 20, 35; *DeBow's Review*, VII, 217, 218.

did Stephen A. Douglas, who did so much to get through Congress the compromise measures and the bills for a Lakes to the Gulf railroad, see fit at that time to introduce a Pacific railroad bill. It possibly could have passed along with the other measures when the spirit of compromise was in the air. In spite of differences of opinion there were at that time strong supporters even in the Northeast and in the South of a central or compromise route.[6] Had a central railroad been put under process of construction at that time, it might have strengthened the influence and solidarity of the Ohio valley and the Middle Atlantic region, which held the balance of political power between the northeastern and southeastern extremes. Furthermore, the two extremes, the upper North and the lower South, through their interest in this national line of transportation and through their anticipations of economic gain therefrom would possibly have been brought closer together. But this was not tried out. For a few years following 1850 the question of the Pacific railroad along with those questions supposed to have been settled by the compromises in that year were not so much agitated.

The period proved to be, however, only a truce. In 1853 the Pacific railroad question revived in all its fury. Senator William M. Gwin of California early in the session of 1852-53 introduced a bill for a southern trunk line to the Pacific with branches in the direction of the principal cities in the Mississippi valley contesting for the honor of serving as the eastern terminal of such a road.[7] In spite of

6. *Proceedings of the Friends of a Railroad to San Francisco* (Boston, 1849), 3.
7. *U. S. Senate Journal,* 32 Cong., 2 sess. [serial 657], pp. 50, 95, 153, 154; *Senate Bills,* 32 Cong., 2 sess., no. 560; *Cong. Globe,* 32 Cong., 2 sess., vol. XXVI, pp. 125, 126, 280, 281, 353.

this last feature, the bill was more favorable to the South, inasmuch as the trunk road was directly in line with a point on the Mississippi between Memphis and Vicksburg. Senator S. P. Chase of Ohio proposed a central route with its eastern terminus on the lower Missouri. Senator Thomas J. Rusk of Texas brought before the Senate a proposal to leave to the president the responsibility of selecting the route and of making contracts for the building of the Pacific road.[8] This, too, would have favored the South inasmuch as the new president would undoubtedly have decided on a route in line with Memphis.[9] The differences of opinion were such, however, that the best that Congress could do in that session was to appropriate money for a series of surveys to be made by the Secretary of War and to be reported back to it, and this was done.[10]

President Pierce in his first annual message of December, 1853, urged upon Congress the necessity of providing for a better means of communication with the Pacific coast.[11] The Senate was, however, so divided on that question that it had difficulty in even deciding to which committee that part of the message should be referred. In due time two companion bills were introduced, one in the Senate and one in the House, providing for a road without designating any eastern terminus but leaving the selection to the contractor.[12] Another bill was introduced, proposing

---

8. *Cong. Globe,* 32 Cong., 2 sess., vol. XXVI, pp. 431, 458, 489; *U. S. Senate Journal,* 32 Cong. 2 sess. [serial 657], pp. 142, 171, 221; *Senate Bills,* 32 Cong., 2 sess., no. 396.

9. *Cong. Globe,* 32 Cong., 2 sess., vol. XXVI, p. 341.

10. 32 Cong., 2 sess., ch. 98, sec. 510, in *Statutes at Large of U. S.* (Boston, 1855), X, 219.

11. Richardson, *Messages and Papers,* V, 221.

12. *Cong. Globe,* 33 Cong., 1 sess., vol. XXVIII, pt. 2, pp. 876, 1333, 1381; *U. S. Senate Journal,* 33 Cong., 1 sess. [serial 689], pp. 256, 374, 738;

to build from one to three roads.¹³ Other measures were introduced but the session came to a close without any Pacific railroad bill passing.

There was not merely a division between the North and the South. As in the years between 1845 and 1849 the West was itself again divided because of local interests. One group preferred a route from Lake Superior through Minnesota, another wanted a road from Chicago through Iowa, the Ohio valley for the most part favored a route westward from St. Louis, while still farther south groups favored routes on the parallels of Memphis, Vicksburg, New Orleans, or Galveston. Members of the national lower house usually reflected these local interests in their voting. Members of the upper house had a more difficult time in knowing how to vote inasmuch as their constituencies frequently embraced two different interests. The South and Southwest had several advantages in this contest. The land acquired as a result of the Mexican war had been granted territorial or state governments by the compromise of 1850 and was to that extent ready for occupation by settlers. If the Federal government granted land to a southern road, this land as well as that retained by the government near the road could be sold more advantageously to settlers and thus not only furnish the money with which to build the road but also lay the basis for soon providing the road with business. The South, too, was ably and actively represented in President Pierce's administration by Jefferson Davis, the Secretary of War,

---

Senate Bills, 33 Cong., 1 sess., no. 273; *U. S. House Journal,* 33 Cong., 1 sess. [serial 709], pp. 495, 994, 1404; *House Bills,* 33 Cong., 1 sess., no. 295.

13. *U. S. House Journal,* 33 Cong., 1 sess. [serial 709], p. 443; *House Bills,* 33 Cong., 1 sess., no. 290.

the dominant figure in the cabinet, and possibly the most influential advisor of the President. In his report of the surveys already referred to, the Secretary of War distinctly expressed his preference for a southern route near the thirty-second parallel.[14] To improve the possibilities of the southern route, the president, on advice of his Secretary of War, late in 1853 sent James Gadsden, the former president of the Louisville, Cincinnati and Charleston and of the South Carolina railroads, and an ardent advocate of the consolidation of the South, to buy from Mexico a strip of land south of the Gila river that was claimed by the engineers to be necessary for the best possible southern route. Gadsden secured this land.[15]

Thoroughly convinced that the South had already fallen behind in industry, commerce, and population, and that it would soon fall behind in its weight in the Federal government, the leaders of the South were more aggressive than northern leaders. By 1854 southern men in the cabinet, at foreign diplomatic posts, in Congress, and in private life were trying in different ways to acquire more slave territory by annexing Cuba, Nicaragua, or Mexico.[16] In that year all the southern states except Texas sent delegates to a so-called southern commercial convention that met at Charleston. It was there proposed by Albert Pike and approved by other delegates that a confederation of southern states within the United States be formed for the

14. *Reports of Explorations and Surveys,* in *U. S. Sen. Ex. Docs.,* 33 Cong., 2 sess., vol. XIII, pt. 1, no. 78 [serial 758], p. 29.

15. P. N. Garber, *The Gadsden Treaty* (Philadelphia, 1923), 23. Mexico's consent to American ownership of the Messela river valley also necessary to the southern route and claimed by the American government under the terms of the treaty of Guadaloupe Hidalgo was also secured by the Gadsden treaty.

16. W. O. Scroggs, *Filibusters and Financiers* (New York, 1916), 6.

purpose of receiving from the Federal government a donation of land and of building a southern railroad through to the Pacific.[17] It was also there proposed to improve the Atlantic harbors of the Southeastern railroads connecting with the proposed southern Pacific railroad and to take steps to revive the trade of those ports with European countries and with South and Central America by subsidizing steamship lines. The members of the convention believed that closer commercial relations with Brazil, the only other important slave-holding country, should be established and that southern manufacturing and education should be fostered.[18] The seriousness of forming such a confederation, such a state within a state, was pointed out by men in the convention and by critics of the movement on the outside who discerned the beginning of the end of the Union in such a confederacy.[19]

Contrast with these conditions the situation in the North. In the beginning of 1854 the great Nebraska country, through which a road westward from Lake Superior, Lake Michigan, or St. Louis would have to pass, was still without territorial government. Moreover southern congressmen were for the most part determined to keep it as an unorganized region in order to discourage the ingoing of settlers from the North and of foreigners. Before the close of the year 1854, however, the region had been promised a territorial government by the passage of the Kansas-Nebraska act which organized the region into two terri-

17. *Journal of the Preceedings of the Commercial Convention of the Southern and Western States* (Charleston, 1854), 64.
18. *Commercial Conventions, Direct Trade, A Chance for the South* [n. p., n. d.], 19, 21.
19. *Journal of the Proceedings of the Commercial Convention,* 71, 113; *The Mississippi River and its Great Tributaries* (Washington, 1856), 11, 13.

tories, one lying west of Missouri and one west of Iowa and Minnesota. But in doing this, the sponsor for the measure, Stephen A. Douglas of Illinois, the most conspicuous member in Congress from the Old Northwest at that time, had seen fit to assume that the Missouri Compromise, which had prohibited slavery in that region, had been repealed by the Compromise of 1850.[20] The author of the Kansas-Nebraska Act now introduced in the Senate at the next session of Congress a bill providing for a possible three roads, a northern, a southern, and a central with its eastern terminal either in Missouri or Iowa.[21] He also quickly induced James A. McDougal in the House and Gwin in the Senate to accept such amendments to their bills introduced in the preceding session as would make them conform in substance with his bill.[22] These amended bills then became the storm centers during the early months of 1855. Douglas possibly hoped that his scheme could be further amended by his friends into a project for a single road that would be acceptable. Such a method of procedure had been successfully employed a few years before by him in the Illinois Central project. In the House the McDougal amended bill was further amended into a measure for a single central road and

20. For a discussion of possible relations between the Kansas-Nebraska act and the Pacific railroad bill, see F. H. Hodder, "Genesis of the Kansas-Nebraska Act," in *Proceedings of State Historical Society of Wisconsin for 1912*, 69-85 and P. O. Ray, "Genesis of the Kansas-Nebraska Act," in the *American Historical Association Report for 1914*, 1, 261-80.

21. *U. S. Senate Journal*, 33 Cong., 2 sess. [serial 745], pp. 103, 120; *Senate Bills*, 33 Cong., 2 sess., no. 537, p. 2; *Cong. Globe*, 33 Cong., 2 sess., vol. XXX, pp. 210, 748, 750.

22. *U. S. Senate Journal*, 33 Cong., 2 sess. [serial 745], p. 265, S. B., no. 273; *U. S. House Journal*, 33 Cong., 2 sess. [serial 776], pp. 200, 203, H. B. no. 295; *Cong. Globe*, 33 Cong., 2 sess., vol. XXX, pp. 281, 319.

passed but was recommitted on reconsideration.[23] The Gwin bill amended into the substance of the Douglas bill also passed the Senate[24] but failed in the House. It possibly could have passed had it not been for the opposition of Benton of Missouri, now a member of the House, and some of the members of the southern part of the Old Northwest who wanted the middle route or none at all and who possibly distrusted the manipulations of Douglas.[25] The failure to agree upon a Pacific railroad in 1855 was practically the end of serious effort in that direction until after the outbreak of the Civil War. Many petitions continued to come to Congress from the northeastern and northwestern states.[26] Everybody agreed in theory that there should be a Pacific railroad. Both political parties in 1856 in their platforms approved of such a road, and the new president in 1857 both in his inaugural and in his first annual message favored one. But an agreement as to just which route was to be followed seemed then out of the question until after the outbreak of the war, when the northern states were free to go on alone. The urge toward the westward, however, went on without the Pacific railroad. The repeal of the Missouri compromise in connection with the organization of Kansas and Nebraska led to some noisy migration into Kansas from the Northeast and the Southeast, but for the most part Kansas was occupied by the people of Missouri and of the Ohio valley. It was a case of the middle region extending itself westward,

23. *Cong. Globe*, 33 Cong., 2 sess., vol. XXX, pp. 316, 330; *U. S. House Journal*, 33 Cong., 2 sess. [serial 776], pp. 203, 209, 225, 235.
24. *U. S. Senate Journal*, 33 Cong., 2 sess. [serial 745], p. 289, S. B. no. 273; *Cong. Globe*, 33 Cong., 2 sess., vol. XXX, p. 814.
25. *Cong. Globe*, 33 Cong., 2 sess., Appendix, vol. XXXI, p. 200.
26. *U. S. Senate Journal*, 34 Cong., 1 & 2 sess. [serial 809], pp. 168. 182, 199, 225, 231, 239, 243, 296, 301, 313, 314, 335, 380, 386.

while the northern extreme sent its surplus into Minnesota, and the southern extreme into Texas.[27]

Between the close of 1853 and the end of 1857, only a few new developments in the routes that served as outlets for the Old West were perfected. The Pennsylvania Company had in 1854 completed its own road over the mountains[28] to replace the Portage railroad and had in 1857 bought the main line of the Pennsylvania canals and railroads between Pittsburgh and Philadelphia.[29] It thereafter used the canals chiefly for the transportation of coal and lumber and operated the railroad from Columbia to Philadelphia as a part of its through line. The Pennsylvania railroad seems, however, to have been still hampered by the requirement of paying to the state a tonnage tax of three mills per ton per mile, which was the equivalent of a dollar and sixteen cents for every ton shipped from Pittsburgh to Philadelphia.[30] This naturally placed the Pennsylvania at some disadvantage in meeting competition through the lowering of freight rates. In 1857 the Baltimore and Ohio company had completed the Northwestern Virginia railroad, thus securing a terminus on the Ohio river at Parkersburg, about a hundred miles down the river from Wheeling, the other western terminal of the Baltimore and Ohio. The additional western terminal was

27. W. O. Lynch, "Population Movements in Relation to the Struggle for Kansas," in *Studies in American History* (Bloomington, 1926), 388-89.

28. *Eighth Annual Report of the Pennsylvania Railroad Company* (Philadelphia, 1855), 3.

29. *Eleventh Annual Report of the Pennsylvania Railroad Company* (Philadelphia, 1858), 9.

30. *Seventh Annual Report of the Pennsylvania Railroad Company*, 11, 34; *Ninth Annual Report of the Pennsylvania Railroad Company* (Philadelphia, 1856), 14; *Tenth Annual Report of the Pennsylvania Railroad Company* (Philadelphia, 1857), 11; *Twelfth Annual Report of the Pennsylvania Railroad Company* (Philadelphia, 1858), p. 20.

a considerable advantage during the low water season on the Ohio.[31] Competition between the Erie canal and the New York railroads induced the canal commissioners to steadily lower the toll rates during the fifties, but the reduction in toll rates, the expense of enlarging the canal and building new canals, and the corruption connected with managing them continually resulted in deficits.[32] To take care of the deficits, the New York Assembly then began the practice of imposing special property taxes varying from year to year from a half-mill to a mill on all property in the state.[33] The railroad owners had to pay this tax along with the other property owners, but they made strenuous objections to paying for the upkeep of the canals, their competitors. This tax amounted in the case of the New York Central to about the same as a tonnage tax of one and one-half mills per ton per mile on all tonnage carried.[34] This would have been equivalent to a tax of about seventy-five cents on every ton carried by rail from Buffalo to New York City. The railroads were, in spite of this, slowly reducing rates, and the freight rate on the New York and Erie railroad was reduced from an average of 2.58 cents per ton per mile in 1854 to 2.46 cents in 1857. This was equal to reducing the rate on a bushel of wheat from Lake Erie to New York City from about 33

31. *Thirty-first Annual Report of the Baltimore and Ohio Railroad* (Baltimore, 1857), 10.
32. *Report of the Auditor of the Canal Department*, in *N. Y. Assembly Docs.*, 1854, no. 145, p. 186; *Annual Report of Canal Commissioners*, in *N. Y. Assembly Docs.*, 1859, no. 40, p. 58; Whitford, *History of the Canal System*, I, 200-42; *Transportation Routes to the Seaboard*, in *U. S. Senate Reports*, 43 Cong., 1 sess., vol. III, pt. 1, no, 307 [serial 1588], Appendix p. 168.
33. *Laws of New York*, 1857, ch. 363; *Ibid.*, 1858, ch. 353; *Ibid.*, 1859, ch. 149.
34. *N. Y. Assembly Docs.*, 1861, vol. V, no. 93, p. 12.

cents to about 31 cents. The Erie canal was carrying wheat during that same period from Buffalo to Albany at from 13 to 17.5 cents per bushel and corn at from 10 to 15 cents.[35] With such difference in freight rates the railroads could not compete with the canal in the carrying of grain except while the canals were frozen up.

The St. Lawrence canals between Lake Erie and Montreal had been completed one after the other in the years between 1826 and 1856 so that the smaller lake vessels could now go all the way from Chicago to Montreal.[36] A few even went during these years from Chicago to Europe.[37] But the lower St. Lawrence outlet did not play a prominent part before the American Civil War.[38] The Canadians had, however, also been building railroads that could play a part in carrying the products of the Old Northwest to the seaboard. Early in 1854 the Great Western railroad was opened and ran eastward from Windsor opposite Detroit through Hamilton to Suspension Bridge, a little north of Buffalo. Another road ran northeastward from Hamilton on the Great Western to Toronto on Lake Ontario.[39] Before the close of 1856 the Grand Trunk railroad had been opened from Stratford near Lake Huron eastward through Toronto to Montreal, Quebec, and Portland, Maine. Early in 1855 the Canadian Northern railroad had been opened from Collingwood on the southern

---

35. Aldrich, *Report on Wholesale Prices*, pt. 1 [serial 3074, pt. 1], pp. 523, 616. The rates given included tolls and freight.

36. Whitford, *History of Canals*, I, 1441-45.

37. *Cleveland Herald's First Annual Statement of the Trade and Commerce of Cleveland for 1858* (Cleveland, 1859), 14.

38. *Report of the Chief Engineer of Public Works on the Navigation of the River St. Lawrence between Lake Ontario and Montreal* (Ottawa, 1874), 11.

39. The Hamilton and Toronto R. R.

end of Georgian Bay southward to Toronto, a point on the Grand Trunk.[40] Goods could thus be carried from Detroit across the river to Windsor or from Cleveland across the lake to Port Stanley and then be transported over the Port Stanley and London railroad and over the Great Western to Suspension Bridge whence, after passing a short distance by the Buffalo, Niagara Falls and Lewiston R. R., they could proceed either by the New York Central road or by the Erie canal or by Lake Ontario steamer. Instead of going all the way to Suspension Bridge, the goods could be transferred at Hamilton for Toronto and then be carried by the Grand Trunk to Montreal, Quebec, or Portland, Maine. Goods from Chicago could go by rail or lake to Detroit and follow the above named routes, or they could go from Chicago by lake to Collingwood on the Georgian Bay and proceed by the Northern railroad to Toronto, where they could either transfer to the Grand Trunk and proceed to Montreal or could transfer to a steamer on Lake Ontario and proceed either to Oswego, another terminus of the Erie canal, to Ogdensburg, a terminus of the Northern New York, or to Montreal. A large quantity of wheat exported from the Old Northwest found its way to the Northeast over these Canadian routes.

In the Old Southwest a few developments had occurred in lines of transportation. Nashville on the Cumberland river after 1854 and Memphis on the Mississippi from the first part of 1857 both had connections by rail through Chattanooga with Charleston and Savannah. Goods could be carried by steamboats from Evansville and Cairo up the Cumberland river to Nashville, or up the Tennessee river

---

40. *Board of Railway Commissioners of Canada,* Report of Samuel Keefer (Toronto, 1861), 24; Appleton, *Railway and Steam Navigation Guide* (New York, Dec., 1857).

to Tuscumbia, or down the Mississippi to Memphis and then be shipped by rail from either of those three points through Chattanooga and Atlanta to Charleston and Savannah. Charleston and Savannah never became seaports for the exports of the West, but commodities passed from the West over these routes and were distributed over the South as far as the Atlantic sea coast.

Within the Old Northwest several important connecting railroads were completed during the period 1854-57. Before the close of 1857 an all-rail route ran from Illiniostown, nearly opposite St. Louis, through Cincinnati to Marietta, nearly opposite Parkersburg, one of the western terminals of the Baltimore and Ohio.[41] Another fairly direct route after 1855 connected Cincinnati with Bellaire, across the Ohio from Wheeling, the other western terminal of the Baltimore and Ohio.[42] Two fairly direct lines after 1856 connected Cincinnati with Pittsburgh, the western terminal of the Pennsylvania road.[43] A direct route from 1856 connected Pittsburgh with Chicago;[44] a fourth,

---

41. The Mississippi and Ohio Railroad, from Illinoistown to Cincinnati; the Cincinnati and Marietta, from Cincinnati to Marietta.

42. The Little Miami, from Cincinnati to Morrow; the Cincinnati, Wilmington, and Zanesville, from Morrow to Zanesville; the Central Ohio, from Zanesville to Bellaire.

43. The Ohio and Pennsylvania, from Pittsburgh to Rochester; the Cleveland and Pittsburgh, from Rochester to Bellaire; then same as in above note. The Ohio and Pennsylvania, from Pittsburgh to Rochester; the Cleveland and Pittsburgh, from Rochester to Steubenville; the Steubenville and Indiana, from Steubenville to Newark; the Central Ohio, from Newark to Columbus; the Xenia and Columbus, from Columbus to Xenia; the Little Miami, from Xenia to Cincinnati.

44. The Ohio and Pennsylvania, from Pittsburgh through Rochester and Alliance to Crestline; the Ohio and Indiana from Crestline to Ft. Wayne; the Ft. Wayne and Chicago from Ft. Wayne to Plymouth; The Cincinnati, Plymouth, and LaPorte from Plymouth to LaPorte; the Michigan Southern and Northern Indiana from LaPorte to Chicago. In 1856 the

Cleveland with Alton, nearly opposite St. Louis;⁴⁵ and a fifth, Toledo with Alton.⁴⁶ Some half dozen roads running west from Chicago connected that place with Prairie du Chien, Dunleith, Galena, Fulton, Rock Island, Burlington, Quincy, Alton, Illinoistown, and Cairo, all on the Mississippi.⁴⁷ The New Albany and Salem railroad now made a rail connection between Michigan City near Chicago and New Albany on the Ohio. These new roads added to those completed by 1853 made a fairly complete network in the Old Northwest. Before the close of 1857 there was a continuous rail route from a point opposite St. Louis, through Cincinnati and through Parkersburg or Wheeling to Baltimore; from the same point opposite St. Louis through Cincinnati and Pittsburgh to Philadelphia and New York City; from the same point opposite St. Louis through Indianapolis, Cleveland, and Buffalo to New York City and

first three lines consolidated into the Pittsburgh, Ft. Wayne, and Chicago and ran from Plymouth to Chicago over their own road from 1858.

45. The Cleveland, Columbus, and Cincinnati, from Cleveland to Crestline; the Bellefontaine and Indiana and the Indianapolis and Bellefontaine, from Crestline to Indianapolis; the Terre Haute and Richmond from Indianapolis to Terre Haute; the Alton and Terre Haute from Terre Haute to Alton.

46. The Toledo, Wabash, and Western, from Toledo to eastern State Line of Illinois; the Great Western from State Line to Springfield; and the Chicago, Alton, and St. Louis from Springfield to Alton.

47. The Galena and Chicago Union from Chicago to Freeport; the Illinois Central from Freeport to Galena and Dunleith; the Galena and Chicago Union from Chicago to Fulton; the Rock Island from Chicago to Rock Island; the Galena and Chicago Union from Chicago to Aurora; the Chicago, Burlington and Quincy from Aurora to Burlington and Quincy; the Rock Island from Chicago to Joliet; the Chicago, Alton, and St. Louis from Joliet to Alton; the Illinois Central from Chicago to Cairo. The above data is based upon Dinsmore, *American Railway Guide*, and *Appleton Railway Guide*—both issued monthly with maps and time tables of roads in operation.

Boston. There was also a continuous route from Chicago, through Pittsburgh to Philadelphia and Baltimore; from Chicago through Toledo, Dunkirk, or Buffalo to New York City; from Chicago through Detroit and Hamilton to Montreal. These routes were, however, in every case composed of at least two end-for-end roads, with breaks in gauge in some cases, and with breaks at large rivers. There were as yet no railroad bridges at Wheeling, Parkersburg, Cincinnati, Louisville, Cairo, or St. Louis. There were, however, bridges across the Allegheny at Pittsburgh and across the Mississippi at Rock Island from 1856.[48] The large suspension bridge at Wheeling was not a railroad bridge.[49]

A comparison of the total exports of the Old West in 1857 with those of 1853 indicates an average increase of only about 30% of the former amount. The total export of flour had increased by 30%, wheat and corn by 50% each, whiskey by 70%, live hogs by more than 200%, and live cattle by over 350%. But the total export of salt pork had declined by 25% and salt beef by 40%. If, however, the flour be considered as wheat, the total surplus of wheat and wheat products amounted to thirty-six million bushels, or an increase of 29%. If the salt pork, salt beef, live hogs and cattle, and whiskey be counted as corn, the total export of corn and corn products amounted to forty-two million bushels, or an increase of about 30% over 1853.

The total export of wheat had risen from a little over eleven million bushels in 1853 to more than sixteen and a half million bushels in 1857. Of the latter export 90% went by the northeastern gateway, 9% by the southern,

48. *Tenth Annual Report of the Pennsylvania Railroad*, 18.
49. Appleton, *Railway Guide,* Dec. 1857, p. 67.

and considerably less than 1% by the eastern. The quantity of wheat exported to the south because of unusual conditions in financial affairs and in river navigation was higher in that year than ever before or after. The total export of flour from the interior had risen from over three million barrels in 1853 to nearly four million in 1857, 47% of the total going by the northeastern gateway, 32% by the southern, and 20% by the eastern. The quantity of flour going by the northeastern route thus showed an absolute decline of 23% as well as a relative decline of 15%. The southern gateway took 50% more than in 1853 and the eastern 100% more. Nearly twelve million bushels of corn were exported as against a little less than eight million in 1853. About the same quantity went south as in the former year, while the quantity going northeastward had doubled and now amounted to over 66% of the total. The total export of salt meat from the interior had fallen from a little below a million and a half barrels in 1853 to a little over a million in 1857 and the export by each of the three outlets showed an absolute decline since 1853. Over 52% of the total still went south, 25% east, and 23% northeast. The total export of live hogs and cattle had, however, risen from less than fifty thousand tons in 1853 to more than three times that amount in 1857. This tonnage of live stock consisting of over eight hundred thousand hogs and over one hundred sixty thousand cattle would have made good the half million barrel decline in the export of salt meat during the period and would have converted the loss to a gain of perhaps 30%. Three-fourths of the live stock went northeast and the remainder went east, largely to Baltimore. The decline in the total export of tobacco was reflected in decreased export to the south, while the export eastward was stationary. The southern outlet, however, still took 83% of the total, while the eastern took 16% and the northeastern only 1% of the total export of tobacco from the West. The southern avenue in 1853 had taken 73% of all the whiskey exported and in 1857 took 46% of the total, while the eastern in 1853 had carried 14% and in 1857, 39%.[50]

Of the goods arriving at New Orleans from the interior, Cincinnati supplied about 42% of the beef, 16% of the pork, 8% of the flour, and 62% of the whiskey.[51] St. Louis supplied 20% of the beef, 19% of the pork, 85% of the flour, and 85% of the corn.[52] Smaller quantities went from Evansville and the Falls Cities[53] and other points on the Ohio, the Wabash, the Cumberland, the Tennessee, and the upper Mississippi. A considerable part of the export of Evansville and the Wabash river went up the Tennessee and Cumberland rivers. The St. Louis exports came

50. Based upon tables compiled from statistics given in: *Tableaux du Commerce et de la Navigation de la Province du Canada pour l'annee 1857* (Toronto, 1858), 216-18; *Eighth Census, 1860,* Agriculture, pp. CLI; Hunt, *Merchants' Magazine,* vol. XXXVIII, pp. 356, 641, 693-704 and vol. XL, pp. 547, 599, 600; *U. S. House Ex. Docs.,* 50 Cong., 1 sess., vol. XX, no 6, pt. 2 [serial 2552], pp. 216-18; *N. Y. Assembly Docs.,* 1858, vol. V, no. 155, pp. 105-09; *Eleventh Annual Report of the Pennsylvania Railroad Company,* pp. 100-01; *Thirty-first Annual Report of the Baltimore and Ohio,* pp. 77-83, 88; *Statement of the Trade and Commerce of Detroit for 1857* (Detroit, 1858), 7-23; *Statistics of Foreign and Domestic Commerce,* in *U. S. Senate Ex. Docs.,* 38 Cong., 1 sess., vol. I, no. 55 [serial 1176], pp. 162-65; *Monthly Summary of Commerce and Finance of the U. S.,* Jan. 1900, in *U. S. House Docs.,* 56 Cong., 1 sess., vol. LV, no. 15, pt. 7 [serial 3942], p. 1960.

51. *Annual Statement of the Trade and Commerce of Cincinnati for the Commercial year ending Aug. 31, 1857* (Cincinnati, 1857), 31.

52. *Annual Review of the Commerce of St. Louis for 1857* (St. Louis, 1858), 6, 33.

53. *Annual Report of the Board of Trade of Evansville, Indiana,* for 1857 (*Evansville Journal,* Evansville, 1868), 23; Ben Casseday, *History of Louisville* (Louisville, 1852), 206, 233, 235.

chiefly from Missouri, Iowa, and the Illinois river valley; the Evansville exports came from southwestern Indiana, and the Cincinnati exports from southwestern Ohio, southeastern Indiana, and northern Kentucky.

Of the total of two hundred forty thousand tons of exports eastward through Pittsburgh, Wheeling, and Parkersburg, the Pennsylvania and the Baltimore and Ohio railroads each carried about half. Of this total Cincinnati sent by river alone 14% of the flour, 16% of the salt meat, 35% of the whiskey, 60% of the wheat, and 66% of the other grain, chiefly corn.[54] Of the one hundred twenty thousand tons of freight going eastward over the Baltimore and Ohio from Parkersburg and Wheeling to Baltimore, all of the seventeen thousand tons taken on at Parkersburg had come by Ohio river steamboats. At Wheeling another seventeen thousand tons had come from the river and eighty-six thousand tons from the Central Ohio railroad.[55] Of these eighty-six thousand tons from the Central Ohio, twenty-five thousand tons had come through from Cincinnati.[56] Most of the remaining tonnage had come from south central Ohio. In other words, of the one hundred twenty thousand tons carried eastward by the Baltimore and Ohio, thirty-four thousand tons had been brought by steamboats from all the western waters, but chiefly from Cincinnati and the Ohio valley, twenty-five thousand tons had come by rail from Cincinnati, the most important forwarding point for goods pro-

54. *Annual Statement of the Trade and Commerce of Cincinnati for the commercial year ending Aug. 31, 1857*, p. 31.
55. *Thirty-first Annual Report of the Baltimore and Ohio*, 11, 77-83, 88.
56. *Report of the Committee appointed by the Holders of the Second Mortgage Bonds of the Central Ohio Railroad Company* (Baltimore, 1858), 14.

150   THE OLD NORTHWEST

duced in the central Ohio valley, and sixty-one thousand tons was largely made up of the railroad freight of south central Ohio. Of a total of one hundred twenty thousand tons sent eastward from Pittsburgh over the Pennsylvania road,[57] about eighty thousand tons, or two-thirds of the total, were brought there from northern Ohio and northwestern Indiana by the Pittsburgh, Ft. Wayne and Chicago road. This included twenty-eight thousand tons of live stock and nineteen thousand tons of flour and grain and constituted all the live stock and half of all the flour and grain that the Pennsylvania carried from Pittsburgh.[58] In other words, two-thirds of the one hundred twenty thousand tons exported over the Pennsylvania road came from northern Ohio and northern Indiana and had been deflected from the northeastern gateway. Very little came from the Cleveland and Pittsburgh railroad. This left only forty thousand tons, or one-third the total shipment over the Pennsylvania railroad eastward from Pittsburgh, to come from the vicinity of Pittsburgh and from the Ohio river. To sum up, of the total exported through the eastern gateway one-third (84,000 tons) was brought to Pittsburgh by the Pittsburgh, Ft. Wayne and Chicago railroad and was the product largely of northern Ohio and northwestern Indiana, a little over a third (86,000 tons) was brought by the Central Ohio to Wheeling and was the product largely of south central Ohio, and a little less than a third (74,000 tons) came by Ohio river steamboats to Parkersburg, Wheeling, and Pittsburgh and was the prod-

57. *Eleventh Annual Report of the Pennsylvania Railroad Company,* 98.

58. *First Report of the Board of Directors of the Pittsburgh, Ft. Wayne and Chicago Railroad Company for 17 months ending Dec. 31, 1857* (Pittsburgh, 1858), 54.

uct of the entire interior, but chiefly of the upper Ohio valley.

Of the fifteen million bushels of wheat exported northeastward in 1857, northern Illinois alone produced 56%, Wisconsin 16%, northern Indiana 11%, northern Ohio and southern Michigan each 5%. The ports exporting this wheat were Chicago 63%, Milwaukee 17%, Toledo 9%, Cleveland and Detroit each 3%, indicating that about seven-eighths of the wheat exported from Toledo and a small part of that exported from Chicago had originally come from northern Indiana. Of the million and three-quarter barrels of flour exported northeastward, Ohio produced 30%, northern Illinois and Wisconsin each 16%, Michigan 15%, and northern Indiana 13%. The cities forwarding this flour were Detroit 23%, Cleveland 19%, Chicago 15%, Milwaukee 13%, and Toledo 11%[59]. Of something over eight million bushels of corn exported northeastward, northern Illinois produced 78%, northern Indiana 13%, Ohio 6%. By ports, the proportions furnished stood: Chicago 80%, Toledo 16%, Cleveland 2%. Some of the Chicago meat export went to lumbering camps in the northern parts of the Old Northwest. Of the two hundred sixty thousand barrels of pork and beef going northeast, 23% went from Chicago and included only half the total beef export from that place, 25% went from Toledo, and 15% went from Cleveland.

---

59. That part of the Detroit export that had come in by railroads from Chicago is not here credited to Detroit, but to Chicago. *Statement of the Trade and Commerce of Detroit for the year 1857*, pp. 7-23; *Fourth Annual Statement of the Trade and Commerce of the City of Milwaukee for the year 1861*, . . . by the Chamber of Commerce (Milwaukee, 1862), 6, 14; *Annual Review of the Trade and Commerce of Chicago for 1857*, Democratic Press (Chicago, 1858).

Of over one hundred fifty thousand cattle and six hundred thousand live hogs, 20% of the cattle and 20% of the hogs went from Chicago and Joliet; 35% of the cattle and 25% of the hogs from Toledo; 40% of the cattle and 30% of the hogs from Cleveland. Of the sixty thousand barrels of whiskey and spirits 60% went from Cleveland and 30% from Toledo. The Chicago surplus of whiskey went to the northern lumber camps.[60]

The commodities exported from Chicago came for the most part from the northern third of Illinois. Of the ten million bushels of wheat and the half million barrels of flour exported from Chicago, three-fourths came by the Galena and Chicago Union; the Chicago, Burlington, and Quincy; and the Rock Island railroads alone from the northwestern third of Illinois. Very little passed from the Mississippi river over these roads to Chicago. Of the seven million bushels of corn exported from Chicago, over half came from the Illinois and Michigan canal from northern Illinois, and practically all of the other half of the corn came by the above three named roads from northwestern Illinois. Of the live hogs nearly 80% came in by wagons from northern Illinois and northwestern Indiana, and 18% came by the above three roads from northwestern Illinois. The Illinois Central and the Chicago, Alton, and St. Louis, the only two roads entering Chicago that passed through any part of southern or central Illinois, together brought only about 10% of the wheat, 4% of the flour, 3% of the hogs, and 56% of the cattle imported into Chicago.[61] Even these importations, relatively small

60. *Tableaux du Commerce*, 1857, pp. 216-18; Hunt, *Merchants' Magazine*, XL, 549, 600; see also annual commercial reports of cities cited in notes below.
61. *Annual Review of the Trade and Commerce of Chicago for 1857.*

in quantity in every case except that of cattle, came almost entirely from stations along the northern halves of the Illinois Central and the Chicago and Alton railroads. The Chicago, Alton, and St. Louis carried approximately the same quantities of flour, corn, and whiskey to St. Louis as to Chicago. But it carried about four times as much wheat and about a fourth as many live hogs to Chicago as to St. Louis.[62] In other words, the products brought to Chicago by the Illinois Central and by the Chicago, Alton, and St. Louis came from the northern third of Illinois. Taking the Illinois and Michigan canal and the Illinois river as another continuous line of communication between Chicago and St. Louis, Chicago drew from little more than the northern third of Illinois. In 1856 St. Louis received from the Illinois river more than four times the flour, one and one-half times the wheat, twenty-five times the whiskey, fourteen times the pork, seven hundred times the beef, and fifteen times the potatoes that the Illinois and Michigan canal conveyed to Chicago. The canal, however, conveyed ten times as much corn to Chicago as the river carried toward St. Louis.[63] One-half of this corn brought by the canal to Chicago was, however, produced north of LaSalle, the southern terminus of the canal, within a hundred miles of Chicago.[64] Comparatively small

62. *Annual Review of the Commerce of St. Louis for the year 1857*, pp. 6, 33; *Annual Review of the Trade and Commerce of Chicago for 1857*, pp. 10-12.

63. *Fifth Annual Review of the Commerce of Chicago . . . for the year 1856* (Chicago, 1857), 29; *Annual Review of the Commerce of St. Louis, for the year 1856*, Missouri Republican (St. Louis, 1857), 7.

64. *Twelfth Annual Report of the Board of Trustees of the Illinois and Michigan Canal for the year ending Nov. 30, 1856*, p. 119, in *Reports Made to the General Assembly of Illinois at its Twentieth Session* (Springfield, 1857), 689. In 1857 half the wheat and corn and all the pork carried on

quantities of whiskey, pork, and beef were brought into Chicago by the canal. They were manufactured there.

Of the goods exported from Toledo in 1857, practically the whole came from southern Michigan and the northern third of Indiana. Of the half million barrels of flour exported from Toledo, over 50% was brought by the Michigan Southern railroad from the extreme northern counties of Indiana and southern counties of Michigan; 31% was brought by the Wabash canal from the valleys of the Maumee and the upper Wabash, a region just a little farther south than the counties just referred to; and the remaining 15% came from the same valleys by way of the Toledo and Wabash railroad.[65] Flour brought to Toledo by the Wabash and Erie canal and by the Toledo and Wabash railroad came almost entirely from the Wabash valley in Indiana between Attica and Ft. Wayne. Only small quantities came by the Toledo and Wabash railroad from east central Illinois or by canal from west central and northwestern Ohio.[66] Of the two and a half million bushels of wheat exported from Toledo, over 50% came by canal from the upper Wabash valley in Indiana, 13% by the Toledo and Wabash railroad from the same region, and 36% by the Michigan Southern and Northern Indiana railroad from northern Indiana and southern Michigan.

the canal was produced north of LaSalle, the southern terminus of the canal. *Thirteenth Annual Report of the Board of Trustees of the Illinois and Michigan Canal for the year ending Nov. 30, 1857*, pp. 36-38, in *Reports to the General Assembly of Illinois* at its Twenty-first session (Springfield, 1859), 372-74.

65. Hunt, *Merchants' Magazine*, LX, 699, 703.

66. *Third Annual Report of the Toledo and Wabash Railway Company* (Toledo, 1861), 25; *Annual Report of the Trustees of the Wabash and Erie Canal* for 1857, pp. 198-217, in *Reports of the Officers of the State to the Governor for 1857* (Indianapolis, 1857), pt. II, no. 4. Statistical tables shows at what points commodities were shipped.

Of the two million bushels of corn exported from Toledo, nearly 50% came by the Wabash and Erie canal from the upper Wabash valley in Indiana, 40% by the Toledo and Wabash railroad from the same valley, and only a little over 10% by the Michigan Southern. Of the fifty thousand barrels of pork and bacon exported from Toledo, nearly 50% came by the Michigan Southern and more than 50% came by the Toledo and Wabash railroad and the Wabash and Erie canal from the Maumee and upper Wabash valleys. About 54% of the hogs and 70% of the cattle came by the Toledo and Wabash railroad, the remainder coming from the Michigan Southern road. In the case of the hogs and cattle coming by the Toledo and Wabash railroad, about half the hogs and nearly all the cattle came from a region lying north of east central Illinois. Of the commodities received at Toledo by canal from western Ohio, no commodities except wheat and flour came from any point farther south than Piqua, and these came in entirely negligible quantities. Other goods cleared on the Miami Extension canal at Piqua and at points farther south went to Cincinnati.[67] Wheat moved northward on the Miami and the Miami Extension canals from as far south as Cincinnati, but the wheat cleared over the canals between Piqua and Cincinnati amounted to less than 1% of the wheat exported from Detroit. Flour and bacon moved northward on the canals from as far south as Dayton, but in small quantities.

Of the exports of Cleveland for 1857 the greater part came from two lines of transportation, the Ohio canal, and

---

67. *Nineteenth Annual Report of the Board of Public Works to the Governor of Ohio for the year 1857*, in *Message and Reports Made to the General Assembly and Governor of the State of Ohio for the year 1858* (Columbus, 1858), pt. 1, no. 12, pp. 546-75.

the Cleveland, Columbus, and Cincinnati railroad. Both these routes tapped regions to the south and southwest of Cleveland. Only small quantities of agricultural commodities came into Cleveland over the Cleveland and Toledo railroad from Toledo or from the southern shore of Lake Erie to the West. Negligible quantities of agricultural products came by way of the Cleveland and Pittsburgh railroad from the southeast of Cleveland. Still smaller quantities came over the Cleveland and Erie railroad from the east or over the Cleveland and Mahoning road from the south. Practically no agricultural products came to Cleveland by way of Lake Erie. Of a little more than a million bushels of wheat received at Cleveland for milling and for re-export, 25% came from the Ohio canal and 58% from the Cleveland, Columbus, and Cincinnati railroad. The total of Cleveland's import of wheat had dwindled, was only half that of Chicago, and less than half of this was for re-export. Of a little over a half million barrels of flour coming to Cleveland, the canal and the Cleveland, Columbus, and Cincinnati railroad each brought 38%. Of less than a half million bushels of corn the canal brought 57% and the railroad brought 17%. Of eighty thousand barrels of pork, 76% came from the Cleveland, Columbus, and Cincinnati railroad and 20% from the Cleveland and Toledo road. Of a half million live hogs 60% came from the Cleveland, Columbus, and Cincinnati and 40% from the Cleveland and Toledo railroad. About half the receipts from the latter road, however, had been forwarded by Toledo and came originally from north Indiana and Illinois. Of more than a hundred thousand cattle 66% came from the Cleveland, Columbus, and Cinnati and 33% from the Cleveland and Toledo railroad.[68]

68. *The Cleveland Herald's First Annual Statement of the Trade and Commerce of Cleveland for the year 1858,* 5, 6.

Cleveland got practically all of the relatively small quantities of flour and wheat that was put on the Ohio canal, although some of the wheat stopped off at places on the way to be converted into flour. In 1857 half of the wheat that was put upon the canal came from points south of Newark. By 1858 two-thirds of the wheat put upon the canal cleared from Newark and points to the south. Over four-fifths of the flour arriving by canal at Cleveland came from the northern half of the canal, but it was in part the product of wheat originally cleared from the southern end of the canal.[69] The corn brought to Cleveland by canal in 1857 and 1858 came from the north central part of the state and was shipped by the region between Dover and Newark. Cleveland got only a small part of the corn put upon the canal since the quantity that was cleared from Newark south was three or four times as large as that cleared to the north. In 1857 three times as much corn arrived by canal at Portsmouth on the Ohio as arrived by canal at Cleveland. Pork and bacon were no longer being shipped in any considerable quantity by canal. The larger part of the pork was put upon the southern end of the canal chiefly at Chillicothe and Circleville and left the canal at Portsmouth and Cleveland in almost equal quantities. At Circleville, at Columbus, and at Newark, pork, bacon, and whiskey left the canal for the railroads which intersected the canal at these points. The whiskey that came by canal to Cleveland was largely the product of points along the northern half of the canal and constituted less than a fourth of the whiskey shipped over the canal. Portsmouth, Cleveland, and Columbus in 1857 each got 20,000 barrels by canal. By 1858 Cleveland had just a little more than held her own, Portsmouth had de-

69. *Ohio Executive Documents, Annual Reports Made to the Governor of the State of Ohio for the year 1859* (Columbus, 1860), pt. 1, pp. 664-99.

clined to a little more than one-half, while Circleville received nearly four times as much as in 1857.[70] The pork and whiskey taken from the canal at Circleville evidently passed over the Cincinnati, Wilmington, and Zanesville railroad and thence over the Central Ohio road to Bellaire and thence to the Baltimore and Ohio railroad at Wheeling. The whiskey, pork, and beef leaving the canal at Columbus went in part over the Cleveland, Columbus, and Cincinnati to Cleveland and in part over the Central Ohio to Bellaire, and thence to the Baltimore and Ohio railroad.

While the total exports from the West in 1857 showed an increase of about 30% over those of 1853, total imports into the West had increased by less than 10% in the same period and stood at about eight hundred and seventy thousand tons. The imports of salt, coffee, molasses, groceries, drygoods, hardware, iron, and furniture had all increased normally, whereas the import of sugar from the south and of railway iron from the northeast had apparently declined a little.[71] Imports through the northeastern gateway had fallen off, those through the southern outlet had a little more than held their own, and those through

---

70. *Nineteenth Annual Report of Board of Public Works . . . of Ohio for the year 1857*, p. 179 and *Ohio Executive Docs. for 1859*, pt. 1, pp. 664-99; *The Cleveland Herald's First Annual Statement of the Trade and Commerce of Cleveland for 1858*, pp. 5, 6.

71. Among the quantities of goods imported the following quantities are definitely accounted for but do not constitute the total of some commodities and account for only half the total tonnage of imports: salt, 169,261 tons; sugar, 94,221; coffee, 49,874; dry goods, 40,631; groceries, 21,080; molasses, 41,097; iron, 17,966; hardware, 5,164; furniture, 3,471; railroad iron, 43,676. Since the goods carried westward by the New York Central and the New York and Erie were not included in the above, the quantity of dry goods given above should no doubt be doubled and other items like coffee, hardware, and furniture considerably increased.

the eastern had more than doubled. About four hundred thousand tons, or about half the total imports, still came by the northeastern gateway, two hundred twenty-five thousand by the eastern, and two hundred forty thousand by the southern. The eastern gateway had gained more at the expense of the northeastern than had the southern. The four hundred thousand tons brought through the northeastern gateway came over the Welland canal, the Erie canal, the New York Central railroad, and the New York and Erie railroad in approximately equal quantities. With the exception of eighty-five thousand tons of salt and forty thousand tons of railroad iron brought westward over the canals, the importations consisted of general merchandise.[72]

Of the importations through the eastern gateway the Pennsylvania brought a hundred sixty-two thousand tons and the Baltimore and Ohio between sixty-four thousand and one hundred two thousand.[73] Two-thirds of the ton-

---

72. *Report of the State Engineer and Surveyor on the Railroads for year ending Sept. 30, 1857*, in *N. Y. Assembly Docs.* (Albany, 1858), no. 89, pp. 153, 157, 167; *N. Y. Assembly Docs.* (1858), vol V, no. 155, p. 110; *Tableaux du Commerce et de la Navigation de la Province du Canada pour l'annee 1857*, pp. 216-18; *Report of the President of the N. Y. and Erie Railroad Company for the year ending Sept. 30, 1858* (N. Y., 1858), 22; *Annual Report of the N. Y. Central Railroad Company for the year ending Sept. 30, 1857*, to the State engineer (Albany, 1857), 24. Through tonnage west on the N. Y. and Erie was 80,271 tons; on the N. Y. Central, 113,230; arrivals at Buffalo on the Erie canal, 94,172; westbound freight on the Welland canal, 78,993 to Americans and 7,470 to Canadians.

73. In the case of the Pennsylvania R. R. the figures are total arrivals at Pittsburgh; in case of the Baltimore and Ohio the sixty-four thousand is westward through freight and the hundred two thousand is estimated arrivals at western terminals. *Eleventh Annual Report of the Pennsylvania Railroad Company*, 98, 100, 101; *Thirty-first Annual Report of the Baltimore and Ohio*, 60, 92. Included in the commodities brought to the West by these two railroads was 12,198 tons of coffee, 21,080 tons of groceries, 40,631 tons of dry goods, 11,441 tons of iron, and 5,164 tons of hardware.

nage brought to Pittsburgh by the Pennsylvania railroad was carried westward into northern Ohio and northern Indiana by the Pittsburgh, Fort Wayne, and Chicago road.[74] About one-third to one-half of all the tonnage brought by the Baltimore and Ohio to its western terminals was transferred to the Central Ohio railroad and distributed by it and connecting lines through southern Ohio, one-half going to Cincinnati and four thousand tons going as far west as Indiana. The other two-thirds were carried down the Ohio river by the steamboats.[75] The two eastern roads together brought more than twice as much as they had brought in 1853. Among the commodities brought in from the east by the two railroads were forty thousand tons of drygoods, twelve thousand tons of coffee, and twenty-one thousand tons of other groceries.

The southern gateway supplied over eighty thousand tons each of sugar and salt, and over thirty-five thousand tons each of coffee and molasses.[76] Of the eighty thousand tons of sugar shipped northward from New Orleans, Cincinnati took twenty-eight thousand and St. Louis twenty-three thousand. Of the thirty-five thousand tons of coffee St. Louis took nine thousand and Cincinnati imported a little less.[77] In general St. Louis and Cincinnati each took

---

74. *First Report of the Pittsburgh, Ft. Wayne, and Chicago Railroad Company*, 36.

75. *Ninth Annual Report of the Central Ohio Railroad for the year 1856-57* (Zanesville, 1857), 24; *Report of the Committee appointed by the Holders of the second mortgage bonds of the Central Ohio Railroad Company*, 10, 21. The Central Ohio took 34,179 tons from the Baltimore and Ohio road.

76. *DeBow's Review*, XXIII, 350, 367, 371; XXIX, 524.

77. *Annual Review of the Commerce of St. Louis for 1857*, pp. 6, 33; *Annual Statement of Trade and Commerce of Cincinnati for the year ending Aug. 31, 1857*, p. 31; *Annual Statement of the Commerce of Cincinnati, 1861*, p. 43; Hunt, *Merchants' Magazine*, XXVIII, 224.

a little more than a fourth of the total quantity of each commodity forwarded northward by New Orleans. The remaining and lesser half of the shipments northward from New Orleans were distributed among several hundred ports and landings on the Mississippi and its tributaries north of Memphis.[78] The Baltimore and Ohio brought to Wheeling and Parkersburg nine thousand tons of coffee. Some of this was distributed along the Ohio river, but the greater part was carried into eastern Ohio by the Central Ohio railroad and distributed along its course and along the canals that it intersected.[79] Cincinnati distributed its coffee along the Miami canal and the Miami Extension and the Wabash and Erie canals as far north as Toledo and from that canal over the Wabash and Erie as far as Ft. Wayne.[80] Cincinnati also sent commodities over the railroads into southeastern Indiana, northern Kentucky, and southwestern Ohio. St. Louis re-exported the coffee, sugar, and molasses to the upper Mississippi and into the Old Northwest as far as Chicago.[81] In general, then, the direction of the movement of outgoing and incoming commerce was about the same in 1857 as before. The new transportation lines in the West had conferred local benefits in the particular regions through which they ran and had enlarged old trade tendencies rather than created new ones. Improvements in transportation lines leading from the interior to the outside markets were not

78. For distribution of sugar see A. P. Champomier, *Statement of the Sugar made in Louisiana in 1852-53* (New Orleans, 1853), 51.
79. *Ohio Executive Documents . . . for the year 1859*, pt. 1, p. 710.
80. *Nineteenth Annual Report of the Board of Public Works for the year 1857*, in *Messages and Reports to the General Assembly and Governor of Ohio*, 236.
81. *Annual Review of the Trade and Commerce of Chicago for 1857*, p. 29.

replacing one another but were competing more and more with one another. For certain particular localities in the West, particular gateways still had decided advantage for import or export of most commodities. Thus while St. Louis could and did export through all the gateways, most commodities could be carried more cheaply at most seasons down the river to New Orleans and then by sea vessels to New York or Europe than by any other route. In the same way the northeastern canals and railroads still had the natural advantage in carrying the bulk of the exports and imports of Cleveland and Detroit.

On the other hand some places like Chicago and Cincinnati were showing tendencies of being able to conduct their intercourse with the outside world almost equally well through all three of the great gateways. More properly speaking these two great forwarding and distributing centers of the interior found it generally preferable to send or receive one type of commodity over one route and another type over another route. Chicago at most seasons received her sugar and molasses from New Orleans and her salt from Buffalo. Ordinarily almost all her grain passed through the northeastern outlet. Her live stock went equally well over the eastern and northeastern railroads. Cincinnati by 1857 seemed to be able to export almost equally well her pork, flour, and whiskey through the southern or through the eastern outlet. To be still more specific, during one week a commodity could be more advantageously exported by one route, while in another week the same commodity might be sent by the other route, depending upon freight rates and prices. In 1856, when the Louisiana sugar crop was short, Chicago did not as usual get practically all her sugar from there but imported more through New York and the northeastern gateway. In 1857, when the season of navigation on the Mississippi was exceptionally long and favorable, Chicago did not send all of her grain exports northeastward, but exported some through New Orleans.[82] Shipping points lying between Cincinnati and Chicago such as Columbus, Ohio; Indianapolis, Indiana; and Springfield, Illinois, were in a still more pivotal position, exporting now more in one direction and now in another according to prices and freight rates in different directions on different commodities.

Freight rates on corn, wheat, flour, and pork from LaSalle, Illinois, and Lafayette, Indiana, to Liverpool by way of New Orleans back as early as 1849 had helped to determine freight rates on the Illinois and Michigan, on the Wabash and Erie, on the Welland, and on the Erie canals and vice versa.[83] By 1854 the freight rates of the Erie and of the Welland canals on flour, pork, coffee, and sugar were helping to determine the rates on the same commodities on the New York and Erie and on the New York Central railroads and thereby affecting rates on other roads.[84] By 1857 the rates on the New York railroads were not only helping to fix rates on the Pennsylvania railroad but were affecting the rates on roads within the West. By this time the Pittsburgh, Fort Wayne, and Chicago road was attempting to deliver the exports of Chicago to the Pennsylvania road at Pittsburgh, while the Michigan Southern and Northern Indiana railroad was

82. *Annual Review of Trade and Commerce of Chicago for 1857.*
83. *Annual Report of the Trustees of the Wabash and Erie Canal for 1849*, p. 260.
84. *Proceedings of the Meeting of Railroad Superintendents held at the St. Nicholas Hotel, New York, Sept. 26, 1854* (Philadelphia, 1854), 6; freight rates from New York to Cincinnati during canal navigation were fixed at $1.40 per cwt. for first class.

just as valiantly struggling to convey the same goods to roads that would deliver them to the New York Central road.[85] The rates on the Pennsylvania were in turn reacting upon those of the Baltimore and Ohio railroad since both had their terminals upon the upper Ohio river and rates on both these roads, and western roads were directly affected by freight rates from Pittsburgh, Wheeling, and Cincinnati to New York and Liverpool by way of New Orleans. Navigation on the Ohio and Mississippi had never been cheaper or more dependable for so large a part of the year as in 1857, and it was forcing freight rates down.[86] The four great trunk railroads leading from the West to the Atlantic seaboard in co-operation with their feeder lines in the West entered into ruinous cut-throat competition with one another during a large part of 1857.[87] The operators of the railroads held numerous conferences and conventions and made numerous agreements fixing

85. *First Report of the Pittsburgh, Fort Wayne, and Chicago*, 52-53. Of all the grain carried eastward on the road, only 5% left the road at Fort Wayne for Toledo and 5% at Crestline for Cleveland. About 99% of the pork, live stock, and whiskey that got on to the road went through to Pittsburgh.

86. *First Report of the Pittsburgh, Fort Wayne, and Chicago*, p. 23; "Navigation on Ohio river for all months in 1857 unprecedented. Lowest river rates ever." Receipts of P., Ft. W. ,and C. reduced for that reason; *Proceedings of an Adjourned Meeting of the Convention of Representatives of various Railroad Companies between the Seaboard and the Western States held at Cleveland, Oct. 1, 1856* (Cleveland, 1856), 15: "Where a railroad competes with a rail and water route the railroad rate shall be same as rail and water rate;" *Proceedings of the General Railroad Association of the Eastern, Middle and Western States held at Pittsburgh, March 13, 1855* (Philadelphia, 1855), 18: "Rates between Boston, New York, Philadelphia, and Baltimore to western point to be same unless there is water competition;" Aldrich, *Report*, pt. 1, p. 616.

87. *Report of President of New York and Erie Railroad to Stockholders for the year ending Sept. 30, 1857* (New York, 1857), 10.

freight rates to and from western cities so situated that they had a choice between different railroads or between railroads and rivers, lakes, or canals. None of these agreements before the Civil War were kept for more than a few months at a time.[88] When the canals were frozen up or the rivers were too low and there was business enough for all the roads, the railroads would refrain for a while from cutting rates. They might even temporarily raise them. At other times the fight went on. All this tended to raise prices of the commodities that the farmer of the West had to sell and lowered prices of merchandise that he wished to buy. Not only had the prices of agricultural products in the West risen but they tended to become more steady because of this choice between competing routes and markets.[89] It was not merely a question of whether freight rates to Liverpool were cheapest by way of Boston, New York, Philadelphia, Baltimore, Charleston, or New Orleans. The strength of the market in these American ports because of local conditions varied from time to time with respect to one another regardless of Liverpool

88. *Proceedings of an Adjourned Meeting of the Convention of Representatives of Various Railroad Companies between the Seaboard and the Western States held at Cleveland, Oct. 1, 1856*, p. 12: The Baltimore and Ohio refused to send representatives because of the "known facility with which former contracts have been broken;" *Report of the New York and Erie for 1857*, p. 10, 11; *Ibid for 1858*, p. 5; *First Joint Report of the Bellefontaine Line for 1856* (Cleveland, 1857), 16: "Efforts have been made to fix rates at conferences for several years. It is easy to agree but impossible to keep."

89. *Annual Statement of Trade and Commerce of Cincinnati for year ending Aug. 31, 1857*, pp. 12, 13, 19, 22, 25. Average price of wheat had risen from about $.83 in 1853 to about $1.09 in 1857. Before the financial crash in the latter part of 1857 the price of wheat had not been below $.90 for two years. The prices of corn were high and the prices of provisions, cattle, and tobacco had never been higher. See also Aldrich, *Report*, pt. 2, p. 61.

prices. If prices declined a little at one outlet, they might hold firm at another. No wonder that the people of the West were anxious to keep all the lines of communication with the outside world open, and if possible to have them still more improved and to see others added to them.

In politics they had frequently found it to their advantage to play one section against the other. In their economic life they were beginning to find it just as helpful to be able to play one commercial outlet against another.

CHAPTER VII

The Old Northwest During the Lean Years of 1857-1860

THE DIVISIVE tendencies so apparent in the period from 1853 to 1857 continued during the period from 1857 to 1860. The period was ushered in by a panic that was followed by two years of extensive crop failures. All of the railroads of the Old Northwest except four ceased paying dividends and the majority passed into the hands of receivers. Cutting of freight rates at points that had a choice of transportation lines and raising them at other points brought criticism and dissatisfaction. Towns and individuals that had subscribed to local railroads were uncertain of the future of their investments. The last gap in the great trunk line from Chicago to New Orleans was completed by the first part of 1860 with the exception of the break at the river between Cairo and Columbus. But no new steps were taken to cement the political bonds between the North and the South by laying an economic basis through the building of more north and south lines of transportation. Railroad conventions continued to be held in the North and commercial conventions in the South. But there was little contact between the two series of meetings. The southern conventions were still interested in direct trade with Europe and in commercial retaliation against the North. The southern conventions as time went on were becoming political rather than commercial. The Knoxville convention of 1857 took up the question of reopening the foreign slave trade. The Montgomery convention of 1858 was speedily turned by the radicals into a secession convention.

In the three years from the end of 1857 to the close of 1860 there was then little further material development in the routes of transportation affecting the Old Northwest. In the routes connecting the Old Northwest with the outside world only minor developments occurred. In Canada the Buffalo and Lake Huron road had been completed in June, 1858, from Goderich on Lake Huron to Ft. Erie opposite Buffalo. This road crossed the Grand Trunk at Stratford and the Great Western at Paris. Late in 1858 a branch road was completed connecting Sarnia, a port at the southern outlet of Lake Huron, with Komoka on the Canadian Great Western line; and near the close of 1859 a road was completed connecting Sarnia with St. Mary's on the Grand Trunk line. These lines gave Wisconsin, Michigan, and northern Illinois additional competing routes through Canada to the Northeastern gateway. About the middle of 1859 the Welland railroad was opened between Lake Erie and Lake Ontario. There were thus by the opening of 1860 railroads running southward from Collingwood on Georgian Bay, eastward from Goderich and from Sarnia on Lake Huron, as well as roads running eastward from Windsor on the Detroit river and northward from Port Stanley on Lake Erie, all connecting with the New York roads at Buffalo and Suspension Bridge and connecting also with the Canadian Grand Trunk at different points which in turn followed the northern shore of the St. Lawrence to the head of ocean navigation at Montreal and from that place to Portland, Maine.[1]

The southern outlet of the Old Northwest had been much improved by the first part of 1860 by the completion of two railroad lines. One of these ran down the Missis-

---

1. *Board of Railway Commissioners of Canada*, 24-25. Appleton, *Railway and Steam Navigation Guides*, 1860, gives maps and time tables.

sippi valley from Columbus, Kentucky, to New Orleans. This route was composed of three roads, but these were so connected as to give through service.[2] Connection between Cairo, Illinois, the southern terminus of the Illinois Central, and Columbus, Kentucky, the northern terminus of the Mobile and Ohio, was made by steamboats. By the opening of 1860 the Illinois Central railroad company could and did advertise the fact and illustrate the fact by map that Chicago, the great grain market of the Northwest, had two complete double transportation lines to the seaboard, each entirely independent of the eastern, northeastern, and southeastern states of the Union.[3] Each double line was made up of one complete rail line and of one complete water line. The northern rail route as thus advertised was composed of the Michigan Central road from Chicago to Detroit, and of the Great Western road and the Grand Trunk road from Windsor opposite Detroit through Canada to Montreal and Quebec. This rail route supplemented an all water route made up of lakes, Canadian canals, and rivers from Chicago to the Atlantic. The other double route thus advertised ran from Chicago to New Orleans. The rail line of this southern route was made up of the Illinois Central, the Mobile and Ohio, the Mississippi Central, and the New Orleans, Jackson, and Great Northern. The water route from Chicago to New Orleans was composed of the Illinois and Michigan canal, the Illinois river, and the Mississippi river. From

2. The Mobile and Ohio from Columbus, Kentucky, through Jackson, Tennessee; the Mississippi Central, from Jackson, Tennessee, to Canton, Mississippi; the New Orleans, Jackson and Great Northern, from Canton to New Orleans; Appleton, *Guide* (Sept., 1859), 261; *Ibid.* (June, 1860), 247, 252, 256; *Ibid.* (Oct., 1860), 260-61, map and time table; Dinsmore, *Guide* (June, 1860), 148, 150, 151.

3. See Appleton, *Guide* (Jan., 1860), 276.

Grand Junction on the Mississippi Central in Tennessee there was also railroad connection through Chattanooga with Richmond, Charleston, and Savannah.[4]

Another route to the South from the Old Northwest was made by the opening in 1859 of the Louisville and Nashville railroad between the two cities from which the road took its name.[5] That road with the Nashville and Chattanooga railroad made possible a better connection between the Ohio river and the east-and-west line of railroads that ran from Memphis through Chattanooga to the southern Atlantic seaports than the connections between that line and the Ohio river afforded by the Mississippi, the Tennessee, and the Cumberland rivers. Cincinnati forwarded goods to Louisville by the Ohio river and by the Covington and Lexington and the Louisville and Lexington railroads. Louisville and Cincinnati were forwarding to the South more freight in 1860 over the Louisville

---

4. One route was made up of the Memphis and Charleston from Grand Junction to Stevenson, the Nashville and Chattanooga from Stevenson to Chattanooga, the East Tennessee and Georgia from Chattanooga to Knoxville, the East Tennessee and Virginia from Knoxville to Bristol, the Virginia and Tennessee from Bristol to Lynchburg, the Petersburg and Lynchburg from Lynchburg to Burkesville, the Richmond and Danville from Burkesville to Richmond; a second route was made up of the first route as far as Chattanooga and then the Western and Atlantic (owned by Georgia) from Chattanooga to Atlanta, the Macon and Western from Atlanta to Macon, the Central Georgia Railway from Macon to Savannah; the third route was made up of the second route as far as Atlanta and then the Georgia Railway, from Atlanta to Augusta, the South Carolina Railway from Augusta to Charleston; the Atlanta and West Point from Atlanta to West Point, the Montgomery and West Point from West Point to Montgomery. Montgomery is on the Alabama River and West Point on the Chattahoochee. Appleton, *Guide* (Oct., 1860), 25, 228, 232, 242, 248, 250, 253, 256, 257, 259.

5. *Annual Statement of the Commerce of Cincinnati for year ending Aug. 31, 1860* (Cincinnati, 1860), 8.

and Nashville road than the road could handle.⁶ Over three hundred thousand bushels of grain and flour alone were carried southward by this road during the first year that it was in operation.⁷ As in the case of the goods that passed over the Memphis and Atlantic seaboard line of railroads from rivers in 1857, so was it with the goods from the Old Northwest shipped south over the Louisville and Nashville railroad in 1860. Such goods reached the South-Atlantic seaports in only small quantities, but they were distributed throughout the South. The railroads and canals leading from the northeastern gateway through New York and the railroads leading from the eastern gateway through Pennsylvania and western Virginia had undergone little change between 1857 and 1860. The work of enlarging the New York canals, which had been in progress for some fifteen years, was nearing completion in 1860.

Within the Old Northwest little change had taken place in the physical aspects of the routes of transportation. The Dayton and Michigan railroad had been completed in 1859 and made with the Cincinnati, Hamilton, and Dayton a direct all rail route between Toledo and Cincinnati.⁸ The Toledo, Wabash, and Western had in 1859 made connection with a town on the Mississippi⁹ and had secured what amounted to an important branch feeder

6. *Annual Statement of the Commerce of Cincinnati for* . . . *1860*, p. 8.
7. *Annual Report of the President and Directors of the Louisville and Nashville Railroad Company, Oct., 1859 to Oct. 1, 1860* (Louisville, 1860), Exhibit B.
8. Appleton, *Guide* (Oct., 1860), 212-13.
9. The Toledo, Wabash and Western connected with the Great Western of Illinois at State Line and the Great Western connected with The Toledo and Quincy. The last named road had its terminus at Quincy on the Mississippi. Appleton, *Guide* (Oct., 1860), 224-25.

172   THE OLD NORTHWEST

line in two affiliated end-for-end roads extending westward from Logansport on its own line to Burlington on the Mississippi river.[10] The Detroit and Milwaukee had been completed from the former place to Grand Haven on the western shore of Lake Michigan opposite Milwaukee.[11]

While there had been little development in the physical sense in the lines of transportation, there had been developments of another kind. In the period between 1857 and 1860 the railroads in the Old Northwest had been hard hit by the general financial situation and by the continued crop failures. Only a few of the better situated roads like the Little Miami and the Galena and Chicago Union made any money during the period.[12] The railroads were one of the causes of the financial troubles that affllicted the country during the closing years of the fifties and were in turn most seriously affected by it. Hard times brought keener competition. Ruinous competition led to efforts to eliminate competition through agreements and consolidation. This consolidation as is always the case took one of two forms. Either it consisted in consolidation of end-for-end or supporting lines or else of parallel or competing lines. Both forms of consolidation were attempted in this period. Throughout the period the stronger roads in the Old Northwest were buying, as far as they were able, the stocks and bonds of weaker feeder roads and entering into

10. The Logansport, Peoria, and Burlington from Logansport to Peoria; the Peoria, Oquawka, and Burlington from Peoria to Burlington. The roads had the same president. Appleton, *Guide* (Dec., 1859); (Oct., 1860), 225.

11. Appleton, *Guide* (Sept., 1859), 222-23.

12. *Little Miami Railroad Company and Columbus and Xenia Railroad Company, Second Joint Annual Report for the year 1857* (Cincinnati, 1858), 11; *Eleventh Annual Report of the Galena and Chicago Union Railroad Company for 1857* (Chicago, 1858), 45.

agreements with them to route traffic over one another's lines. Where there was not real legal consolidation there were interlocking directorates and administration. These consolidated end-for-end lines within the Old Northwest in turn were in some cases gradually becoming linked up to and becoming extensions of the great eastern trunk lines such as the Pennsylvania, the Baltimore and Ohio, and the New York Central, that ran eastward from the eastern or northeastern gateways. As early as 1853 an arrangement had been made whereby the Little Miami and the Columbus and Xenia, two practically end-for-end roads, were to be operated by one superintendent as one road from Cincinnati to Columbus, Ohio. In 1857 the Columbus and Xenia in turn loaned its credit to the extent of $20,000 to the Steubenville and Indiana road in the hope of perfecting its own connections by means of that line with the Pennsylvania railroad at Pittsburgh.[13]

Soon after the Madison and Indianapolis road was completed, construction was begun upon railroads radiating from Indianapolis to the north, east, and west. By 1852 John Brough, the president of the Madison and Indianapolis, reported that his road was operating in connection with the Indianapolis and Bellefontaine, running northeastward from Indianapolis, as well as with the Indianapolis and Peru which ran northward from Indianapolis. He also reported that the Terre Haute and Indianapolis and the Indianapolis and Lafayette would be run in con-

13. *The Little Miami Railroad Company and Columbus and Xenia Railroad Company, Second Joint Annual Report for 1857*, p. 5. The Central Ohio ran from Columbus through Newark and Zanesville to Bellaire opposite Wheeling. The Steubenville and Indiana ran from Newark to Steubenville; The Cleveland and Pittsburgh, through Steubenville to Rochester; the Ohio and Pennsylvania, through Rochester to Pittsburgh.

nection with his line and would send their exports over his line to the Ohio river.[14] By 1853 the connection between the Madison and Indianapolis and the Indianapolis and Bellefontaine had resulted in the election of Brough as president of both roads.[15] In 1856 an agreement was made by the Indianapolis and Bellefontaine, by that time known as the Indianapolis, Pittsburgh, and Cleveland, with the Bellefontaine and Indiana railroad to run the two roads as one continuous line between Cleveland and Indianapolis with Brough as president of both roads.[16] These roads were together thereafter known as the Bellefontaine line. In 1860 this Bellefontaine line made further arrangement with the Terre Haute and Richmond,[17] the Terre Haute, Alton, and St. Louis, and the Indiana Central to operate all these roads as a continuous line between Cleveland and St. Louis by using cars of a compromise gauge so that freight cars might be sent through without being unloaded.[18] In 1856 the Ohio and Pennsylvania owned stock in the Ohio and Indiana and the latter, in the Ft. Wayne and Chicago road. All three were unable to meet their financial obligations, and the last named road was not yet completed. They were reorganized and consolidated into the Pittsburgh, Ft. Wayne, and Chicago railroad, thus spanning the entire distance between Chicago and Pittsburgh by means of a single road.[19]

14. John Brough, *A Brief History of the Madison and Indianapolis Railroad*, 12.
15. Dinsmore, *Guide* (Nov., 1853), 110, 112.
16. *First Joint Annual Report of the Bellefontaine Line for the year 1856* (Cleveland, 1857), 19.
17. Road between Terre Haute and Indianapolis.
18. *Twelfth Annual Report of the Terre Haute and Richmond for 1860* (Terre Haute, 1861), 7; Appleton, *Guide* (Oct., 1860), 200.
19. *First Report of the Board of Directors of the Pittsburgh, Ft. Wayne*

As has already been stated not only was the process of linking up end-for-end or feeder roads going on within the Old Northwest but also the trunk lines leading out from that section to the Atlantic ports were seeking to enlarge their business by assisting or controlling feeder roads within the Old Northwest. The Pennsylvania railroad company had begun, even before it had completed its own road, to assist railroads in Ohio that were so built as to bring freight to Pittsburgh, its western terminus. In 1852 the directors of the Pennsylvania agreed to purchase with Pennsylvania railroad bonds five thousand shares of the stock of the Ohio and Pennsylvania railroad already mentioned above, a feeder and connecting line running west from Pittsburgh.[20] In 1853 the directors of the Pennsylvania railroad company were authorized by the stockholders to buy stock in the Marietta and Cincinnati, in the Ohio and Pennsylvania, and in the Springfield, Mount Vernon, and Pittsburgh railroad companies with bonds of the Pennsylvania railroad company[21] and to secure promises to operate the "whole line sympathetically with our own." All these were expected to become feeders for the western terminal of the Pennsylvania. In 1854 the directors of the Pennsylvania company were authorized by the stockholders to guarantee to the amount of $500,000 the bonds of the Steubenville and Indiana,[22] a road that was to run from Steubenville on the Ohio river a little below

and Chicago Railroad Company for the seventeen months ending Dec. 31, 1857, pp. 5, 6, 8.

20. *Fifth Annual Report of the Pennsylvania Railroad Company* (Philadelphia, 1852), 21. The Ohio and Pennsylvania was to run from Pittsburgh through Rochester in Pennsylvania to Crestline in Ohio.

21. *Sixth Annual Report of the Pennsylvania Railroad Company,* 5, 6, 8, 22, 23, 24, 25.

22. *Seventh Annual Report of the Pennsylvania Railroad Company,* 6.

Pittsburgh to Newark, a station on the Central Ohio railroad, which in turn made connections at Columbus with the Columbus and Xenia and the Little Miami railroads for Cincinnati. In 1854 the directors of the Pennsylvania reported that they had bought $750,000 worth of the stock of the Marietta and Cincinnati railroad and $300,000 worth of the stock of the Ohio and Indiana railroad, exchanged $100,000 worth of the shares of the Marietta and Cincinnati for the Maysville and Big Sandy stock,[23] bought $300,000 worth of stock of the Ohio and Pennsylvania and $100,000 worth of the stock of the Springfield and Mt. Vernon, and had endorsed the bonds of the Steubenville and Indiana to the extent of $500,000, a total investment of $1,450,000 in western roads.[24] These roads were one and all looked upon as feeders or parts of feeder lines for the Pennsylvania at Pittsburgh. By February of 1855 the directors of the Pennsylvania began to record their disappointments in some of these western roads. The directors of the Marietta and Cincinnati had run out of money before they had their main line completed and had used up the subscription of the Pennsylvania company in completing the main line instead of building a branch road up the river from Marietta to connect with the Pennsylvania line.[25] By 1856 the Ohio and Indiana and the Springfield and Mt. Vernon were again needing help. The Pennsylvania directors then decided to cease helping the latter road and to give more support to the Steubenville and Indiana as part of a more direct route from Pittsburgh to

23. *Seventh Annual Report of the Pennsylvania,* 17. The Ohio and Pennsylvania railroad was to extend from Pittsburgh to Crestline and the Ohio and Indiana was to extend from Crestline to Ft. Wayne.

24. *Seventh Annual Report of the Pennsylvania,* 15; *Eighth Annual Report of the Pennsylvania,* 15, 17, 18.

25. *Eighth Annual Report of the Pennsylvania,* 17.

THE LEAN YEARS OF 1857-60 177

Cincinnati instead.[26] Later that year the Pennsylvania directors were able to exchange their Springfield and Mt. Vernon stock for Steubenville and Indiana stock on releasing the latter company from an obligation to change to the Pennsylvania gauge.[27] In 1857 the directors of the Pennsylvania complained that the direct route from Pittsburgh to Steubenville and the Marietta and Cincinnati road were still incomplete, although the funds were again exhausted.[28] At the time that the Ohio and Pennsylvania, the Ohio and Indiana, and the Ft. Wayne and Chicago were consolidated in 1856 into the Pittsburgh, Ft. Wayne, and Chicago, the Pennsylvania held $769,850 worth of the stock of the consolidated company.[29] In 1858 the directors of the Pennsylvania reported that their subscriptions to western roads were largely without result because the Pittsburgh, Ft. Wayne, and Chicago road and the Pittsburgh and Steubenville road were not yet completed. The attempt of the Pennsylvania railroad to consolidate the Hempfield railroad with the Marietta and Cincinnati and thus give the Pennsylvania a southern branch to Cincinnati also failed.[30] In 1859 the Pennsylvania Company charged to profit and loss its subscription of $750,000 to the Marietta and Cincinnati and that of $100,000 to the Springfield and Mt. Vernon and other accounts aggregating $1,182,982.95.[31] During 1858 the Pennsylvania company had sold to the Pittsburgh, Ft. Wayne, and Chicago

26. *Ninth Annual Report of the Pennsylvania*, 23, 24.
27. *Tenth Annual Report of the Pennsylvania*, 22.
28. *Tenth Annual Report of the Pennsylvania*, 23.
29. *Tenth Annual Report of the Pennsylvania*, 22. The Ohio and Pennsylvania from Pittsburgh to Crestline, the Ohio and Indiana from Crestline to Ft. Wayne, the Ft. Wayne and Chicago from Ft. Wayne to Chicago.
30. *Eleventh Annual Report of the Pennsylvania*, 15.
31. *Twelfth Annual Report of the Pennsylvania*, 10.

some old material with which to complete the road from Plymouth, Indiana, to Chicago and had taken in return $650,000 of the first mortgage bonds of that road.[32] During 1860 the Pittsburgh, Ft. Wayne, and Chicago, in spite of all this help, had to be reorganized. In October of that year it was sold by the United States marshall to a committee appointed by creditors and shareholders. The Pennsylvania railroad held bonds to the value of a million dollars and stock to the value of nearly a million more in the reorganized company.[33] For some time past there had been interlocking of administration between those two roads. In 1857 the Board of Directors of the Pittsburgh, Ft. Wayne, and Chicago had elected J. Edgar Thomson chief engineer.[34] In 1858 they had elected him president of their road. He was already president of the Pennsylvania railroad[35] as well as of the Southern Pacific. The result of this manipulation was that before the end of 1860 the Pennsylvania may be considered for traffic purposes as practically extending westward through Pittsburgh over the Pittsburgh, Ft. Wayne, and Chicago as far as the city of Chicago. The Pennsylvania was at the same time reaching out for Columbus, Ohio, through her control of the Steubenville and Indiana road, but from Rochester to Steubenville her cars still passed over the road of the Cleveland and Pittsburgh and from Newark to Columbus over the Central Ohio, a road run in harmony with the Baltimore and Ohio. The

32. *Twelfth Annual Report of the Pennsylvania*, 13.

33. *Fifteenth Annual Report of the Pennsylvania Railroad Company* (Philadelphia, 1862), 11.

34. *First Report of the Board of Directors of the Pittsburgh, Ft. Wayne, and Chicago Railroad Company, for seventeen months ending Dec. 31, 1857*, p. 21.

35. *Annual Reports of the Pennsylvania Railroad*—Fifth to Twenty-second Annual Reports; Appleton, *Guide* (Oct., 1860), 55.

THE LEAN YEARS OF 1857-60

Pennsylvania's other approach to Cincinnati was over the Pittsburgh, Ft. Wayne, and Chicago as far as Crestline and then over three roads that the Pennsylvania officials believed to be owned by men who considered the interests of the Pennsylvania as secondary to her northern competitors.[36]

The Baltimore and Ohio had not been quite so active as the Pennsylvania in forming alliances with the roads in the Old Northwest, but it had accomplished something in that way. It still counted much upon its connection with the Ohio river. In the latter part of 1854 the Baltimore and Ohio had decided to loan $400,000 worth of the Northwestern Virginia railroad bonds to the Central Ohio railroad company to enable the latter to complete its road from Columbus through Newark to Bellaire nearly opposite Wheeling,[37] one of the western terminals of the Baltimore and Ohio railroad. By 1855 it appears that more than that sum had been loaned to that road.[38] From September of 1854 to October of 1855 the city of Wheeling opposed in the courts of Virginia the connection of the Central Ohio with the Baltimore and Ohio at Benwood, trying to force the connection at Wheeling.[39] This merely delayed and did not prevent the connection. From 1855 the Baltimore and Ohio may be considered as extended for all practical purposes by the Central Ohio through Bellaire and Newark as far as Columbus, Ohio.

---

36. *Tenth Annual Report of the Pennsylvania*, 19. The three roads were were the Cincinnati, Columbus, and Cleveland, the Columbus and Xenia, and the Little Miami.

37. *Twenty-eighth Annual Report of the Baltimore and Ohio*, 15.

38. *Twenty-eighth Annual Report of the Baltimore and Ohio*, 15, 17; *Twenty-ninth Annual Report of the Baltimore and Ohio Railroad Company* (Baltimore, 1855), 8, 11.

39. *Twenty-ninth Annual Report of the Baltimore and Ohio*, 8.

The Little Miami and the Columbus and Xenia were because of largeness of their local traffic in a powerful and strategic position. They were financially interested because of their stock investments in keeping open three competing routes all running eastward from their eastern terminal at Columbus so they could send traffic first through Columbus over the Central Ohio road to Bellaire or Wheeling, a terminal of the Baltimore and Ohio, second over the Steubenville and Indiana road to Steubenville and thence to Pittsburgh, a terminal of the Pennsylvania railroad, or finally over the Cincinnati, Columbus, and Cleveland road to Cleveland on the important lines of railways and waterways running through the northeastern gateway. Parallel roads not financially tied up got only local business. The Cincinnati, Wilmington, and Zanesville railroad provided a much shorter route from Cincinnati to Zanesville than did the route by way of Columbus. But the former line got practically none of the through traffic for the simple reason that it connected the town of Morrow on the Little Miami and the town of Zanesville on the Central Ohio, roads that were financially linked together.[40] The Marietta and Cincinnati, a still shorter route between Cincinnati and Parkersburg, the southwestern terminus of the Baltimore and Ohio, got only a small share of the through traffic east, simply because the Little Miami, over whose tracks the Marietta and Cincinnati railroad entered Cincinnati, could send freight to Wheeling, another terminal of the Baltimore and Ohio, over a route made up of practically the whole length of its own line, of the Columbus and Xenia, and of

40. *Ninth Annual Report of the Central Ohio Railroad for 1856-57*, p., 12.

the Central Ohio, roads affiliated with the Little Miami.⁴¹ The Pennsylvania had begun the assistance of the Marietta and Cincinnati with the purpose of making it a connecting link between its own western terminal and Cincinnati but had abandoned the project. Now the Cincinnati and Marietta railroad was left with only one eastern outlet, the Baltimore and Ohio.⁴² The latter road did not have to favor the former to get its traffic and instead made concessions to the Central Ohio road and to the Ohio river steamboats, where there was danger of losing traffic to the Pennsylvania. From a half to two-thirds of all the westbound freight brought by the Baltimore and Ohio to its western terminals was carried away by Ohio river steamboats. Both the Baltimore and Ohio and the Pennsylvania down to the close of 1860 were bidding for the river trade by giving better rates to goods brought by river.⁴³ The explanation offered was that the river-borne freight paid insurance, but at least a part of the reason of course was that the Ohio river trade, if not favored, could go either to Pittsburgh, Wheeling, or New Orleans. Furthermore up to 1858 the freight brought by the Ohio river steamboats was considered more important than all that could be brought by the western railroads. The Pennsylvania directors even as late as 1856 favored improvement of the Ohio river.⁴⁴

The competition between parallel lines within the Northwest and the competition between the parallel trunk

41. *Report of the Committee appointed by the Holders of the Second Mortgage Bonds of the Central Ohio Railroad Company*, 13.
42. *Special Report of the Marietta and Cincinnati Railroad Company* (Cincinnati, 1858), 81.
43. *Fourteenth Annual Report of the Pennsylvania Railroad Company* (Philadelphia, 1861), 4.
44. *Ninth Annual Report of the Pennsylvania*, 30.

lines leading out to the Atlantic seaboard had resulted, then, first of all in a number of end-for-end roads in the west combining with one another and in some cases with an eastern trunk line. Only for a short time did the eastern trunk roads try to get western parallel roads to bid against one another or did western roads try to get eastern roads to bid against one another. Competition after that went on against rival parallel systems and against unconnected roads. Freight rates were cut and traffic was routed to keep it from rivals. Only in one case was there a successful combination of parallel or competing lines. That case was one of two groups of rival lines in the Old Northwest and will be referred to again.

The competition between the parallel trunk lines that led from the Old Northwest to the Atlantic ports resulted in many attempts to unite in associations for the purpose of fixing freight and passenger rates by gentlemen's agreements or conferences. In 1854, the very year after the Baltimore and Ohio and the Pennsylvania had completed their roads, a conference of officials of these two roads and of the New York Central, of the New York and Erie, of the Hudson River railroad and of the Philadelphia and Wilmington was held in New York City to fix rates and abolish passes.[45] The agreement, however, was not long kept. During the next two years the compact or gentlemen's agreement between the presidents of these big trunk lines was often renewed and as often broken.[46] It was also soon discovered that these agreements could scarcely be kept without the co-operation of the roads in

---

45. *Twenty-eighth Annual Report of the Baltimore and Ohio*, 12.
46. *Proceedings of an Adjourned Meeting of the Convention of Representatives of the Various Railroad Companies between the Seaboard and Western States held at Cleveland, October 1, 1856*, p. 12.

the Old Northwest. It was at points in the Old Northwest like Chicago, Indianapolis, and Columbus from which freight could be routed over the western roads to the western terminals of either of the four great trunk lines that freight rates on through traffic to New York City were cut to a ruinously low figure. It was to these western cities that the officials of the trunk lines sent their runners to solicit business, to distribute free passes to shippers, and to plaster buildings with broadsides advertising the advantages and disadvantages of different roads. An association of the eastern, middle, and western railroads was therefore formed. At the second meeting of the association in March, 1855, sixty-three delegates representing thirty-eight roads were present. Committees reported on a number of subjects of general interest, but the question of competition was avoided at the formal sessions.[47] The next year, 1856, similar conventions were held at Cincinnati in September and at Cleveland in October. At the last meeting twenty-one of the roads of the Old Northwest were represented along with eight eastern, northeastern, and Canadian roads. The Baltimore and Ohio refused to send a representative for the reason that it had already entered into too many agreements that were never kept.[48] The convention, however, attacked the problem of competition with earnestness. John Brough and William Dennison, presidents of two western roads, took the most conspicuous parts. Freight was divided into four classes and the rate on each class was fixed from Cincinnati, Columbus,

47. *Proceedings of the General Railroad Association of the Eastern, Middle, and Western states; Also of the General Ticket agents Association, Pittsburgh, March 13, 1855* (Philadelphia, 1856), 6, 7.
48. *Proceedings of an Adjourned Meeting of the Convention of the Representatives of Various Railroads, Oct. 1, 1856*, pp. 3, 12.

Indianapolis, and Chicago to New York and vice versa. Resolutions were adopted restricting the use of passes and condemning the practice of advertising by posters.[49] It was also agreed that violations of the agreement were to be referred to the presidents of the four great trunk lines and the president of the Western of Massachusetts who were to meet at New York City and whose decisions were to be final unless reversed by a convention. Roads violating the agreements were to be disciplined by other roads refusing to sell through tickets or to send through freight over the lines of the former roads.[50] In spite of all the agreements and administrative machinery the objectionable practices not only continued but grew worse.

By the next year, 1857, the officials of an important western line in referring to the many efforts at fixing rates during the past several years could only admit that agreements were easy to make but almost impossible to keep.[51] The presidents of the New York Central and of the New York and Erie again met in conference and again agreed to eliminate the evils. A little later in that year the representatives of these two roads met those of the Pennsylvania and of the Baltimore and Ohio and entered into a similar agreement.[52] But it was not kept. The panic of '57 brought down the prices of farm products. Farmers refused to sell their crops, hoping for a recovery of prices. In 1858 the crops were short through a large part of the Northwest and the farmers had less to export. Railroad

49. *Ibid.*, 7, 18.
50. *Ibid.*, 16, 17.
51. *First Joint Annual Report of the Bellefontaine Railroad Line*, 16.
52. *Report of the President of the New York and Erie Railroad to the Stockholders for the year ending Sept. 30, 1857*, pp. 10, 11; *Thirty-second Annual Report of the Baltimore and Ohio Railroad Company* (Baltimore, 1858), 22.

operators became nervous and began to bid for one another's business. Even before the close of 1857 complaints were made of violations of the compact. The directors of the Pittsburgh, Ft. Wayne, and Chicago railroad complained in 1857 of hard times, competition with the Ohio river, and low freight rates on goods within the range of competition of the four big east and west roads.[53] In June, 1858, the New York and Erie openly announced its reduced rates. From August to October in that year not only the big trunk roads but also the western roads were cutting rates to a point below the cost of transportation.[54] In most cases the roads because of crop shortage were carrying a traffic reduced in quantity at a reduced rate.[55] Many roads were fast approaching bankruptcy. But the worse their financial plight the more urgent was their need for attracting business by further reducing rates.

The presidents of the four big trunk lines bethought themselves of another conference. They met late in September of 1858 in New York City and formed and published the famous St. Nicholas agreement named after the hotel in which they met. They once more abolished free passes, runners, and freight agents in the West except at lake and river ports. Agents were to allow freight to follow its own natural course. The difference between the rail and water rate and the all rail rate from New York to Cincinnati was to be reduced to eight cents per hundred pounds on first and second class freight and to five cents

53. *First Report of the Board of Directors of the Pittsburgh, Ft. Wayne, and Chicago Railroad Company for the year ending December 31, 1857,* p. 23.
54. *Annual Report of the President and Directors of the Ohio and Mississippi Railroad (Eastern Division) for 1857-58 and 1858-59* (Cincinnati, 1859), 12.
55. *Report of the President of the New York and Erie* (1858), 5.

on third and fourth class freight. The New York Central and the New York and Erie were not to make a lower rate between New York City and Columbus and points southwest of that place than between New York City and Cleveland. S. M. L. Barlow, president of the Ohio and Mississippi railroad, was made umpire to judge of infractions of the agreement.[56] The representatives of the trunk lines continued to hold frequent conferences under this agreement in New York City and Washington City and the compact was at least formally kept for five months and twenty days. There is no doubt that for a time the transportation situation was improved. An attempt was made at a convention of western railroads to bring them into harmony with the St. Nicholas compact, but the requisite number failed to ratify and the remainder, therefore, considered it not binding.[57]

The officials of the New York Central soon became dissatisfied with the compact. They argued that freight rates from western points to New York City, Philadelphia, and Baltimore should be the same. They complained that because of lower freight rates to the last two points, products of the West were going to those cities instead of to New York. The officials of the other trunk lines in turn accused the New York Central of breaking the agreement by carrying through freight from Chicago and Indianapolis at a rate as low as 22 cents per hundred.[58] The New

---

56. *Twelfth Annual Report of the Pennsylvania*, 19; Hunt, *Merchants' Magazine*, XXXIX, 621, 622; J. L. Ringwalt, *Development of Transportation in the United States* (Philadelphia, 1888), 153.

57. *First Joint Annual Report of the Bellefontaine Line for the year 1856*, p. 16.

58. G. W. Cass, *New York Central Road. The Buffalo Convention and the St. Nicholas Compact. To the Directors of the Pennsylvania Railroad Company* (April 11, 1859), 2, 10.

The Lean Years of 1857-60   187

York and Erie served notice that it would withdraw from the compact on March 20, 1859, and would make no more agreements with the New York Central while it remained under the management of the men that were then in control. Officials of all the four trunk lines indulged in accusations and personal vituperation of the bitterest kind in pamphlets and newspapers.[59] Roads again cut rates to suit their own business results.[60] The Baltimore and Ohio lowered its rates on coffee, sugar, and other westbound freight but maintained its former rates on eastbound agricultural products till late in 1859.[61] Before the close of that year the rate wars and the reduced business because of crop failures and poor management had driven the New York and Erie, one of the trunk lines, and the Pittsburgh, Ft. Wayne, and Chicago, the most important feeder of the Pennsylvania, into the hands of receivers. A great number of the western roads had for some time been in that predicament. Under these conditions the representatives of the four great trunk roads and those of the Grand Trunk railroad of Canada held conferences in New York City in October of 1860 and in Washington City in January of 1861 and readopted with some amendments the articles of their former agreements. Rates from western competing points to New York City routed over either of the four lines were to be the same.[62]

59. G. W. Cass, *Letter to the New York Times in Reply to New York Central Railroad Company* (April 25, 1859), 1; *New York Tribune*, April 1, 1859, article by "New York."
60. *Thirteenth Annual Report of the Pennsylvania Railroad Company* (Philadelphia, 1860), 3.
61. *Thirty-third Annual Report of the Baltimore and Ohio Railroad Company* (Baltimore, 1859), 17, 48.
62. *Proceedings of an Adjourned Meeting of the Presidents of the Five Atlantic Trunk Lines held at Willards Hotel in Washington City, Jan. 21,*

Among all the charges and accusations hurled back and forth, it appears that three of the trunk lines practically agreed that the officers of the New York Central were the most unscrupulous and most given to breaking their agreements. The president of the Pennsylvania in his report of 1860, however, went one step beyond this and pointed out that the real cause of the trouble was the competition between the New York Central and the Erie canal. Undoubtedly it was a very important factor in forcing the rates on the New York Central down. The river and ocean route by New Orleans was also a factor. As a result of all these rate wars and in spite of the many agreements average freight rates had been much reduced. The average rate per ton per mile had steadily fallen each year on the Pennsylvania from 5.42 cents in 1852 to 1.96 cents in 1860. On the New York Central the average rate had declined from 2.95 cents in 1854 to 2.06 in 1860 and on the New York and Erie from 2.57 cents to 1.81 cents during the same time. The average rate on the Pittsburgh, Ft. Wayne, and Chicago for 1860 was, however, lower than any of these and stood at 1.67 cents. The average freight rate and tolls on the Erie canal had, however, continuously been lower than any of these. It stood at 1.1 cents in 1856, dropped as low as .7 cents in 1858, and had risen again by 1860 to 1.1 cents.[63]

Within the Old Northwest the competition between parallel lines had led in one case after several attempts to an agreement that was faithfully kept for many years. This,

---

1861 (New York, 1861), 3, 4; *Fourteenth Annual Report of the Pennsylvania*, 4.

63. *Transportation Routes to the Seaboard*, pt. 1, appendix, p. 61; Aldrich, *Report*, pt. 1, p. 616; Ringwalt, *Development of Transportation in the United States*, 244.

however, went farther than a mere gentleman's agreement. The roads concerned, while keeping their separate organizations, agreed to place their earnings on through business into a common fund or pool and divide in accordance with prearranged ratios. From 1851 there existed two parallel rail routes each made up of end-for-end roads from Cincinnati to ports on Lake Erie. Competition between the rival lines at once resulted in the cutting of freight rates by 20%.[64] By the first part of 1853 freight was carried from Cincinnati to Cleveland, a distance of 254 miles, for $4.40 a ton or less than 2 cents per ton per mile. In April, 1853, the companies constituting these two parallel lines entered into a written agreement for ten years. The Cincinnati, Hamilton, and Dayton, the Mad River and Lake Erie, and the Junction railroad were denominated the west line from Cincinnati to Cleveland. The Little Miami, the Columbus and Xenia, and the Cincinnati, Columbus, and Cleveland constituted the east line. Rates on through freight and passenger business between Cincinnati and Cleveland were to be the same over both lines. Each line was to retain 50% of the gross earnings on through business for running expenses and the remainder was to be pooled and then divided in the ratio of 60 for the east line to 40 for the west line. It was agreed that after February 1, 1855, any company should have the right once each year to demand a reconsideration of the basis of dividing the earnings on through business. In case the presidents of the different roads disagreed on any questions they were to appoint a referee. The arrangement lasted just about a year. Before the middle of 1854 the members of the west

64. *Ninth Annual Report of the Little Miami Railroad Company* (Cincinnati, 1851), 20.

line were accused of denouncing the members of the east line as unfair, abandoning the contract, and cutting rates.[65] For several years nothing further was attempted. In December, 1858, a convention of western railways was held at Cleveland for the purpose of eliminating ruinous competition by agreement.[66] As a result in September, 1859, the Cincinnati, Hamilton, and Dayton; the Sandusky, Dayton, and Cincinnati; the Springfield, Mt. Vernon, and Pittsburgh; and the Cleveland, Columbus, and Cincinnati entered into a contract to send freight from the Sandusky, Dayton, and Cincinnati railroad eastward from Springfield to Delaware, a town on the Cleveland and Columbus road, over which road it would then be carried northeastward to Cleveland instead of its being carried northward to Sandusky over the Sandusky, Dayton, and Cincinnati.[67] In February, 1860, the Cincinnati, Hamilton, and Dayton broke its agreement, entered a new agreement with a parallel rival line composed of the Little Miami and the Columbus and Xenia and with the Dayton, Xenia, and Belpre, leased by the Little Miami, for operating their roads on joint account for a period of twenty years.[68] Rates between Cincinnati and Columbus were to be the same over both routes and annual earnings were to be divided

65. *Little Miami Railroad Company, Explanatory Letter to the Stockholders* (Cincinnati, 1854), 14, 16.
66. *Little Miami Railroad Company and Columbus and Xenia Railroad Company, Third Joint Annual Report for the year 1858* (Cincinnati, 1859), 5.
67. *Report of the Stock and Bondholders of the Sandusky, Dayton and Cincinnati* (Late Mad River) (Sandusky, 1860), 6.
68. *Report of the Sandusky, Dayton, and Cincinnati* (1860), 7; *Tenth Annual Report of the Directors of the Cincinnati, Hamilton, and Dayton* (Cincinnati, 1860), 10; *The Little Miami Railroad Company and the Columbus and Xenia Company Fifth Joint Annual Report for 1860* (Cincinnati, 1861), 51, gives the contract.

on a pre-arranged ratio. The change of arrangement signified that instead of all goods carried by the Cincinnati, Hamilton, and Dayton road from the vicinity of Cincinnati going to Cleveland, it was to be first carried to Columbus, from where it could go either to Cleveland over the Cincinnati, Columbus, and Cleveland or to Pittsburgh or to Wheeling over the Central Ohio. This contract was faithfully kept for many years.

The commerce of the Old Northwest with the outside world in 1860 showed fair improvement over 1857. The total export of flour had increased by more than 20%. The export of wheat and corn had each doubled. The total export of salt meat had increased by 50%. The export of live hogs had declined by 25% and that of live cattle had increased by 85%. The export of whiskey had increased by 25%. If the flour be considered as wheat and the salt pork, hogs, and whiskey be counted as corn, it will be found that the total export of wheat had increased by 50% and amounted to more than fifty millions of bushels and that the total export of corn had increased by more than 40% and stood at nearly sixty million bushels.

Of a total export of more than five and a half million barrels of flour more than 62% passed through the northeastern gateway in 1860 instead of 47% of the total as in 1857. Only 21% of the total passed south instead of 32% as in 1857. Of a total export of twenty-nine million bushels of wheat about 98% passed through the northeastern gateway and the remainder went east. Of a total export of twenty-four million bushels of corn 80% passed to the northeast and only 20% went south. While the southern outlet received a million bushels more of corn in 1860 than in 1857, the southern outlet took 10% less of the total export than it did in 1857. Of a total export of over a million and a half barrels of salt meat, 38% went south, 33% went east, and 28% went northeast. While the southern outlet took more salt meat in 1860 than in 1857, it took 17% less of the total export than it had in the earlier year. Of the live hogs almost as many went through the eastern gateway as through the northeastern, but of the cattle more than four-fifths went through the latter. Live stock was carried entirely by railroad and, of course, none went south except 3% to Louisville. Of a total export of five hundred thousand barrels of whiskey, 38% went south and 52% went east. The southern outlet took almost exactly the same amount in 1860 as in 1857, but it took 8% less of the total in 1860 than in 1857.[69] Some of the outstanding facts may be summarized. There was an enormous increase in the production of corn, wheat, flour, and cattle in the northern part of the Old Northwest. This increase was of course exported for the most part through the northeastern outlet, the grain going largely by lake and canal and the flour and cattle going by railroad. More than twice as much of every commodity went over the canals and railroads running eastward from Buffalo as passed over the railroad eastward from Dun-

69. *Tables of the Trade and Navigation of the Province of Canada for the year 1860* (Quebec, 1861), 10-125, 242-44; *N. Y. Assembly Docs.* (1861) vol. V, no. 93, p. 184; *Statistics of Foreign and Domestic Commerce of the United States*, in *U. S. Sen. Ex. Docs.*, 38 Cong., 1 sess., no. 54 [serial 1176], p. 159, 162, 163; *Monthly Summary of Commerce and Finance, Jan. 1900*, p. 1960, 1962; *Eighth Census*, 1860, Agriculture, CLI and CLVIII; Hunt, *Merchants' Magazine*, XL, 734; *First Annual Report of the Directors of the Erie Railway Company for the year ending Dec. 31, 1862* (New York, 1863), 3; *Thirty-fourth Annual Report of the Baltimore and Ohio Railroad Company* (Baltimore, 1860), 106-09, 115; *Fourteenth Annual Report of the Pennsylvania*, 108-10; *U. S. House Ex. Docs.*, 50 Cong., 1 sess., vol. XX, no. 6, pt. 2 [serial 2552], pp. 200-02, 216-18.

kirk and the railroads and canals of Canada. While the South and the southern outlet took more of every commodity except flour in 1860 than in 1857, it had declined relatively in every case. The gain of the eastern outlet was most pronounced in the forwarding of whiskey, salt pork, and live stock. Of the first two the eastern outlet took as much as the southern and in the case of the live stock was at least becoming a worthy rival of the northeastern outlet.

The centers forwarding the products of the Old Northwest and the sections producing them in each case can be accurately determined. The products exported through the northeastern gateway were forwarded almost entirely by five lake cities and were produced almost entirely in the northern parts of the Old Northwest. Of the twenty-nine million bushels of wheat exported northeastward, Chicago forwarded 42%, Milwaukee 26%, Toledo 14%, Detroit 6%, and Cleveland ½%.[70] Of the three million barrels of flour exported northeastward, Chicago and Milwaukee each sent 15%, Toledo and Detroit each 22%, and Cleveland 17%. Of the twenty million bushels of corn Chicago forwarded 68%, Toledo 25%, Detroit, Cleveland, and Milwaukee together less than 5%. Of the half million live hogs Cleveland sent 35%, Chicago 25%, Toledo 15%, Detroit 2%, and Milwaukee none. Of a quarter of a million of live cattle Cleveland forwarded 36%, Chicago 26%, Toledo 13%, and Detroit 11%. Of three hundred thousand barrels of salt pork Chicago for-

70. Wheat originally exported from Chicago over the Michigan Central to Detroit and over the Michigan Southern to Toledo was re-exported from the latter places but is credited above to Chicago. Likewise wheat exported from Toledo over the Cleveland and Toledo road to Cleveland has been deducted from the Cleveland total export.

warded 47%, Cleveland 35%, Toledo 14%, Detroit 14%, and Milwaukee 9%. The whiskey practically all went from Chicago.

The regions from which these cities drew the commodities that they exported can be determined with a nicety. Milwaukee's export naturally came from the southern half of Wisconsin.[71] Relatively very little came to her from beyond the Mississippi. Chicago's export came almost entirely from the northern third of Illinois. The Galena and Chicago Union alone brought to Chicago a third of all the wheat; the Chicago and Rock Island brought nearly half the whiskey; the Chicago, Burlington, and Quincy, nearly half the cattle and a third of the corn; and the Chicago and Northwestern, a third of the flour exported from Chicago. These four roads together brought four-fifths of all the flour, two-thirds of all the wheat, and more than half the corn and hogs that entered Chicago. These roads received these products from a relatively small part of Illinois lying to the west, southwest, and northwest of Chicago. The remainder of the products were brought by the Illinois Central railroad; the Chicago, Alton, and St. Louis railroad; and the Illinois and Michigan canal. The Illinois and Michigan canal brought about a fourth of all the corn and a tenth of all the wheat. A careful study of the annual reports of the Chicago and Alton and of the Chicago branch of the Illinois Central indicates that relatively small quantities of commodities placed upon these lines south of Springfield and Mattoon

---

71. *Third Annual Statement of the Trade and Commerce of Milwaukee for the year 1860*, pp. 6, 14, 17, 19, 20, 21; *Monthly Summary of Commerce and Finance, Jan. 1900*, p. 1966; *Eighth Census, 1860*, Agriculture, p. CL; G. G. Tunnell, "Statistics of Lake Commerce," in *U. S. House Docs.*, 55 Cong., 2 sess., vol. LI, no. 277 [serial 3679], p. 55.

The Lean Years of 1857-60   195

near the center of the state found their way to Chicago. Likewise relatively small quantities of commodities came from Wisconsin over the Chicago and Northwestern and the Chicago and Milwaukee and from Iowa over the Chicago and Rock Island.[72]

The great bulk of the commodities exported by Detroit were brought by the Michigan Central from the southern fourth of the state of Michigan. The Detroit and Milwaukee brought a half million bushels of wheat from the northern part of southern Michigan.[73] In the case of Toledo after deducting from the total exports the commodities brought there by the Michigan Southern and Northern Indiana railroad that the road had brought through from Chicago, the remainder is found to have come largely from northern Indiana, with somewhat less from north central Illinois and still less from northwestern Ohio and southern Michigan. The Michigan Southern railroad from extreme

---

72. *Third Annual Statement of the Trade and Commerce of Chicago for the year ending Dec. 31, 1860, Reported to the Chicago Board of Trade by Seth Catlin* (Chicago, 1861), 16, 17, 33, 35; *First Half-Yearly Report of the Receivers of the St. Louis, Alton and Chicago Railroad to the Trustees from Dec. 3, 1859 to June 30, 1860* (Chicago, 1860); *Second Half-Yearly Report, of the Receivers of the St. Louis, Alton and Chicago Railroad*, 27; *Illinois Central Railroad Company Report and Accounts for the Year ending Dec. 31, 1860*, pp. 11, 12.

73. *Annual Statement of the Trade and Commerce of Detroit for the year 1860*, by J. E. Scripps (Detroit, 1861), 16, 20, 29; *Third Annual Statement of the Trade and Commerce of Chicago for the year ending Dec. 31, 1860*, pp. 19, 22, 39; *Monthly Summary of Commerce and Finance, January, 1900*, p. 1966; *Statistics of Foreign and Domestic Commerce*, 157. After deducting from Detroit's exports the commodities brought there by the Michigan Central which had originally been exported from Chicago and the commodities brought there by the Detroit and Milwaukee which had originally been exported from Milwaukee across the lake to Grand Haven, the Western terminal of that road, it is clear that the remaining exports of Detroit came from the southern half of Michigan.

southern Michigan and extreme northern Indiana, the Toledo and Wabash railroad from the Wabash valley of northern Indiana and the Wabash and Erie canal from the same region each brought one-third of the wheat and flour. The latter two lines, however, brought nearly all the corn and this came from the upper Wabash region in Indiana. The flour, wheat, and corn that the canal brought was for the most part produced in the Wabash valley between Lafayette and Ft. Wayne. The Toledo and Wabash railroad drew most of its freight from the same part of that valley, but it received a sixth of the grain, a third of the hogs, and over half of its large consignment of cattle from the Great Western, which in turn brought them from north central Illinois.[74] The Toledo and Wabash railroad also drew rather heavily from the Logansport and Peoria feeder line from northwestern Indiana and northern Illinois, but received very small quantities from the intersecting north and south roads such as the Peru and Indianapolis and the Lafayette and Indianapolis. Commodities from these roads went largely through Indianapolis to the Ohio river towns.

From the total exports of Cleveland must, of course, be deducted the commodities brought there from Toledo by the Cleveland and Toledo. The remaining exports of Cleveland will, then, be found to have come for the most

74. *Toledo Blade's (Third) Annual Statement of the Trade and Commerce of Toledo for the year 1860* (Toledo, 1861), 18; *Second Annual Report of the Toledo and Wabash Railway Company for the year ending August 31, 1866* (Toledo, 1860), 22; Hunt, *Merchants' Magazine*, XLV, 573 and XLVI, 365, 366; *Eighth Census*, Agriculture, p. cxlix; *Statistics of Foreign and Domestic Commerce*, 155, 156; *Reports of the Officers of State of the State of Indiana for 1859 and 1860*, pt. 1 (Indpls., 1860), 326-43; *Documents of the General Assembly of Indiana at Forty-first session* (Indianapolis, 1861), pt. 1, pp. 273, 285.

THE LEAN YEARS OF 1857-60

part from north central Ohio and from the southern parts of northwestern Ohio and northeastern Indiana. The commodities forwarded from Cleveland entered the place chiefly over three lines, the Ohio canal, the Cleveland, Columbus, and Cincinnati railroad, and the Cleveland and Toledo railroad. The canal still brought from its course through north central Ohio a fourth of all the flour and wheat that entered Cleveland.[75] Of the commodities brought by the Cleveland, Columbus, and Cincinnati, one-third came from the Bellefontaine line, considerably more than a third from its own way stations between Cleveland and Columbus, and considerably less than a third from the Columbus and Xenia and other lines running into Columbus from the west, and from the Pittsburgh, Ft. Wayne, and Chicago line crossing at Crestline.[76] The Bellefontaine line brought about half of its contribution through from Indianapolis. Of the commodities brought by the Cleveland and Toledo, about two-thirds had been forwarded from Toledo, but the road was bringing in some wheat, flour, and hogs from the way stations between the two ports.[77] The Cleveland and Erie and the Cleveland and Pittsburgh naturally brought few agricultural commodi-

---

75. McClelland and Huntington, *Ohio Canals*, 175, 176.

76. *Tenth Annual Report of the Directors of the Cleveland, Columbus and Cincinnati Railroad Company to the Stockholders for the year 1860* (Cleveland, 1861), 17, 18; *Little Miami Railroad Company and the Columbus and Xenia Railroad Company Fifth Joint Report, for 1860*, pp. 44, 45; *Fifth Joint Annual Report of the Bellefontaine Railroad Line for the year 1860*, etc. (Cleveland, 1861), 15, 27; *Third Annual Report of the Pittsburgh, Ft. Wayne and Chicago for 1859* (Pittsburgh, 1860), 86; *Fourth Annual Report of Pittsburgh, Ft. Wayne and Chicago Railroad Company, for the year ending Dec. 31, 1860* (Pittsburgh, 1861), 35.

77. *Report of the Directors of the Cleveland and Toledo Railroad Company*, etc. (Cleveland, 1861), Statement F.

ties although the latter did bring some wheat and flour.[78] Practically nothing came by lake to Cleveland in 1860. Relatively nothing except some flour and cattle reached Cleveland from the region between Columbus and Cincinnati. In general Cleveland was falling decidedly behind both relatively and absolutely as a forwarding center. With Ohio's increase of population there was much less of a surplus for export than formerly.[79] Southern Ohio was exporting eastward and southward, while Toledo and Chicago on the other hand were tapping regions increasing in production enormously year by year.

The four hundred thousand tons of commodities transported eastward through the eastern gateway passed through Pittsburgh and thence over the Pennsylvania railroad or through Wheeling or Parkersburg and thence over the Baltimore and Ohio. Of the hundred and fifty thousand tons transported eastward over the Baltimore and Ohio, 38% had been brought to its western terminals by the Ohio Central railroad, 15% by the Marietta and Cincinnati railroad, and 37% by the Ohio river.[80] The Ohio Central in turn received this freight from its own way stations, from the Little Miami and Columbus and Xenia line, and from the Cincinnati, Wilmington, and Zanesville road.[81] These roads stretched

78. *Thirteenth Annual Report of the Cleveland and Pittsburgh Railroad Company* (New Haven, 1861); *Ninth Annual Report of the Cleveland and Pittsburgh Railroad Company* (New York, 1857), Statement B.

79. *Memorial of the Union Merchants Exchange of Saint Louis to the 43rd Congress*, etc. (St. Louis, 1874), 9.

80. *Thirty-fourth Annual Report of the Baltimore and Ohio*, 58, 60.

81. *Tenth Annual Report of the Cleveland, Columbus and Cincinnati*, etc., 17; *Fifth Joint Annual Report of the Little Miami Railroad Co. and Columbus and Xenia*, 44-45; *Receivers Report to Circuit Court of U. S.-vs.-Cincinnati, Wilmington & Zanesville R. R. Co. and others for the year ending April 30th, 1859* (Cincinnati, 1859), 15, 18.

across the state from Wheeling to Cincinnati and drew from a zone that may be called the northern part of southern Ohio. The Marietta and Cincinnati ran through Ohio just south of these roads and drew from the southern part of southern Ohio.[82] Some of the flour and pork carried eastward by these railway lines from Cincinnati had been originally brought to that place by the railroads from southeastern Indiana and southwestern Ohio. The exact quantity of each commodity brought by the railroads to the western terminals of the Baltimore and Ohio cannot now be stated but it apparently included some hundred fifty thousand barrels of flour from the Little Miami and the Central Ohio, some fifteen thousand tons of live stock from the Central Ohio and the Marietta and Cincinnati, and some three hundred thousand bushels of wheat and corn from the latter. The Ohio river naturally brought some commodities from its entire course but for the most part from its more eastern end. About half of the three hundred thousand barrels of flour and of the twenty-three thousand tons of livestock and nearly all of two hundred forty thousand barrels of salt meat and of the hundred twenty-five thousand barrels of whiskey carried eastward by the Baltimore and Ohio had come to its terminals by steamboats. The Baltimore and Ohio was very distinctly an outlet for the Ohio valley.

Of the nearly two hundred fifty thousand tons of commodities that passed eastward from Pittsburgh over the Pennsylvania railroad, more than one-half was brought by

82. *Thirty-third Annual Report of the Baltimore and Ohio*, 21, 51; *Report of the President and Directors of the Marietta and Cincinnati Railroad Company* (London, 1861), 10; *Annual Report of the President and Directors of the Ohio and Mississippi Railroad Company (Eastern Division) to the stockholders for the years 1860-61* (Cincinnati, 1861), 33.

the Pittsburgh, Ft. Wayne, and Chicago road, now controlled by the Pennsylvania; and less than half came by the Steubenville and Indiana railroad and the Cleveland and Pittsburgh road and Ohio river steamboats. Practically every bit of the eight hundred thousand bushels of grain and the fifty-four thousand tons of livestock carried eastward by the Pennsylvania was brought to Allegheny and Pittsburgh by the Pittsburgh, Ft. Wayne, and Chicago line. More than half of the four hundred thousand barrels of flour and one-fifth of the three hundred thousand barrels of meat came from the same road.[83] This road crossed northern Illinois, northern Indiana, and northern Ohio and drew its freight from those sections. Approximately one-half of the flour and the pork that it delivered to the Pennsylvania at Pittsburgh had been carried through from Chicago; the other half came onto the road at Crestline from the Bellefontaine road running from Indianapolis to Crestline. The grain and livestock was picked up all along the way stations of the road from Chicago to Pittsburgh. It was a noteworthy fact that this road succeeded in keeping all the commodities except a little of the grain once got onto the road from being transferred to roads that crossed its course and delivered practically the whole amount of its eastbound freight to the Pennsylvania road. The Steubenville and Indiana brought to the Pennsylvania some commodities from its local stations in eastern Ohio but little from farther west. Its western terminus was Newark, a way station on the Ohio

83. *Fourth Annual Report of the Pittsburgh, Ft. Wayne and Chicago Railroad Company, etc.*, 35; *Third Annual Report of the Pittsburgh, Ft. Wayne and Chicago*, 86; *Fourteenth Annual Report of the Pennsylvania Railroad Company*, 108, 110; *Fifth Annual Report of the Pittsburgh, Ft. Wayne and Chicago Railroad Company for the year ending Dec. 31, 1861* (Pittsburgh, 1862), 42.

Central, which carried most of its freight through from Columbus to Bellaire opposite Wheeling, one of the western terminals of the Baltimore and Ohio. The Cleveland and Pittsburgh railroad brought even less. A large part of its freight consisted of iron and coal and merchandise and was carried from Pittsburgh to Cleveland. The two roads together brought to the Pennsylvania road not over a tenth of its eastbound traffic. The Ohio river still contributed nearly half the tonnage or a little over one hundred thousand tons. Half of the four hundred thousand barrels of flour and nearly all of the three hundred thousand barrels of meat and nearly all of the hundred thirty thousand barrels of whiskey carried eastward by the Pennsylvania railroad had been brought by river to Pittsburgh. That is, to the western terminals of the Pennsylvania and of the Baltimore and Ohio, the steamboats brought about three hundred fifty thousand barrels of flour, ten thousand tons of livestock, four hundred fifty thousand barrels of salt meat, and two hundred fifty thousand barrels of whiskey.

The exports southward from the Old Northwest in 1860 passed through several channels; down the Mississippi to Memphis and to New Orleans as formerly, over the newly completed Louisville and Nashville railroad southward from Louisville, and up the Cumberland and Tennessee rivers. The commodities going up these latter rivers came largely from Evansville and the lower Wabash valley.[84] They supplied a local market in western Kentucky and

84. *Annual Report of the Board of Trade of Evansville, Indiana, for 1867*, etc. (Evansville, 1868), 23, 51; *Evansville Journal* for 1860 gives statistics of city's river trade with the Wabash, Green, and Tennessee rivers; *Annual Report of the President and Directors of the Louisville and Nashville Railroad Company, Oct. 1, 1859 to Oct. 1, 1860*, Exhibit B, shows 300,000 bushels of grain shipped southward.

were comparatively limited in quantity. Agricultural commodities shipped out of Louisville over the Louisville and Nashville to Nashville and beyond had reached Louisville by steamboats, by railroad from Covington opposite Cincinnati, and by packets from Madison, New Albany, and other river terminals of southern Indiana railroads. More freight was offered than the road could handle.[85] The commodities going to New Orleans were forwarded largely by St. Louis, Cincinnati, and Louisville, with smaller shipments by Evansville and Cairo. St. Louis forwarded practically all of the million barrels of flour and the four million bushels of corn that reached New Orleans. Cincinnati still forwarded directly seventy-five per cent of all the whiskey that New Orleans received. St. Louis supplied the greater part of the remainder of the whiskey. Cincinnati, St. Louis, and Louisville each supplied a little less than a third of the pork. Cincinnati forwarded a third of all the beef.[86] Cincinnati, Louisville, and St. Louis in each case drew their commodities from the country lying around them in a radius of a hundred and fifty miles. Cincinnati pretty well dominated southwestern Ohio, southeastern Indiana, and northern Kentucky.[87] Louisville just as completely controlled the central part of southern Indiana. St. Louis was the market for south-

---

85. *Annual Report of the President and Directors of the Ohio and Mississippi Railroad Company (Eastern Division) to the Stockholders for the year 1860-1861*, p. 14. Complains that most of the hogs fattened along its line were taken by the north and south roads to their river terminals; *Annual Statement of the Commerce of Cincinnati for the commercial year ending August 31, 1860*, p. 8.

86. *Annual Statement of the Trade and Commerce of St. Louis, for 1865* (St. Louis, 1866), 22, 80; *Annual Statement of the Commerce of Cincinnati for the commercial year ending Aug. 31, 1860*, p. 44.

87. *Little Miami Railroad Company, Twelfth Annual Report*, 14.

western Illinois as far north as Springfield, for the Missouri river valley and parts of the upper Mississippi valley.[88] That part of southern Illinois usually known as Egypt was exporting over the Illinois Central railroad through Cairo and sent twelve steamboats to New Orleans in 1860.[89] Cincinnati, Louisville, and St. Louis each drew a considerable part of her commodities from regions lying outside the Old Northwest. Cincinnati was the chief market for agricultural products for the region extending northward to Indianapolis and Columbus and southward to Lexington. The greater quantity of the wheat and corn and nearly all the hogs transported upon the Little Miami and the Columbus and Xenia found its ways to Cincinnati. The flour, whiskey, and pork from the way stations of that line, however, went east and northeast.[90] The greater part of the livestock, the pork, and the grain outside of wheat from the way stations of the Cincinnati, Wilmington, and Zanesville passed westward to Cincinnati.[91] Indianapolis was shipping commodities northeastward to Cleveland over the Bellefontaine line; eastward to Pittsburgh over the Bellefontaine; southeastward to Cincinnati over the Indiana Central and the Cincinnati, Hamilton, and Dayton; and southward to Lawrenceburg, Madison, and Jeffersonville over the Indianapolis and Cincinnati, the Madison and Indianapolis, and the Jefferson-

---

88. *First Half Yearly Report of the Receivers of St. Louis, Alton and Chicago Railroad, etc.* (Chicago, 1860), 14. Tables indicate that wheat and oats shipped at Atlanta, Illinois, on this line went southward.

89. *U. S. House Ex. Docs.*, 50 Cong., 1 sess., vol. XX, no. 6, pt. 2 [serial 2552], p. 214.

90. *Little Miami Railroad Company and the Columbus and Xenia, Fifth Joint Annual Report*, 44, 45.

91. *Receiver's Report . . . the Cincinnati, Wilmington and Zanesville Railroad* (Cincinnati, 1859), 15, 17, 18.

ville and Indianapolis railroads respectively. Practically all agricultural products put upon the three last named roads sought the Ohio river terminals instead of going northward to Indianapolis.[92]

In general that part of the Old Northwest lying south of a line running through Wheeling, Columbus, Indianapolis, and Springfield exported its surplus through the southern and the eastern gateways. In this region as a whole increased production had for a decade little more than kept ahead of increase of population so that the surplus had increased but little in comparison with the northern part of the Old Northwest.[93] As an avenue for the disposal of

[92]. *Report of the Indianapolis and Cincinnati Railroad Company for the year 1859* (Cincinnati, 1860), 31, 32; *Annual Report of . . . the Ohio and Mississippi . . . for the year 1860-61*, p. 14; *Seventh Annual Report of the President and Directors of the Indiana Central Railway Company* (Richmond, 1859), 5. Nearly all agricultural products carried by the latter road went to Cincinnati.

[93]. Tabulation based upon the census of 1840, 1850, 1860:

POPULATION AND PRODUCTION STATISTICS—NORTHERN AND SOUTHERN PARTS OF THE OLD NORTHWEST IN 1840, 1850 AND 1860

(The following figures are given in thousands)

		Population	Swine Produced	Swine Surplus
Northwest 1840	Northern part	1316.9	4380.0	3063.1
	Southern part	1364.4	2678.6	1314.2
Northwest 1850	Northern part	2028.8	2880.3	1069.5
	Southern part	1791.3	3264.0	1472.7
Northwest 1860	Northern part	3118.4	4228.2	1109.8
	Southern part	2283.4	3626.8	1341.4

		Wheat Produced	Wheat Consumed	Wheat Surplus
Northwest 1840	Northern part	10224.6	8218.3	2006.3
	Southern part	11891.5	9550.8	2340.7
Northwest 1850	Northern part	21074.2	14201.6	6772.8
	Southern part	9042.0	12539.1	−3397.3
Northwest 1860	Northern part	34845.7	21828.8	13016.9
	Southern part	20959.5	15983.8	4975.7

the surplus of this southern part of the Northwest the southern gateway was only a little more important by 1860 than was the eastern. In gross quantity they stood almost equal. Even after making allowance for the fact that half the tonnage carried eastward by the Pennsylvania line came from the northern part of the Northwest and that Cincinnati, Louisville, and St. Louis drew considerable portions of their exports from regions outside the Old Northwest, the two outlets still stand about equal in importance.

The total imports into the Old Northwest had risen from a little over seven hundred thousand tons in 1857 to a little over eight hundred thousand in 1860. At the northeastern gateway the situation was almost exactly that of 1857. The four hundred thousand tons entering there was brought by the Erie canal to Buffalo, by the Erie canal to Oswego and thence by the Welland canal to Lake Erie, by the New York Central railroad to Buffalo, and by the New York and Erie railroad to Dunkirk in almost equal parts. The canal and the railroads terminating at Buffalo in each case had only a trifle the advantage of the other two. Of the two hundred twenty thousand tons sent westward over the Erie and the Welland canals, a hundred thousand consisted of salt and the remainder consisted of general merchandise of which sugar and railroad iron held first place in tonnage, each comprising about a sixth of the total.[94] Illinois took a third of all the merchandise transported westward by the northeastern canals. Indiana, on the other hand, received less than 5% from that source. Of a little over two hundred thousand

---

94. *N. Y. Assembly Docs.* (1861), vol. V, no. 93, pp. 139, 224; *Tables of the Trade and Navigation of the Province of Canada for the year 1860*, pp. 242-44.

tons brought by the New York Central and the New York and Erie to Buffalo and Dunkirk, practically the entire quantity was listed as merchandise.[95] About two-thirds of the tonnage brought to Dunkirk by the Erie railroad was carried west by the Lake Shore railroad and the remainder was carried by lake steamers to Cleveland and Toledo.[96]

Of a little more than three hundred thousand tons brought to the eastern gateway, the Pennsylvania brought three-fourths to Pittsburgh; and the Baltimore and Ohio brought one-fourth to Wheeling and Parkersburg. In the two hundred thirty thousand tons brought by the Pennsylvania, the largest items were seventy thousand tons of iron of all descriptions, thirty thousand tons of coal, thirty-two thousand tons of drygoods, and fourteen thousand tons of groceries.[97] The Baltimore and Ohio brought an additional thirteen thousand tons of drygoods and nine thousand tons of groceries.[98] Besides groceries in general the two roads together brought over sixteen thousand tons of coffee, two-thirds of this coming over the Baltimore and Ohio road. Of the two hundred thirty thousand tons brought to Pittsburgh by the Pennsylvania, almost two-thirds was carried westward and distributed through northern Ohio and Indiana by the Pittsburgh, Ft. Wayne, and Chicago.[99] A little less than five thousand tons of this found its way over the Bellefontaine line as far south as

95. *Annual Report of the New York Central Railroad Company for the year ending Sept. 30, 1860* (Albany, 1860), 18, 21; *Statistics of Foreign and Domestic Commerce,* 126, 127, 133, 134.

96. *First Annual Report of the Directors of the Erie Railway Company for the year ending Dec. 31, 1862,* p. 30.

97. *Fourteenth Annual Report of the Pennsylvania Railroad,* 108-10.

98. *Thirty-fourth Annual Report of the Baltimore and Ohio,* 100.

99. *Fourth Annual Report of the Pittsburgh, Ft. Wayne and Chicago Railroad for the year ending Dec. 31, 1860,* p. 35.

Indianapolis.[100] The other third of the tonnage brought to Pittsburgh by the Pennsylvania was for local consumption in Pittsburgh, for shipment northward over the Cleveland and Pittsburgh railroad, for shipment westward into Ohio over the Steubenville and Indiana, and for shipment down the Ohio river by steamboat. It would perhaps not be far off to estimate that these four means of disposal divided eighty thousand tons almost equally.[101] Much of the coal and iron was for Pittsburgh consumption.

Of the seventy-five thousand tons brought by the Baltimore and Ohio from Baltimore to its western terminals, a little more than half was carried westward into southern Ohio by the Central Ohio railroad and by the Cincinnati and Marietta. The Central Ohio received over thirty-six thousand tons and the Marietta and Ohio took a little over nine thousand.[102] Of the tonnage transferred to the Central Ohio, one-half went to Cincinnati and a third was for distribution along the way stations of the Central Ohio. Trifling quantities were carried as far west as Indianapolis.[103] A little less than half of the total tonnage brought to the western terminals by the Baltimore and Ohio was for consumption at Wheeling and Parkersburg and for transport down the Ohio river by the steamboats. About four thousand tons were consumed in Wheeling,[104] and twenty-five thousand tons were carried away by the

---

100. *Fifth Joint Annual Report of the Bellefontaine Railroad Line*, 27.
101. *Eighth Annual Report of the Cleveland and Pittsburgh Railroad Company* (Cleveland, 1856), 24 opposite table C; *Thirteenth Annual Report of the Cleveland and Pittsburgh Railroad Company*, gives no statistics on freight.
102. *Thirty-fourth Annual Report of the Baltimore and Ohio*, 58, 60.
103. *Ninth Annual Report of the Central Ohio Railroad*, 24.
104. *Thirty-fourth Annual Report of the Baltimore and Ohio*, 59.

Ohio river steamboats. From Pittsburgh the river boats brought only slightly smaller quantities, making the total carried down the Ohio from the eastern gateway by the steamboats about fifty thousand tons.

Of the imports into the Old Northwest from the southern gateway, sugar and molasses, coffee and salt were still the most important items. Of some sixty-six thousand tons of sugar brought up the Mississippi, St. Louis took twenty-five thousand tons, Cincinnati fifteen thousand tons, Louisville, Evansville, and other Ohio river towns took much smaller quantities.[105] Of the coffee forwarded from the south, St. Louis received and distributed a little more than seven thousand tons and Cincinnati a little less than that amount. Almost as much coffee was now entering through the eastern gateway. Cotton was coming up the Mississippi in 1860 in large enough quantity to attract attention. Over a hundred thousand bales came northward from Memphis alone. Most of this was used by manufacturers in the Old Northwest, but a little was also carried to the East over the trunk line railroads.[106] In general the years 1857-59 were marked by hard times and many crop failures and the people of the Old Northwest were holding their importations down pretty nearly at the same level throughout the period.

105. *DeBow's Review,* XXIV, 524; *Annual Statement of the Trade and Commerce of St. Louis* (St. Louis, 1866), 22, 80; *Annual Statement of the Commerce of Cincinnati for the commercial year ending Aug. 31, 1860,* p. 44.

106. *Thirty-fourth Annual Report of the Baltimore and Ohio Railroad,* 66.

CHAPTER VIII

The Two Extremes Against the Middle, 1860-1861

AT LEAST three things in 1860 tended to keep the region lying between the Great Lakes and the Ohio river together. First, the region had had a sufficient community of interest in its dealings with the national government to constitute in some respects a distinct section of the country. The people of the Northwest had on more than one occasion shown evidences of a consciousness of the fact that in some respects their interests were one. The politicians of the Northeast and of the South had for years taken that fact into consideration when intertwining issues in presidential elections and combining interests in national legislation. Second, of the five political divisions of the Old Northwest three touched, with their northern boundaries, the Great Lakes and, with their southern boundaries, rested upon the Ohio. Together they reached from the eastern limits of the region to the Mississippi. Third, the entire area was free soil and its people had no intention of changing that status. The region had first been made free by legislation by the central government, had been so maintained by state enactment, and had practically been put beyond the possibility of change by climatic conditions and by having been settled by people who did not want to hold slaves or were financially unable to do so. The few inhabitants who desired to introduce slavery have attracted attention out of all proportion to their importance.

Three facts tended to cause the Old Northwest to pull apart somewhere along the old National road. First, the northern part lay, in general, within the valley of the Great Lakes, while the southern part lay within the valley of the Ohio river. Hence most of the northern part was in the glaciated area, and was almost universally adapted to grain production on a fairly large scale. The southern part, on the other hand, had a far greater proportion of hill land, whose soil was more quickly exhausted and not so well adapted to large scale agriculture. Second, the northern part was settled extensively by people of New England ancestry, while the southern part had a large proportion of the southern upland stock.

There were, of course, important exceptions to this generalization. But the people of the northern part looked with consideration upon northeastern culture, institutions, and leaders. They had not entirely outgrown some of the mental traits of their ancestors and took themselves fairly seriously. Looking upon themselves as their brothers' keepers, many felt called upon to do what they could to restrict the spread of slavery everywhere. In the southern part were many who were bound by ties of blood and sentiment to people in the South. As individualists, however, they did not look for inspiration to the southerners or to anyone besides themselves. They were not anxious to settle the slavery question for people living outside the Old Northwest. They had as little use for the New England Yankees as the latter had for them. The rapid development and prosperity of the lake region in comparison with the western end of the Ohio Valley during the twenty-five years preceding the Civil War had not lessened this mutual feeling.

Third, the two parts had different commercial connections and interests. The northern part exported its surplus through the northeastern and eastern gateways of the Old

Two Extremes against the Middle 211

Northwest, while the southern part exported through the eastern gateway and to the South. The statistics for the exports through the northeastern gateway, over the railways and the canals of upper New York and of Canada, in 1860, indicate an increase over that of twenty-five years before that has seemed to some to require some kind of explanation. During the same period of time the receipts of the same kinds of commodities at New Orleans showed a steady but much smaller rate of increase up to about 1853, and then remained almost stationary. The railroad maps of the Old Northwest for the fifties depict the gradual completion of rail routes connecting lake ports with ports on the Ohio and on the Mississippi. By taking these three facts into consideration, it has been easy to jump to the conclusion that the relatively large increase in the exports through the northeastern gateway was due to the fact that the railroads brought from the Ohio valley commodities that had formerly been transported southward. This conclusion is, however, not justified. The railroads had not weaned the Ohio valley away from its economic connection with the South. The railroads were useful in rerouting the commodities of this valley after the South had been closed during the war, but the change had not yet come in 1860. The people of the Ohio valley did not decide to fight the people of the South so much because they had concluded that they could get along economically without the South as they did because they believed that they could not get along without it. One needs to study carefully the annual reports of railroads and canals to discover the source, destination, and quantity of shipments. From these it appears that the increased export through the northeastern gateway by 1860 was really due to the increased population of the lake region and the region to the west of the lakes. In 1835 the exports northeastward, through or around the eastern end of Lake Erie, went from that part of the lake region that was producing a surplus and from a part of central Ohio that had already been annexed to the lake basin by the Ohio canal. In 1860 the exports northeastward went from the lake region, the region to the west, and from such other areas in northern Ohio, northern Indiana, and northern Illinois as had been annexed by the opening of the Ohio canal, of the Wabash and Erie canal, and of the Michigan and Illinois canal. With trifling exceptions, no region in the Ohio valley was exporting northeastward in 1860 which had once exported southward or eastward. The regions annexed by the canals to the basin of the lakes were annexed before those regions had begun to produce much of a surplus; and while the railroads facilitated commerce, they made no considerable change in the direction of commerce except in one case. That was the deflecting of commerce from the northeastern gateway to the eastern gateway by the Pittsburgh, Ft. Wayne, and Chicago road. In 1835 the Ohio valley, excepting the part annexed by the canals to the lakes, shipped southward, or eastward from the upper reaches of the Ohio. So it was in 1860. Excepting coffee, sugar, molasses, and part of the salt, nearly all imports into the Northwest in 1860 as in 1835 came by the northeastern and by the eastern gateway.

Two changes had, however, taken place that were the result of the opening of the railroads. Meats and live stock made up a far more important proportion of the exports through the northeastern gateway in 1860 than in 1835. It was the railroads of the Northwest and more especially those of upper New York state that had made this change possible. The canals were frozen up during the packing season and could not handle live stock efficiently at any time. Hence the lake region did not go into the live stock production extensively till after the opening of the railroads. The other change applied to the Ohio valley. A considerable proportion of the commodities shipped from the Ohio valley to New Orleans in 1835 was reshipped to places along the Mississippi above New Orleans, to Charleston, to Baltimore, and to New England. By 1860 more places along the lower Mississippi were supplied directly from the Northwest. Goods were also shipped directly to Memphis and thence by rail eastward to Chattanooga and into the interior of the South. Greater quantities than formerly were also shipped up the Cumberland and the Tennessee rivers and over the newly opened Louisville and Nashville railroad. The two last named lines of communication established contact with the railroad running eastward from Memphis to Chattanooga. From the latter place pork and corn were forwarded by rail to Charleston, to Savannah and to other southeastern points. Pork that had formerly gone by New Orleans to Baltimore, or live stock that had been driven eastward over the Cumberland road, in 1860 went for the most part over the Baltimore and Ohio railroad to Baltimore. New England after the completion of her railway connections with the Great Lakes drew her provision imports from that source rather than from the Ohio valley by way of New Orleans. To the Northwest New Orleans was relatively a little less important than formerly, but the South as a whole was as important as ever. The Ohio valley was in 1860 as closely connected economically with the South as in 1835. Southwestern Ohio had during the fifties become more industrial with the result that Cincinnati's prosperity depended in part upon the fact that she was a distributing center for a country a hundred miles around and depended less than formerly upon her export to the lower Mississippi. Yet when the war came, Cincinnati for a time was in economic distress. From August, 1861, to August, 1862, the business outlook was hopeless. By the latter date the effect of orders from the Government and of unprecedented orders from England brought relief.[1] Towns farther down the valley felt even more keenly the effect of losing their trade with the South and through the South. Some managed to hurry their exports south before the trade was forbidden.[2] But when this trade had been pretty effectually stopped, Louisville, Evansville, and St. Louis for a time found their business ruined and for years thereafter felt the injury to their economic life.[3] Louisville, where much of the pork was packed that was produced in south central Indiana, packed only one-third of the quantity in 1861 that she had in 1860. So serious appeared the outlook for a time that Lincoln made special arrangement to relieve the Ohio valley by making purchases of government supplies there.[4] The Illinois Central railroad laid down as much freight at Cairo during each of the first four

1. *Annual Statement of the Commerce of Cincinnati for the year ending August 31, 1861*, pp. 5, 6; *Ibid., 1862*, p. 5.
2. *Annual Statement of the Commerce of Cincinnati for the year ending August 31, 1861*, pp. 6, 38.
3. J. W. Foster, *Report of the Evansville Board of Trade for 1867* (Evansville, 1868), 23, 65; *Annual Review of the Trade and Commerce of Louisville for the Year ending March 31, 1866* (Louisville, 1866), 5; *Annual Statement of the Trade and Commerce of St. Louis for the year 1865*, p. 6.
4. Foster, *Report of the Evansville Board of Trade for 1867*, p. 65; J. G. Nicolay and J. Hay, *The Complete Works of Lincoln* (New York, 1890), VI, p. 286; *Annual Statement of the Commerce of Cincinnati for the year ending Aug. 31, 1862*, p. 5.

months of 1861 as in all the eight remaining months of the year, an evidence of the extent of the regular export from the southern half of Illinois to and through the South.[5] Prior to 1860 Chicago had scarcely shipped anything to the South, but during the year preceding the war she was beginning to ship thence in large quantities and her merchants and packers were congratulating themselves on the acquisition of a new market.[6]

Some of the southern leaders were in 1835 conscious of this economic connection between the Northwest and the South and were seeking to perfect the lines of communication and of transportation both for commercial and for political purposes. By 1860 they were in part closing their eyes to this connection and in part misinterpreting its significance in the event of attempted separation. The so-called southern commercial conventions that were held almost annually during the fifties became more and more political in character as time went on. Together they constituted the sessions of a kind of Congress of the South that envisaged the South as a future economic entity if not as a political entity. The delegates planned direct trade with England and South America. They discussed the building of east-and-west railways through the South with the aid of the Federal Government or of an association of the southern states. They hoped to weaken the economic connection between the Northeast and the South but considered the Northwest hardly at all. When they did, it was usually to point out that the South could produce her own pork and corn or that the Northwest would

5. *Illinois Central Railroad Company, Report and Accounts for the year ending December 31, 1861*, p. 1.
6. *Third Annual Statement of the Trade and Commerce of Chicago for the year ending December 31, 1860*, p. 18.

have to continue to be duly respectful because of its need for the southern market. Southern gentlemen seem to have reasoned that the deference on the part of the people of the Ohio valley, which was really due to a desire to hold the South in the Union, would continue even after the South had left the Union. Lincoln, who had spent most of his life in the Ohio valley or on its fringes, saw more clearly. In 1861 he gave it as his opinion that, if the railway from Charleston to Cincinnati had been built in the years following 1835, secession could never have come, but that even without that road, the Mississippi might be a cross-tie of sufficient strength to hold the Union together ultimately.[7]

All the railroads that had one terminal upon the Ohio river to a certain extent served as cross-ties. The railroads of the Old Northwest were of great service to the Federal government in the Civil War, and the war in turn financially benefitted many of the roads. Inflated prices of agricultural products, the needs of the Federal armies, and the crop failures in England all helped to stimulate shipments. The shipment of government supplies for the army and the frequent transfer of troops increased the business of many of the roads and enabled them to recover from the financial difficulties of the late fifties. The roads in the northern halves of Illinois, Indiana, and Ohio were now transporting to the east and northeast products that had formerly sought the south.[8] The roads in the southern halves of these states were during the first part of the war transporting goods northward and eastward from their

---

7. H. C. Carey, *To the Friends of Union*, etc. [pamphlet], p. 2.
8. *Ohio Executive Documents, Messages and Reports to the General Assembly and Governor of the State of Ohio for the year 1861, pt. 1* (Columbus, 1862), 335.

way stations that they had formerly transported toward the Ohio or the Mississippi. But through traffic because of the loss of connections south of southern terminals was sadly diminished.[9] The officials and stockholders were convinced that if the war stopped with the South permanently out of the Union, the loss of the temporary government business and the diminution of through traffic to and from the South would leave their roads again in financial difficulties. Every railroad in the Old Northwest that had a terminal upon the Ohio had been so built with the expectation of trade with the South. For that reason the officials and owners of those roads almost without an exception united with the business men in a sturdy support of the war. Only a few of the interesting cases can here be mentioned. The directors of the Illinois Central in their annual report for 1861 stated that it would be beyond human power to re-establish the prosperity of the road "until the relations with the South are renewed."[10] Many of the officials of that road played a prominent part in the war. Lincoln had only served as an attorney for the road but he was quite familiar with the needs of the road and with the hopes of its promoters. George B. McClellan was vice president and general superintendent of the road from 1857 to 1860 and traveled between Chicago and New Orleans to increase the business of the road.[11]

9. *Little Miami Railroad Company and the Columbus and Xenia Railroad Company, Sixth Joint Annual Report for 1861* (Cincinnati, 1862), 4.
10. *Illinois Central Railroad Company, Report and accounts for year ending Dec. 31, 1861*, p. 1.
11. W. H. Osborn to G. B. McClellan, January 9, 1857; Samuel Barlow to G. B. McClellan, June 21, 1860, and July 25, 1860; H. A. Alsop to G. B. McClellan, July 14, 1860, and September 26, 1860; G. B. McClellan to W. H. Osborn, New Orleans, June 3, 1858, in McClellan Papers, Library of Congress, MSS. Division.

Nathaniel P. Banks was governor of Massachusetts from 1858 to 1860. He believed that the country would soon be plunged into war and he took steps to prepare his state by forming special military organizations and providing for their military instruction. At the close of his term he accepted the vice presidency of the Illinois Central, vacated by McClellan, and held the position until the call for volunteers in 1861 when he received a command.[12] W. H. Osborn, the president of the road during the Civil War period, had in the period of depression just before the war persuaded British stockholders to loan millions to the road.[13] Richard Cobden and other British free traders were intensely interested in the development of the grain growing West of America, were buying land and railroad stock, were contemplating the establishment of Welsh and English colonies in Illinois, and some of them as the guests of Osborn and McClellan traveled all over the Illinois Central system.[14] These British investors were as much concerned over the effect of an independent Confederacy upon the future of the Illinois Central and upon the West as was Osborn himself. Before the war Osborn had not spent much time in the West, as his wife preferred to live in New York, but the outbreak of the war found him down in the Egyptian part of Illinois doing what he could to make his railroad serve the needs of the government and

12. Appleton, *Guide* (Oct., 1860), 47.
13. Samuel Sturgis to G. B. McClellan, New York, January 26, 1858, in McClellan papers.
14. R. Cobden to G. B. McClellan, New York, May 25, 1859; Cobden to McClellan, Paris, July 28, 1860; L. W. Acland to McClellan, August 28, 1860; Acland to McClellan, Oxford, England, Nov. 28, 1860; W. H. Osborn to McClellan, New York, March 6, 1858; E. E. Etus to McClellan, Lancaster, England, June 16, 1859; N. Caird to McClellan, Baldoon, Scotland, October 27, 1860, in McClellan Papers.

Two Extremes against the Middle   219

wining and dining Grant and Rawlins when the latter two were preparing to maneuver the Confederates back from the neighborhood of Cairo.[15]

George B. McClellan had resigned the vice-presidency of the Illinois Central in 1860 to accept a similar position with the Ohio and Mississippi railroad eastern and western divisions. This road extended from St. Louis to Cincinnati and by means of the Cincinnati and Marietta railroad made connections by ferry at Parkersburg with the Baltimore and Ohio railroad. The Confederate activities in Maryland and western Virginia in May, 1861, stopped transportation on the Baltimore and Ohio road, the most direct outlet for the Ohio and Mississippi railroad. McClellan had offered his services to Governor William Dennison of Ohio and had been put in command of the troops of that state. At the latter's suggestion the Federal government placed McClellan in general control of the troops for the Department of the Ohio.[16] The government gave him discretionary authority to move into western Virginia and Maryland when he deemed the time proper for clearing the Confederates from the route of the Baltimore and Ohio.[17] One of the directors of the Ohio and Mississippi promised to keep McClellan's position with the railroad open for him until his return, and the officials of a dozen of the leading railroads of Ohio presented him with a warhorse and with their best wishes. Both the Federals and the Confederates were anxious to

15. J. A. Rawlins to E. B. Washburn, Headquarters, District of Cairo, December 30, 1861, in Washburn Papers, Library of Congress, M S S. Division.
16. E. D. Townsend to McClellan, May 15, 1861, in McClellan Papers.
17. W. Scott to W. Dennison May 20, 1861, and T. F. Carlile to McClellan, May 30, 1861, in McClellan Papers.

get control of the Baltimore and Ohio for military reasons but were anxious to avoid the criticism of being the first to interfere with traffic on the road. Robert E. Lee gave strict orders that the officers of the road were not to be interfered with in the usual operation of the line.[18] McClellan concentrated some of his troops at strategic points on the Ohio side of the river in order to give the unionist element in western Virginia assurance of protection, but he delayed moving his troops across until after the Wheeling convention had decided upon separation from Virginia and until after the first news arrived that the Confederates had burned some of the bridges on the railroad. As McClellan moved his troops into western Virginia, he issued a proclamation on May 26, naming these two events.[19] From this time and for nearly a year following, traffic over this route was frequently interrupted. Commodities of the Ohio valley that had formerly sought this outlet had to be carried out over more northern lines. Roads in southern Ohio that had used the Baltimore and Ohio as an eastern outlet found their business sadly diminished by the deflection of business.[20]

The three war governors of Ohio were all railroad presidents at one time or another and were vitally interested in the commercial life of the Old Northwest. William Dennison was president of the Columbus and Xenia before the war and remained a director of that road while he was

18. R. E. Lee to G. A. Porterfield, Richmond, May 4, 1861, and Lee to Porterfield, May 24, 1861, in McClellan Papers.
19. Proclamation of McClellan to Union Men of West Virginia, May 26, 1861, and McClellan to Col. B. F. Kelley, Cincinnati, May 26, 1861, in McClellan Papers.
20. *Fourteenth Annual Report of the Directors and Third Annual Report of the Receiver of the Central Ohio Company* (Zanesville, 1863), 9; *Fourteenth Annual Report of the President and Directors of the Cleveland and Pittsburgh* (New Haven, 1862), 22, statement opposite.

governor during the first part of the war.[21] This road with an associated road, the Little Miami, made an important northeast and southwest line between Cincinnati and Columbus that would have probably been adversely affected by a permanent withdrawal from the Union by the slaveholding states. Larz Anderson, brother of the Major Anderson who commanded at Sumter and who later was sent by Lincoln to enroll the Kentucky volunteers, was one of the important stockholders and directors of both the Columbus and Xenia and the Little Miami. David Tod, a Douglas delegate to the Charleston convention who succeeded Dennison as governor, was president of the Cleveland and Mahoning railroad. Governor John Brough was president of the Bellefontaine line, a northeast and southwest road between Indianapolis and Cleveland.[22] Brough played a very important part in the railroad development in Ohio and Indiana as well as an important part in the war. Having served as auditor of Ohio and as editor of the *Cincinnati Enquirer* in the forties, he became in 1848 president of Indiana's first real railroad, the Madison and Indianapolis, and remained in that position till 1853. During that time the Indianapolis and Bellefontaine railroad and the Indianapolis and Peru railroad were built and were operated by the Madison and Indianapolis. The Indianapolis and Terre Haute and the Indianapolis and Lafayette completed in 1852, while operated by separate companies, were run in connection with the Madison and Indianapolis.[23] Thus four roads converging

21. *First Joint Annual Report of the Little Miami and the Columbus and Xenia for 1856* (Cincinnati, 1857), 2; *Sixth Joint Annual Report*, 4; *Seventh Joint Annual Report*, 2.
22. Whitelaw Reid, *Ohio in the War* (Cincinnati, 1868), II, 1021, 1023.
23. John Brough, *A Brief History of the Madison and Indianapolis Railroad*, 12.

upon Indianapolis from the west, north, and east in the early fifties were apparently looked upon by Brough as feeders for the Madison and Indianapolis, over which line farm products would be carried southward to the Ohio. In 1853 Brough was also president of the Indianapolis and Bellefontaine railroad. In 1855 the name of the latter road was changed to that of Indianapolis, Pittsburgh, and Cleveland. In 1856 he became president of the Cleveland and Indianapolis route composed of the former Indianapolis, Pittsburgh, and Cleveland and of the Bellefontaine and Indiana.[24] In 1857 the name of this route was changed to the Bellefontaine Line and President Brough moved from Indianapolis to Cleveland.[25] By 1860 the Bellefontaine Line, the Indianapolis and Terre Haute, the Terre Haute, Alton, and St. Louis, and the Indiana Central were operated as one line.[26] Brough's line did not suffer from the immediate consequences of the Civil War. In fact this northeast and southwest route had been steadily falling behind from 1857 to 1860 while during the war its receipts tripled.[27] In 1863 when Lincoln's administration was looking about for a man to defeat C. L. Vallandigham, the Copperhead candidate for governor of Ohio, John Brough, lifelong Democrat, but a staunch supporter of the war, was drafted to make the race. He was elected governor and the directors of his road not only sanctioned his acceptance of his new office but continued him as president of the road throughout the time that he served as governor.[28]

24. Dinsmore, *American Railway Guide* (Nov., 1853), 110, 112; *Ibid.* (April, 1855), 125.
25. Appleton, *Guide* (September, 1857).
26. Appleton, *Guide* (Oct., 1860), 200.
27. *Third Annual Report of the Bellefontaine Railway Company for 1867* (Indianapolis, 1868), 11.
28. *Ninth Joint Annual Report of the Bellefontaine Railroad Line* (Cleveland, 1865), 2.

Two Extremes against the Middle   223

The people of the Old Northwest in contemplating, in 1860, secession and the formation of a northern and a southern confederacy as an accomplished fact could see only three conceivable positions that the Old Northwest might occupy. First, it might break somewhere along the old National road, the part lying in the Ohio valley joining the southern confederacy and the part lying in the valley of the Great Lakes joining a northern confederacy. This breaking-into of three of the states would have involved a double revolt on the part of the Ohio valley—a revolt against the Federal Government and against three state governments. It would automatically have arrayed against the revolutionists the machinery of their state governments, each moving with a certain momentum in the fulfillment of the ends for which it had been instituted, and using in the struggle for self-perpetuation the resources over which it legally had command. In breaking up a state, the revolutionists could not even have pleaded the southern doctrine of secession. With Richard Yates, tutored in his task by Lincoln, and with Oliver P. Morton, who needed no tutoring from any man, in control of the political machinery and of half the population of two of the states, the breaking up of these two states could not have been accomplished without such active aid from the southern confederacy as could neither have been given nor accepted. Then it would have meant that a small non-slaveholding region north of the Ohio would have been rather more closely joined to a large slaveholding region south of the river than either of those two sections would have relished. A considerable proportion of the people north of the Ohio had originally crossed the river from the south because they did not care to live in a state where they had to compete with slave labor. A large number hated the negro whether free or slave. While the southern states, in appointing commissioners to attend the secession conventions of neighboring states and in every case to urge secession, appointed delegates to every slave state, they appointed delegates to no state north of the Ohio river.[29] Apparently the southern leaders felt quite frankly that they had had enough experience in being yoked up with free states. Finally, it would have meant placing the people of the Ohio valley under the political and economic domination of the South and placing the people of the Lake region in a similar position with respect to the Northeast. They would in neither case have had the numerical power or the importance to have held their own; nor could they as formerly have obtained sectional concessions for themselves by threatening to join one side or the other in the contest between Northeast and South. The Ohio valley would have had the outlet at New Orleans and the southern market; but if the southern confederacy had decided not to spend the money to keep the sand bars and snags out of the Mississippi, the people of the Ohio valley could not as formerly have used their possession of the balance of power to secure their desires through a rivers and harbors bill. Neither could they have threatened to use the northeastern route without first negotiating with a foreign power. The dividing of the Northwest was obviously impracticable.

A second conceivable position in 1860 would be for the Old Northwest to remain together and to become thus a part of either the northern or the southern confederacy. To have joined the southern confederacy would have meant for the lake region to have lost control over its northeastern outlet, part of its eastern market, and pos-

---

29. Statement based upon an examination of the different Journals of the Secession Conventions.

sibly access to the English market. The possibilities of getting the agricultural surplus out of the Old Northwest by the transport lines of the valleys of the St. Lawrence and of the Mississippi in case the Northwest separated from the Northeast were given consideration both in England and in America at that time, but the plans seem not to have been promising. For the wheat-growing lake region the breaking away from the Northeast would have meant nothing less than economic ruin. That region had increased in population and production in the fifties until it could not be carried into the southern camp by the Ohio valley against its consent. Then it would have meant the union with the slave-holding confederacy of a people in the lake region, a majority of whom were opposed to the existence of slavery anywhere. Finally it would have meant for the entire Old Northwest the same subjection to the political domination of the South that would have befallen the Ohio valley in case the valley had gone alone. On the other hand, in case the Northwest as a whole had joined the northern confederacy, the Ohio valley would have lost its southern outlet and southern market. Governors, Congressmen, and business men of the Northwest as well as of Kentucky and Tennessee of that day almost unanimously expressed the opinion that they could never give up the southern outlet. Moreover the Northwest would in that case have been just as truly dominated politically and economically by the Northeast as they would have been in the other case by the South. While the people of the Ohio valley would not have had the qualms of conscience in entering an association with the Northeast that their northern neighbors would have had in joining a slaveholding confederacy, it would have been by no means a union of love. Obviously the Old Northwest could not as a whole join either Northeast or South and it did not.

Third, the Old Northwest conceivably might stand aloof from both the northern and southern confederacy and establish a confederacy of its own. It would, however, have been a landlocked country deprived of every access to the sea except at the pleasure of some foreign power. This would have meant economic strangulation or fighting a way out later on. The plan of an independent northwestern confederacy was considered, but was manifestly the worst possible solution. It would have been better to have had even one line of communication with the outside world than none at all, but as Lincoln pointed out, all of the routes would be better than any one.[30]

All these possibilities contemplating secession as an accomplished fact were considered but all led to insurmountable difficulties. The danger to the commercial lines of the Old Northwest was decisive. On November 16, 1860, Governor B. Magoffin of Kentucky wrote to the editor of the *Kentucky Yeoman*: "To South Carolina and such other States who may wish to secede from the Union, I would say the geography of this country will not admit of a division—the mouth and sources of the Mississippi river can not be separated without the horrors of civil war—we cannot sustain you in this movement merely on account of the election of Lincoln."[31] On the same day Senator Doolittle of Wisconsin wrote to the Republicans of Milwaukee: "We have not purchased Florida to pro-

---

30. Nicolay and Hay, *Complete Works of Lincoln*, VIII, 113-15.
31. *Journal of the Called Session of the House of Representatives of the Commonwealth of Kentucky, beginning Jan. 17, 1861* (Frankfort, 1861), 17, Appendix to Governor's message; H. Greeley, *American Conflict* (Hartford, 1865), I, 340.

tect our entrance into the Gulf of Mexico, nor Louisiana to control the outlet of the Mississippi Valley, nor annexed Texas and defended her against Mexico at the expense of forty thousand lives and one hundred million dollars to suffer them now to pass under a foreign and hostile jurisdiction. It cannot be done." On December 5, 1860, this letter was read by Joseph Lane of Oregon in the United States Senate in the midst of the discussion of secession.[32] On November 22, 1860, Oliver P. Morton, then lieutenant governor elect of Indiana but soon to become governor of that state, said in an address at a celebration of the Rail Maulers at Indianapolis: "And especially must we of the inland states cling to the national idea. If South Carolina may secede peaceably, so may New York, Massachusetts, Maryland, and Louisiana, cutting off our commerce and destroying our right of way to the ocean. We should thus be shut up in the interior of a continent, surrounded by independent, perhaps hostile nations, through whose territories we could obtain egress to the seaboard only upon such terms as might be agreed to by treaty. . . . Can it be possible then that Kentucky, Tennessee, Arkansas and Missouri can ever become so infatuated, so demented as to subscribe to the doctrine that a state has the right to secede, thereby placing their commerce, their peculiar institution, their everything within the power of Louisiana, commanding as she does the outlet of the Mississippi and the entrance to the Gulf."[33]

On December 9 Governor Magoffin of Kentucky in a circular letter to the governors of the slaveholding states sent some propositions to be considered as a basis for an

32. *Cong. Globe,* 36 Cong., 2 sess., pt. 1, p. 9.
33. W. D. Foulke, *Life of Oliver P. Morton* (Indianapolis, 1899), I, 90.

adjustment of the sectional troubles. Among the propositions was one "to amend the constitution so as to guarantee forever to all the States the free navigation of the Mississippi River."[34] The day following, in the House of Representatives of the United States, C. L. Vallandigham of Ohio said: "We of the Northwest have a deeper interest in the preservation of this government in its present form than any other section of the Union. Hemmed in, isolated, cut off from the seaboard upon every side; a thousand miles and more from the mouth of the Mississippi, the free navigation of which under the law of nations we demand and will have at every cost; with nothing else but our other great inland seas, the lakes—and their outlet, too through a foreign country—what is to be our destiny? ... We do not mean to be a dependency or province either of the East or of the South, nor yet an inferior or second rate power upon the continent; and if we cannot secure a maritime boundary upon other terms we will cleave our way to the seacoast with the sword."[35]

On the same day and in the same House McClernand of Illinois said: "What, too, would be the fate of the youthful but giant Northwest in the event of a separation of the slaveholding from the non-slaveholding states? Cut off from the main Mississippi and the Gulf of Mexico on one hand, or from the eastern Atlantic ports on the other, she would gradually sink into a pastoral state and to a standard of national inferiority. This the hardy and adventurous millions of the Northwest would be unwilling to consent to. This they would not do. Rather would they, to the last man, perish upon the battlefield. No

---

34. *Journal of the Called Session of the House of Representatives of the Commonwealth of Kentucky, Jan. 17, 1861*, p. 19.

35. *Cong. Globe*, 36 Cong., 2 sess., pt. 1, 38.

power on earth could restrain them from freely and unconditionally communicating with the Gulf and the great mart of New York. Any attempt to prevent them from doing so would be as vain as the attempt to stay the rushing waters of the great father of rivers by a fisherman's net."[36]

On December 19, 1860, Andrew Johnson of Tennessee said in the United States Senate that Louisiana had been bought and defended in order to secure for the West the free navigation of the Mississippi. Slidell of Louisiana answered that there was not a citizen of any of the southwestern states bordering on the Mississippi who did not "acknowledge the propriety and the necessity of extending to every citizen of the country whose streams flow into the Mississippi the free navigation of the river and the free exchange of all the agricultural products of the valley of the Mississippi." Johnson replied: "Hereafter when a conflict of interest arises; when difficulty may spring up between two separate powers, Louisiana having the control of the mouth of the river might feel disposed to tax our citizens going down there. It is a power that I am not willing to concede to be exercised at the discretion of any authority outside of the Government. The Senator's assurance does not amount to anything."[37] On December 25, Stephen A. Douglas of Illinois wrote: "We can never acknowledge the right of a state to secede and cut us off from the ocean and the World without our consent."[38]

Governor William Dennison in his message of January 7, 1861, at the beginning of the second session of the fifty-fourth general assembly of Ohio said: "Shall the artery

---

36. *Cong. Globe,* 36 Cong., 2 sess., pt. 1, p. 39.
37. *Cong. Globe,* 36 Cong., 2 sess., pt. 1, p. 137.
38. A. Johnson, *Stephen A. Douglas* (New York, 1908), 447.

that gives life to the great valley of the West be at the mercy of hostile communities and subject to be severed from the Gulf Stream through which the interior states reach and embrace their seaboard sisters? If there were nothing else in the interposition of a foreign power upon the grand trunk of the mighty flood whose branches bear the fruit—the riches of the continent—it is enough to array the country against it, that it would break the symmetry, nature has given it for the full development of the vast republic now reaching from ocean to ocean. The right of secession is the right to tear a limb from the body and in the supposed case of secession of states on the lower Mississippi, if the right of domain over all its sources would not attach to the seceding states, it would at least seriously conflict with the free enjoyment of opposing rights and eventually lead to dissention, if not war between the states directly interested in the navigation of that great highway of the world's commerce."[39]

Governor Richard Yates in his inaugural address of January 14, 1861, said: "Can it be for a moment supposed that the people of the valley of the Mississippi will ever consent that the great river shall flow hundreds of miles through a foreign jurisdiction and they be compelled, if not to fight their way in the face of the forts frowning upon its banks to submit to the imposition and annoyance of arbitrary taxes and exhorbitant duties to be levied upon their commerce."[40] Governor Oliver P. Morton in his message of April 24 to the General Assembly of Indiana

---

39. *Ohio Executive Documents for the year 1860* (Columbus, 1861), pt. 1, pp. 561, 562.

40. *Reports to the General Assembly of Illinois*, 22nd session (Springfield, 1861), vol. 1, p. 27; *Journal of House of Representatives* of 22nd General Assembly of Illinois, Regular Sess. (Springfield, 1861), p. 98.

Two Extremes against the Middle 231

expressed again the opinion that he had proclaimed in the public address of the preceding November.[41]

It will be observed that all these statements except the last four were made during the time that South Carolina was considering secession and before the secession conventions of any of the states of the lower Mississippi had convened. The southwestern states had early warning of the attitude of the Northwest. If Louisiana and Mississippi could have refrained from interfering with the trade of the Old Northwest on the lower Mississippi until after the Federal government would have been compelled to stop that trade, the hostility of the Northwest might in part have been directed against the Federal administration. George B. McClellan, writing from Cincinnati late in December, stated that if the South would give the Northwest time, the latter would help them; but if they went off half-cocked, the Northwest would meet them unitedly.[42] But the efficiency of Governor Pettus of Mississippi in military preparations led him to make a serious political blunder. A rumor had been spread in Pittsburgh in December that the Federal government intended to send some cannon from the arsenal there to the South.[43] This rumor spread southward and Pettus became nervous. On January 12 he had an officer of the state militia plant a battery at Vicksburg with orders to stop down-going vessels and search them for government cannon and troops. Several vessels were stopped and one, the *A. O. Tyler* of Cincinnati, was fired upon, January 15.[44] The report of

41. *Indiana Documentary Journal* for 1860-61 (Indianapolis, 1861), 579.
42. G. B. McClellan to L. L. M., Cincinnati, Dec. 27, 1860, in McClellan Papers.
43. Frank Moore, *Rebellion Record* (New York, 1861-63), I, 16.
44. Moore, *Rebellion Record*, I, 15.

this incident, somewhat exaggerated, was quickly spread by telegraph and caused great excitement and anger in Cincinnati. The *Cincinnati Gazette* reported that a mob had planted the cannon at Vicksburg with the avowed purpose of sinking every steamboat that should offer to pass without submitting to search. A citizen of Cincinnati wrote the editor of the *New Orleans Picayune* that the report that the state of Mississippi intended to exercise a military surveillance over the navigation of the Mississippi river had powerfully aroused the Northwestern states. Another wrote the same editor: "Hitherto the great Northwestern states have maintained a calm attitude, a contemptuous tranquility, because they are so conscious of their overwhelming power, but now, when an interruption, or an insult or the slightest obstruction is offered to their commerce, they feel like rising as one man and crushing at once and forever any obstacle which may be in its way." This letter was apparently written by a friend to the South for he asked whether something could not be done to allay the mad excitement of the Mississippians. The editor of the *Picayune* explained and explained again.[45] The governor of Mississippi withdrew the artillery company on the same day that it had fired upon the *A. O. Tyler* and in his message on the same day to the special session of the legislature he explained his act and recommended that "the most prompt and efficient measures be adopted to make known to the people of the Northwestern states, that peaceful commerce on the Mississippi river will be neither interrupted nor annoyed by the authorities or the people of Mississippi. This in my opinion will materially aid in preserving peace between the Northwestern and Southern states, if it can be preserved."

45. *Extracts from the Editorial Columns of the New Orleans Picayune* (New York, 1861), 20, 21.

But the damage had already been done. Every assurance and guarantee of the free navigation of the river after this only served to attract attention to the fact that the people of the southwestern states assumed that they would have it within their power to guarantee that right or refuse to do so. The Mississippi secession convention adopted a resolution that "the people of the state of Mississippi recognize the right of the free navigation of the Mississippi river for commercial purposes in time of peace, by all states occupying its banks and they are willing to enter into proper stipulations to secure the enjoyment of that right."[46] On January 25 the convention instructed the governor to forward promptly to the executives of the northwestern states copies of this resolution.[47] This was intended to be reassuring but the people of the Northwest could not help but observe that they were to enjoy this right only in time of peace and then on condition of entering into stipulations. The secession convention of Louisiana passed a single resolution besides the ordinance of secession and this had to do with the navigation of the Mississippi. The resolution passed on January 26 ran as follows: "We the people of Louisiana recognize the right of the free navigation of the Mississippi river and its tributaries by all friendly states bordering thereon, we also recognize the right of ingress and egress of the mouths of the Mississippi by all friendly powers and hereby declare our willingness to enter into stipulations to guarantee the exercise of those rights."[48] The assurance was as generous as an independent, sovereign state could be ex-

46. *Journal of the Convention and Ordinances and Resolutions adopted in January, 1861* (Jackson, 1861), 24.
47. *Journal of the Convention [Mississippi]*, 68.
48. *Official Journal of the Proceedings of the Convention of the State of Louisiana* (New Orleans, 1861), 10, 18; F. Moore, *Rebellion Record*, I, 26, document no. 27.

pected to make in behalf of a foreign power, but its unsatisfactory characteristics, so far as the Northwest was concerned, were obvious. A resolution assuring "the people of those states lying upon the Mississippi river and its tributaries that it was not the purpose of Louisiana in any event to obstruct or embarass the free navigation of that stream" was introduced but voted down because it promised more than Louisiana could live up to in case of armed conflict.[49]

The state of Alabama did not border upon the Mississippi but her secession convention was the occasion of some enlightening comments and resolutions upon the question of the navigation of that river and of rivers that touched that state. The Tennessee river flowed through that state and emptied into the Ohio. On January 23 a resolution was introduced stating that it was the opinion of the convention that the navigation of the Mississippi should be free to the people of the states and territories lying upon it and its tributaries and that no obstructions to the enjoyment of that privilege should be offered except for protection against a belligerent and unfriendly people. This was, however, going too far, in the opinion of W. L. Yancey. He stated that he was in sympathy with the purpose of the resolution which was to meet a state of public opinion in the Northwest based upon misrepresentation of southern views. Yet he pointed out that restrictions would have to be imposed both to cause the northwestern states to bear their share of the upkeep of lights and buoys and to safeguard the peculiar domestic institution of the South. When a resolution was introduced proposing that rivers formerly under the control of the Federal govern-

---

49. *Official Journal of the Proceedings of the Convention of the State of Louisiana*, 10-12.

ment should remain open to the commerce of the states of the United States, Yancey pointed out that under the new confederacy each state would control the rivers and the commerce within its boundaries. As a result the final resolution passed on January 25 indicated that the subject properly belonged to the sovereign state of Louisiana but that it was the sense of the Alabama convention that the navigation of the Mississippi should remain free and no further restrictions should be imposed except tonnage duties to keep open and safe the navigation of the mouth of the river and for purposes of protection against a belligerent and unfriendly people.[50] The navigable waters of the state were declared free highways for the citizens of Alabama and of such states as might join in forming a southern slaveholding confederacy.[51]

The Congress of the Confederate States soon after its meeting began the consideration of the navigation of the Mississippi and continued its discussion of that question both in open and in secret session until February 22, when it passed an act declaring the peaceful navigation of the Mississippi free to the citizens of any states upon its borders, or its navigable tributaries.[52] This freedom was limited, however, by the proviso that such navigation would be under the police regulations of the several states through which the river passed, that masters would be subject to light money, pilotage, and like charges, and that if the master entered without paying duty on manufac-

---

50. *Ordinances Adopted by the People of the State of Alabama in Convention at Montgomery commencing January 7, 1861* (Montgomery, 1861), 30; W. R. Smith, *The History and Debates of the Convention* (Montgomery and Atlanta, 1861), 188.
51. *Ordinances adopted by the People of the State of Alabama*, 6.
52. *Journal of the Congress of the Confederate States of America*, in *U. S. Sen. Docs.*, 58 Cong., 2 sess., vol. I, no. 234, pp. 9, 60, 67, 68, 75, 76.

tured goods he would have to give bond not to sell the goods within the confederacy.[53] On April 29, 1861, Jefferson Davis in a message to the Confederate Congress notified it that in the treasury department regulations had been devised to put into effect the legislation on the subject of the navigation of the Mississippi and that delay and inconvenience had been avoided as far as possible.[54]

It will be observed that all of these acts and statements except the last one referred to had occurred before the Federal Government had done a single thing to stop the trade of the Old Northwest with the South. After Lincoln's inauguration this delay was deliberate. All the evidence that came to the Old Northwest that its trade with the South and by the southern outlet was in danger was the report of the debates and proceedings in the South. It gave the Northwest time to see that it was the seceding states and not the Federal Government that would thwart them in case of conflict or separation. The Northwest began to realize that it had an interest in a piece of property in the South, the Mississippi river, that was more important than Fort Sumter; and the Confederates were assuming possession in spite of all the assurances that they would allow the people of the Northwest to use it under certain conditions.

On April 25 Governor Yates of Illinois sent General R. K. Swift with some troops from the northern part of that state to occupy Cairo at the confluence of the Ohio

---

53. *Acts and Resolutions of the First Session of the Provisional Congress of the Confederate States held at Montgomery* (Richmond, 1861), 58; *the Statutes at Large of the Provisional Government of the Confederate States of America from February 8, 1861, to February 18, 1862* (Richmond, 1864), 36-38; Moore, *Rebellion Record*, 1, 17.

54. J. D. Richardson, *A Compilation of the Messages and Papers of the Confederacy* (Nashville, 1905), I, 77; Moore, *Rebellion Record*, I, 173.

Two Extremes against the Middle 237

and Mississippi. This action was taken by order of the war department but that fact was by no means heralded about.[55] Yates admitted this fact to the Illinois legislature but to most observers it had the appearance of being an act of the governor of a state.[56] When a state senator of Kentucky protested to Lincoln against the seizure of Cairo, the president had John Hay write the senator that Lincoln said he would not have ordered the movement of troops had he known that Cairo was in the Kentucky senator's district.[57] From this kind of an answer an outsider could scarcely guess whether Lincoln was seriously assuming responsibility or not. On April 26 the steamboat *C. E. Hillman,* laden with munitions and bound from St. Louis to Nashville, was seized at Cairo by Illinois troops. On the other hand other boats bound from St. Louis to ports on the lower Mississippi were searched; and when no munitions were found, were allowed to proceed.[58] When Governor I. G. Harris of Tennessee desired to know whether the *C. E. Hillman* had been seized by government authority, he was sent an unsigned letter from the president stating: "The government has no official information of such seizure, but assuming that the seizure was made and that the cargo consisted chiefly of munitions owned by Tennessee and passing into control of its governor, this government avows the seizure, because the governor of Tennessee disrespectfully refused to furnish troops to quell rebellion."[59] This reply left people still wondering

55. Moore, *Rebellion Record,* I, 44.
56. *Journal of the House of Representatives of the Twenty-Second General Assembly of the State of Illinois at the Second Session begun April 23* (Springfield, 1861), 15.
57. Nicolay and Hay, *Complete Works of Lincoln,* VI, 266.
58. Moore, *Rebellion Record,* I, 47, 49.
59. Nicolay and Hay, *Complete Works,* VI, 258.

whether the president had ordered such seizures or whether he was just assuming responsibility after the event. There seems to have been an occasional complaint that the Illinois troops were interfering with the river borne trade at Cairo, but these complaints were not many.[60] The fact of the matter seems to have been that at the worst the troops were only annoying and not stopping trade. In a conference of Colonel Prentiss, then in charge at Cairo, with Colonel Tilghman in charge of the western division of the Kentucky militia, as late as May 6, the former stated that he was instructed to seize no property unless he had information that such property consisted of munitions of war destined to the enemies of the United States Government. He stated further that in general munitions of war would not even be detained if destined for the authorities of Kentucky.[61] It was no doubt considered far better for the Union cause to allow such few steamboats laden with provisions as were dispatched in spite of public opinion in the North to proceed unmolested so that they might be seized by the Confederates and thus throw the blame upon the southerners. Pillow was seizing steamboats from the North right and left at Memphis during the first part of May.[62]

In the meantime public opinion had effectively checked the shipments southward from several forwarding points in the Old Northwest. As soon as the news of Fort Sumter reached Cincinnati, some of the merchants of that place refused to continue to ship to the South.[63] There were

60. *Illinois State Journal*, May 1, May 22, 1861.
61. Moore, *Rebellion Record*, I, 194, document no. 139.
62. Thomas Sherlock to G. B. McClellan, May 3, 1861, in McClellan Papers.
63. *Cincinnati Daily Commercial*, April 15, 1861.

some merchants whose desire for profit from the southern trade was stronger than their patriotism, but those opposed to shipments were too numerous and too well organized for them and they were forced to stop shipments.[64]

The question speedily arose whether shipments to Kentucky should not be made an exception to the general ban inasmuch as Kentucky professed to be neutral. A delegation of merchants of Louisville visited Cincinnati on April 23 for the purpose of resuming commercial relations between the two cities. The mayor read to the visitors the letter of Governor Dennison of April 23 stating that he could not forbid trade even in arms with a state that had not withdrawn from the Union.[65] The merchants of Louisville returned home satisfied that trade with Cincinnati would be resumed. There was, however, bitter criticism by Northern radicals of the so-called weakness of the mayor and of the governor. Soon after this the citizens of Cincinnati called another meeting and resolved that it was treasonable to trade with a state that did not openly declare for the Union.[66] At Evansville trade had slowed down and with it industry had come to be practically at a standstill by the middle of May.[67]

The second gentle step taken by the Federal Government in stopping trade with the South took the form of an order from the Secretary of the Treasury on May 2 to the

64. *Annual Statement of the Commerce of Cincinnati for the year ending August 31, 1861*, pp. 6, 38.

65. *Messages and Reports to the General Assembly and Governor of the State of Ohio for the year 1861* (Columbus, 1862), pt. 1, p. 412; Reid, *Ohio in the War*, I, 39.

66. Reid, *Ohio in the War*, I, 40; *History of Ohio Falls Cities and their Counties* (Cleveland, 1852), I, 96.

67. John Ingle, President of Evansville and Crawfordsville Railroad, to G. B. McClellan, May 17, 1861, in McClellan Papers.

customs officers to search steamboats and railroads for munitions and provisions with hostile destination.[68] This order seems, however, to have been enforced with discretion. A week after its issue Prentiss at Cairo had no orders to prevent provisions from going to the Confederate states nor even to stop munitions from going to Kentucky. Two steamboats continued to make their regular trips up and down the Kanawha carrying all kinds of freight into the interior of western Virginia during the entire period intervening between the dates of Virginia's secession and of the Wheeling convention, at which time the western part of the state decided to remain with the Union.[69] Inasmuch as Kentucky was still professing neutrality, under the order of the Secretary of the Treasury provisions and munitions could not be prevented from going to Kentucky unless it could be proven that the goods were destined to pass through Kentucky for a more southern state. The Kentucky House of Representatives considered a resolution of protest against the so-called blockade of Louisville but decided to ridicule the whole performance by adding to the resolution an amendment that earnestly protested against a blockade of the Kentucky river by A. Lincoln whereby the free ingress of fish into that river might be interfered with.[70] Provisions continued to cross the Ohio river from Indiana to Louisville and from that place were carried southward by the Louisville and Nashville at the rate of two trains of twenty-five or thirty cars per day.[71]

68. Hunt, *Merchants' Magazine*, XLIV, 786.
69. Simeon Nash to G. B. McClellan, May 15, 1861, Gallipolis, in McClellan Papers.
70. *Journal of the Called Session of the House of Representatives of the Commonwealth of Kentucky begun May 6, 1861* (Frankfort, 1861), 101.
71. Statement of "Jas. A. Gillespie" [detective], May 9, 1861, in McClellan Papers.

This process had about exhausted the stock at Louisville by the end of the first week in June and would have done so entirely but for the supplies brought across from Indiana. James Guthrie, president of the Louisville and Nashville, argued that an embargo upon the railroad would embarrass the Union voters in the coming Kentucky elections.[72] The Congressional election was to occur on June 20 and the election for members of the state legislature on August 4. McClellan also urged that Kentucky be handled delicately until these events had safely passed.[73] On June 24 after the first of these elections the surveyor of the port of Louisville under new instructions from the Federal government took another little step forward by prohibiting shipments over the Louisville and Nashville railroad except upon permits issued from his office. This regulation was contested in the Jefferson Circuit Court, but Judge Muir on July 10 sustained the Federal Government.[74] On the same day Lincoln in a memorandum to General S. B. Buckner stated: "So far I have not sent an armed force into Kentucky nor have I any present purpose to do so." The election for members of the state legislature of Kentucky occurred on August 4 and was a victory for the Union cause. On August 16 President Lincoln issued his formal proclamation forbidding commerce with the states in insurrection.[75] This proclamation came after trade had practically ceased; Lincoln had played a shrewd political game. He had not only helped to keep Kentucky from seceding but he had made the people of the southern part of the Old Northwest feel all

72. Thomas M. Key [Governor Dennison's agent to Governor Magoffin] to G. B. McClellan, June 7, in McClellan Papers.
73. G. B. McClellan to Winfield Scott, June 5, in McClellan Papers.
74. *History of the Ohio Falls Cities and their Counties*, I, 324.
75. Nicolay and Hay, *Complete Works*, VI, 346.

the disadvantages of losing their trade with and through the South without having incurred for his administration much of the odium for having caused that cessation. Most of the indignation because of the course of events was directed against the Confederate states. Now on August 24 Lincoln in writing to Governor Magoffin of Kentucky could admit: "I believe there is a military force in camp in Kentucky acting by authority of the United States. I believe arms have been furnished by the United States. I believe the force consists exclusively of Kentuckians."[76] The way in which Lincoln jockeyed the Confederates into an unfavorable position with respect to the stopping of trade with the Northwest was quite similar to the manner in which the Union government by concentrating its military forces in Missouri across the river from Columbus, Kentucky, frightened Leonidas Polk into hurrying Pillow into seizing Hickman, Kentucky, thus casting upon the Confederates the reproach of having first violated Kentucky neutrality and giving Grant the pretext for seizing Paducah on September 5.[77] The Confederate government was still bidding for the Northwest as well as trying to provide herself with foodstuffs when on August 31, 1861, her Congress put into effect an act exempting from duty bacon, pork, hams, wheat, flour, Indian corn, and practically all the agricultural products of the Northwest.[78] It was then too late. By that time most of the families in the Northwest were represented by their young men in the

---

76. Nicolay and Hay, *Complete Works*, VI, 349.

77. L. Polk to Magoffin, Sept. 1, 1861, in *Orders of the Rebellion*, series I, vol. IV, p. 179; M. J. Thompson to Pillow, Sept. 3, in *Ibid.*, p. 155; Harris [scout]to Polk, Sept. 3, in *Ibid.*, p. 180; Governor I. G. Harris to Polk, Sept. 4, in *Ibid.*, p. 180; Polk to I. G. Harris, Sept. 4, in *Ibid.*, 180; Polk to J. Davis, Sept. 4, in *Ibid.*, p. 181.

78. *Tariff of the Confederate States of America* (Charleston, 1861), 14.

Union armies. The manufacturers at Evansville, Cincinnati, and other cities who had been facing bankruptcy were given government contracts and workmen who had for a time been without bread were glad to go back to work.[79] As the Union line advanced south across Kentucky and Tennessee, the farmers of the Ohio valley enjoyed the best market for their products that they had ever known. For a time in the latter part of 1862 and the first part of 1863 when the military failures convinced some that the South could not be defeated and that the separation of the South must eventually be recognized as permanent, the old division in the Northwest between those who wanted to go with the South and those who wished to go with the Northeast naturally reappeared. Along with this reappeared the movement for a united Northwest apart from either the South or the Northeast. Many people in the Ohio valley then frankly announced that if the separation of the South must be permanent they preferred to go with the Confederacy.[80] There is no doubt, however, that Lincoln in his annual message of 1862 tried to formulate for the people of the Northwest the only tenable attitude. He said: "The great interior has three outlets; one to Europe by way of New York; to South America and Africa by New Orleans; and one to Asia by San Francisco. Anywhere the line is drawn every man of the interior is cut off from some one or more of these outlets. These outlets east, west, and south are indispensable to the well-being of the people inhabiting and to inhabit the vast region.

79. *Annual Statement of the Commerce of Cincinnati for the year ending August 31, 1861*, p. 5; *Annual Report of Commerce of Cincinnati for Year ending August 31, 1862*, p. 5; *Annual Report of the Board of Trade of Evansville, Indiana, for 1867*, pp. 23, 25.
80. Foulke, *Oliver P. Morton*, I, 175, 209-13.

Which of the three may be the best is no proper question. All are better than either; and all of right belong to that people and to their successors forever. True to themselves, they will vow rather that there shall be no such line."[81] The reopening of the Mississippi in the middle of 1863 was hailed by the merchants of Cincinnati as the greatest event of the war so far as the West was concerned. So far as the people of the Northwest were concerned, it was indeed the greatest single objective and when once attained stiffened their determination to hold out and to keep it.

The fact is today apparent as it was to the majority in 1861 that no part of the country was more desperately in need of the preservation of the Union than was the Old Northwest. Putting aside the disintegrating effect of once admitting the right of secession, both the Northeast and the South could have endured as separate entities. But for the Old Northwest, land-locked, economically and culturally divided, drawn to North and to South, existence would have been intolerable. Manifestly it was to the interest of the Old Northwest to maintain the Union and the Constitution unimpaired. It could gain nothing by helping either North or South win the ascendancy in the Federal government. To preserve the balance of power and to preserve it by using that very advantage which they wished to keep was the true interest of the people of the Northwest. To formulate principles of settlement upon which they could agree, get the Federal government to voice those principles as its own, and then support the Federal government in the settlement was the only rational policy. In formulating these principles, the bulk of the people of the Ohio valley could conscientiously have yielded more to the South in the matter of slavery exten-

81. Nicolay and Hay, *Complete Works,* VIII, 113-15.

sion than could either the people of the lake region or the Republican head of the Federal government. This willingness to yield was not an evidence of disunion sentiment, but on the contrary an evidence, in part, of the extreme to which they were willing in their agony to go to save the Union. In part, it was only the outgrowth of their conception of democracy.

While it is now fairly clear that much of the course and outcome of the Civil War turned upon the decision and activities of the Northwest, it is of no particular credit or discredit to the people of that region that they pursued the line of action that they did. They simply could not do otherwise. There was no other way out and most of them had come to realize that fact before the middle of '61. To Buchanan and to Lincoln belong the credit of having delayed for a sufficient length of time, on the one hand, unfortunately to convince many in the South and in the Northeast that the erring sisters would be allowed to depart in peace, and on the other hand fortunately to enable the people of the Old Northwest to mentally explore every avenue of escape only to discover that each was a blind alley and that there was no salvation for them save in union. To Lincoln belongs the credit for having so managed the closing of the Mississippi and of the southern trade frontier that, without having brought upon himself and the administration any of the onus for having caused economic distress in the Ohio valley, he yet brought the people of the valley to a full realization of the certainty and extent of the danger to their commerce in case a foreign power controlled the mouth of the Mississippi. To Lincoln belongs the credit for having shoved into the background every question between the North and the South except that of preserving the Union and for having so managed the Sumter affair that it appeared to the people of the Northwest that the Southerners were the aggressors bent upon destroying the Union. Among others the people of eastern Virginia had for years talked states' rights and the community of southern interests until belief in those things filled their subconsciousness more fully than they perhaps knew. The people of the Northwest had for years realized the importance to themselves of belonging to a great union with a dominion stretching in all directions to the open sea and with a Federal Government strong enough to improve rivers and to help build railroads and to open up the West. In their thinking the Nation, the Union, and the Federal Government loomed large. When Sumter was fired upon, the psychological complex of the people of eastern Virginia was such that, in spite of the sincere desire of many to help save the Union, to many of them it appeared that the Southerners had defended their government or were doing what was best for the interest of the South. The psychological complex of the people of the Northwest was such that, in spite of a sincere desire of many to make concessions, to them it appeared that the Southerners had attacked their government and were breaking up the Union, without which the Old Northwest would be doomed.

Many times since the Civil War the problem of getting to market the agricultural products of the Old Northwest and the regions more remote reasserted itself. There have been frequent revivals of the movements to improve the Mississippi and its tributaries, the great natural outlet to the south. The movement to improve the Great Lakes-Ocean waterway has likewise been perennial. The most determined and at times radical efforts have been made in the Northwest to compel the railroads to serve better the needs of the farmer in the interior. Only the existence of a great Federal Government with authority to assume control of this situation could have brought a peaceful solution. Farmers' alliances, granger movements, agricultural blocks, and grain marketing associations have been in part at least so many manifestations of the desire of the farmers of the interior to get the most of what they needed for what they produced. Had the Civil War resulted in the breaking up of the country, the fundamental conditions for these movements would still have existed. But the movements would of necessity have taken on an international aspect. It would then have been a matter of securing by treaties and wars from a southern confederacy and possibly from a northeastern confederacy the right of access to the sea. The history of central and of east central Europe might have repeated itself on this continent. But the Old Northwest, conscious of such a danger, decided to fight for the integrity of the country and of the government. Very few today would deny that that decision determined the outcome.

248

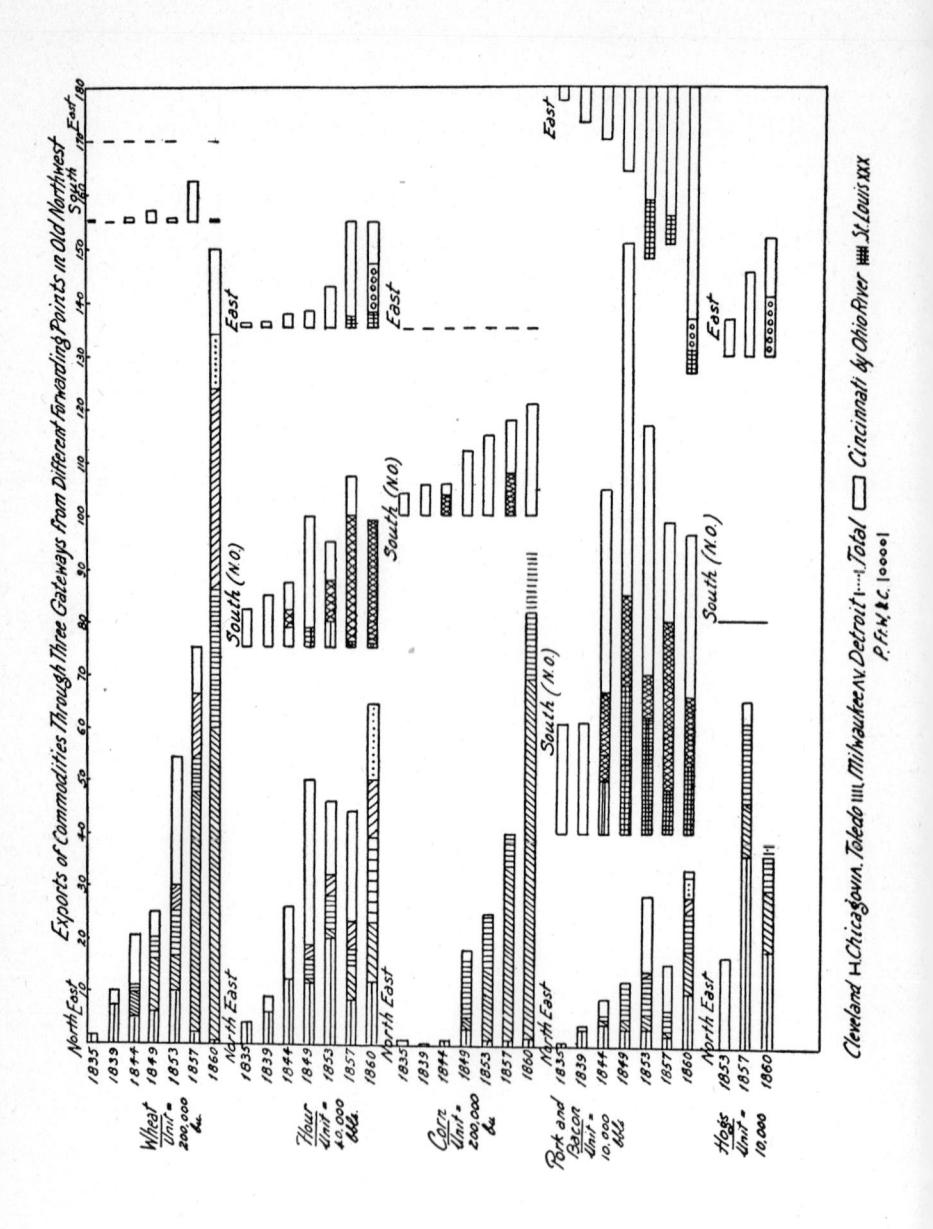

249

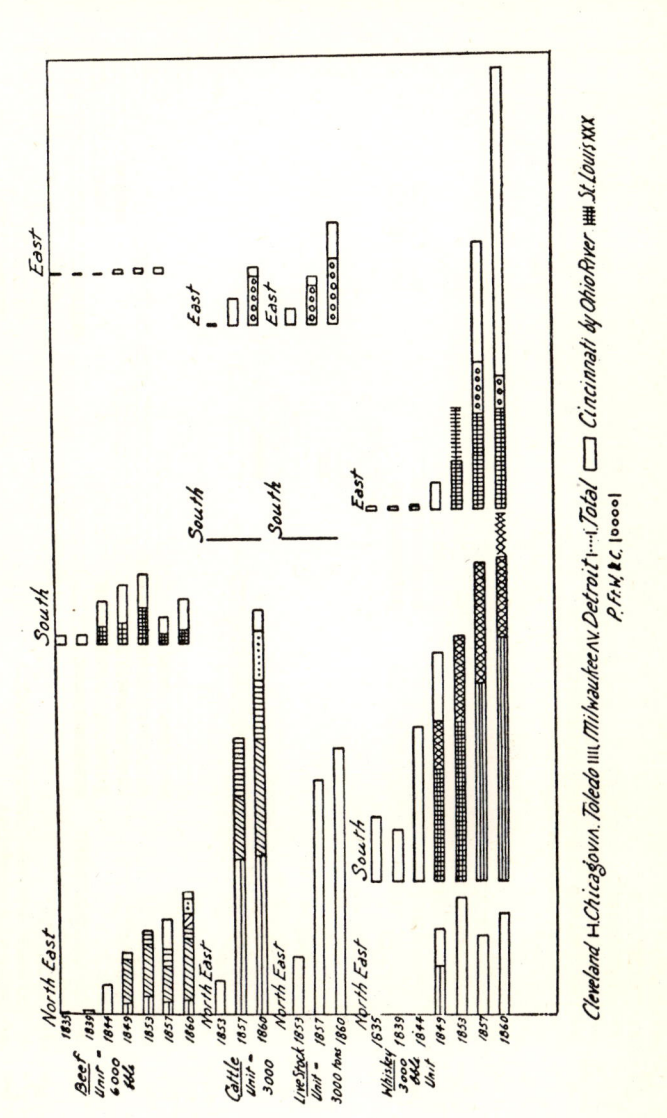

INDEX

Aberdeen, Lord, 61, 63, 66-68, 70, 71
Adams, John Quincy, 10, 11, 12, 74
Albany, N. Y., 6, 7, 15, 40, 41, 142
Allegheny, Pa., 120, 200
Allegheny Portage R. R., 14, 17, 18, 108, 140
Alton, Ill., 110, 145
Alton and Terre Haute R. R., 145
Anderson, Larz, 221
Anderson, Major R., 221
Atlanta and West Point R. R., 170
Attica, Ind., 154
Attica and Buffalo R. R., 41
Auburn and Rochester R. R., 41

Balance of power, 1, 133, 244
Baltimore and Ohio railroad, 26, 108, 112, 114, 116, 120, 125-6, 140, 144, 149, 158-61, 164, 173, 178, 179-84, 187, 198-99, 201, 206-07, 213, 220
Banks, N. P., 218
Barlow, S. M. L., 186
Beaver, Pa., 80
Bellaire, O., 144, 158, 179, 180, 201
Bellefontaine and Indiana R. R., 145, 174, 222
Bellefontaine Line (R. R.), 174, 184, 197, 200, 203, 206, 221, 222
Benton, Thomas H., 36, 43, 61, 70, 72, 73, 74, 131-32, 139
Benwood, Va., 179
Berrien, J. M., 24
Blanding, Abraham, 22, 26, 29, 30
Bloomington, Ill., 122
Bright, John, 65
British investments in N. W., 218
British law of 1831, 34, 45
British West Indies, 8, 9, 12, 45, 47
Brookville, Ind., 32
Brough, John, 47, 173-74, 183, 221-22
Buchanan, James, 59-63, 65, 245
Buckner, S. B., 241
Buffalo, N. Y., 6, 8, 15, 16, 18, 40-41, 46, 89, 112-13, 124, 141-42, 145-46, 162, 168, 192, 205, 206
Buffalo and Batavia R. R., 41

Buffalo and Lake Huron R. R., 168
Buffalo, Niagara Falls and Lewiston R. R., 112, 143
Buffalo and New York City R. R., 107, 112
Buffalo and Rochester R. R., 112
Buffalo and State Line R. R., 109
Burlington, Ia., 145, 172

Cairo, Ill., 143, 145, 146, 167, 169, 202, 203, 214, 219, 236-38, 240
Calhoun, John C., 11, 22, 29, 30, 43, 49, 50, 74, 77, 78
Canada, 8, 9, 12, 13, 33, 34, 45, 46, 48, 69, 79, 80, 125, 168
Canada, trade with, 9, 13, 45-47
Canadian Canals, 169, 193
Canadian Railroads, 142-43, 168, 183
Canadian Northern R. R., 142-43
Carrol, O., 89
Carver, Hartwell, 131
Central America, 137
Central (Georgia) R. R., 109, 170
Central Ohio R. R., 144, 149, 158, 160, 161, 176, 178-81, 191, 198-99, 201, 207
Charleston and Augusta R. R., 25, 29
Charleston and Ohio river railroad movement, 22-29
Charleston convention of 1854, 136; of 1860, 221
Chase, S. P., 134
Chesapeake and Ohio canal, 11
Chicago, 31, 54, 58, 81, 87, 118, 127, 132, 135, 142-46, 151-54, 161-63, 167-79, 174, 178, 183-86, 193-95, 198, 200, 215, 217
Chicago, Alton and St. Louis R. R., 110, 145, 152-53, 194
Chicago, Burlington and Quincy R. R., 110, 145, 152, 194
Chicago and Milwaukee R. R., 195
Chicago and Northwestern R. R., 194-95
Chicago and Rock Island R. R., 194-5

Chillicothe, O., 15-16, 18, 35, 55, 157
Cincinnati, Hamilton and Dayton R. R., 110, 171, 189, 190-91, 203
Cincinnati, Plymouth and LaPorte R. R., 144
Cincinnati, Wilmington and Zanesville R. R., 144, 158, 180, 198, 203
Circleville, O., 88, 157, 158
Civil War, 3, 6, 30, 76, 90
Clay, Henry, 10, 11, 22, 42-44, 102
Cleveland, 14-16, 18, 54, 87-88, 118, 143, 145, 151-52, 155-58, 162, 174, 180, 183, 186, 189, 190-91, 193-94, 196-98, 201, 203, 206, 221-22
Cleveland, Columbus and Cincinnati R. R., 110, 119, 145, 156, 158, 180, 189-91, 197
Cleveland and Erie R. R., 109, 156, 197
Cleveland and Indianapolis R. R., 222
Cleveland and Mahoning R. R., 156, 221
Cleveland and Pittsburgh R. R., 110, 144, 150, 156, 178, 197, 200, 201, 207
Cleveland and Toledo R. R., 156, 196-97
Clinton, DeWitt, 10
Cobden, R., 218
Collingwood, Can., 142-43, 168
Columbia, Pa., 14, 140
Columbus, O., 89, 122, 157-58, 163, 173, 176, 178-80, 183, 186, 190-91, 197-98, 201, 203-04, 221
Columbus, Ky., 167, 169
Columbus and Xenia R. R., 110, 144, 173, 176, 180, 189, 190, 197, 198, 203, 220-21
Compromise of 1850, 99-102, 138
Confederates, 218, 219, 220, 223
Confederate Congress, on Mississippi R., 235
Cotton import in N. W., 208
Covington, Ky., 82, 202
Covington and Lexington R. R., 170
Crestline, Ohio, 179, 197, 200
Cuba, 136
Cumberland road, 9, 213

Davis, Jefferson, surveys, 134, 136
Dayton, Ohio, 14, 32, 40, 56, 80, 88, 155
Dayton and Michigan R. R., 170
Dayton, Xenia and Belpre R. R., 190
Delaware, Ohio, 190
Democrats, 43, 58, 70, 71, 73, 98
Democratic platform of 1844, 60
Dennison, William, 183, 219-21, 229, 239
Detroit, 54, 81, 142-43, 146, 151, 155, 162, 169, 193-95
Detroit and Milwaukee R. R., 81, 172, 195
distribution of proceeds, 42
Doolittle, Sen., 226
Douglas, S. A., 102-04, 133, 138-39, 229
Dover, O., 126, 157
Dubuque, Ia., 104
Dunkirk, N. Y., 107, 109, 113, 124, 146, 193, 205, 206
Dunleith, 145
Dunn, George H., 23

East Tennessee and Georgia R. R., 170
East Tennessee and Virginia R. R., 170
Eaton and Hamilton R. R., 110
"Egypt," 203, 218
England, 4, 12-13, 45-48, 50, 59-70, 72, 74-76, 79, 214-16, 225
English corn laws, 46, 68, 71, 72, 79-80
Erie and Kalamazoo R. R., 109
Erie and Northeast R. R., 109
Erie canal, 7-10, 15-16, 18, 20-21, 31, 34, 37, 39, 41, 46, 51, 54, 82, 94, 112, 124, 141-43, 159, 163, 171, 188, 205
Evansville, Ind., 111, 143, 148, 149, 201, 202, 208, 214, 239, 243
Evansville, Indianapolis and Cleveland Straight Line R. R., 18
Exports,—1825, 4, 7
    1835, 20
    1839, 32-34
    1844, 51-53
    1849, 82-83
    1853, 115-16
    1857, 146-47
    1860, 191
    Chicago, 1833-39, 31
    Michigan, 1835, 31
    Wisconsin, 1841, 51

Index

Falls Cities, 29-148
Far East, 59
Federal aid to railroads, 105
Forbes road, 5
Ft. Erie, 168
freight rates, 140-41, 163-65, 167, 182, 185-89
French Broad river valley, 22, 25
French and Spanish West Indies, 12
Ft. Wayne, Ind., 154, 161, 196
Ft. Wayne and Chicago R. R., 144, 174
Fulton, Ill., 145

Gadsden, James, 22, 136
Galena, Ill., 145
Galena and Chicago Union R. R., 81, 110, 120, 145, 152, 172, 194
Gallatin, Albert, 5
Galveston, Tex., 135
gateways, natural, 2, 6, 211, 226, 243
    inherent difficulties of, 18
    exports by 1839, 33
        1844, 52-53
        1849, 83-85
        1853, 116-17
        1857, 146-48
        1860, 191-93
Gentlemen's Agreements, 164-65, 122, 182-91
Georgian Bay, 143, 168
Goderich (Can.), 168
Gorman, W. A., 102
Grand Haven, Can., 172
Grand Trunk R. R. (Can.), 142-43, 168-69, 187
Grant, U. S., 218
Great Western R. R. (Ill.), 145, 196, 171
Great Western R. R. (Can.), 142-43, 168-69
Green, Duff, 63, 64
Guadaloupe Hidalgo, 130
Guthrie, James, 241
Gwin, W. M., 133, 138, 139

Hall, Judge James, 23
Hamilton, Ont., 142-43, 146
Hamilton and Toronto R. R., 142
Hannegan, Senator Edward, 74

Harmar, O., 56, 121
Harris, I. G., 237
Harris, T. L., 102
Harrisburg, Pa., 5
Harrison, William H., 23-24, 28, 30, 38
Hay, John, 237
Haymond, T. S., 102
Hayne, R. Y., 10, 22, 24-26, 29-30, 38, 78
Haywood, Senator W. H., 70
Hempfield R. R., 177
Hickman, Ky., 242
Hillman, C. E., steamboat, 237
Hollidaysburg, Pa., 14
Houston, Sam, 131
Hudson River R. R., 107, 108-12, 182
Hudson's Bay Company, 71

Illinois Central R. R., 105, 110, 138, 145, 152-53, 169, 194, 203, 214, 217-19
Illinois and Michigan canal, 81, 90, 103, 120, 152-53, 163, 169, 194, 212
Illinois river, 81, 84, 95, 120, 153, 169
Illinois river valley, 20, 117, 122, 149
Illinoistown, Ill., 145
Imports into N. W.
    1825, 7
    1835, 21
    1839, 35-36
    1844, 56-57
    1849, 92-94
    1853, 123-27
    1857, 158-61
    1860, 205-08
improving outlets to N. W.,
    18th century, 5
    1800-25, 6, 7
    1825-35, 14
    1840-44, 41
    1845-49, 80
    1850-53, 103-09
    1853-57, 140-43
    1857-60, 168-71
improving of routes within the Northwest,
    1825-35, 14
    1835-39, 32
    1840-44, 40, 49
    1845-49, 80

1850-53, 109-11
1853-57, 144-46
1857-60, 171-72
Indiana Central R. R., 110, 174, 203, 222
Indianapolis, 90, 122, 145, 163, 174, 183-84, 186, 200, 203-04, 207, 221-22
Indianapolis and Bellefontaine R. R., 145, 173-74, 221-22
Indianapolis and Cincinnati R. R., 110
Indianapolis and Lafayette R. R., 110, 173, 196, 221
Indianapolis and Peru, 173, 196, 221
Indianapolis, Pittsburgh and Cleveland R. R., 173, 222

Jackson, Andrew, 10-12
Jeffersonville, Ind., 203
Jeffersonville and Indianapolis, 110, 204
Johnson, Andrew, 229
Johnstown, Pa., 14
Joliet, Ill., 152
Junction R. R., 189

Kansas-Nebraska Act, 137, 138
(Great) Kanawha river, 5, 36
Kentucky neutrality, 239, 240, 242
Komoka, Ont., 168
Knoxville convention, 26, 167

Lafayette, Ind., 40, 82, 89, 93, 95, 122, 163, 196
Lake Shore R. R., 206
Lane, Joseph, 227
LaSalle, Ill., 93, 122, 153, 163
Lawrenceburg, Ind., 110, 203
Lawrenceburg and Indianapolis R. R., 23, 27
Lee, R. E., 220
Lexington, Ky., 203
Lexington and Frankfort R. R., 111
Lincoln, Abraham, 30, 214, 216, 217, 221-23, 236-37, 241-42, 245
Little Miami R. R., 81, 88, 110, 172-73, 176, 179, 181, 189, 190, 198-99, 203, 221
Liverpool, 36, 80, 163-65
live stock, 113, 212

Logansport, Ind., 172
Logansport, Peoria and Burlington R. R., 171, 196
Louisville, 26, 29, 58, 118, 146, 170, 201-04, 208, 214, 239, 240
Louisville, Cincinnati and Charleston R. R., 22-29, 136, 216
Louisville and Frankfort R. R., 111
Louisville and Lexington R. R., 170
Louisville and Nashville R. R., 170-71, 201, 202, 213, 240-41
Louisville and Portland canal, 15

McClellan, G. B., 217, 219-20, 231
McClellan in Western Va., 219
McClernand, J. A., 102, 228
McDougal, J. A., 138
McLane, L., 62-63, 66, 70
Macon and Western R. R., 109, 170
Madison, Ind., 81, 110, 202-03
Madison and Indianapolis R. R., 81, 89, 110, 173-74, 203, 221-22
Mad River and Lake Erie R. R., 81, 88, 189
Magoffin, B., 226-27, 242
Mansfield, E. D., 23
Marietta, O., 55, 144
Marietta and Cincinnati R. R., 144, 175-77, 180-81, 198-99, 207, 219
Mattoon, Ill., 194
Maumee valley, 40, 154-55
Maysville, Ky., 29
Maysville and Big Sandy R. R., 176
Maysville road bill, 12
Memphis, 78, 132, 134-35, 143-44, 161, 170, 201, 208, 213
Memphis and Charleston R. R., 170
Memphis convention of 1845, 77-78
Mexico, 50, 75-76, 98, 132, 136
Miami canal, 14, 16, 32, 40, 56, 80, 88, 126-27, 155, 161
Miami Extension canal, 32, 40, 56, 80, 88, 155, 161
Michigan Central R. R., 81, 169, 195
Michigan City, Ind., 54, 110, 145
Michigan Southern and Northern Indiana R. R., 82, 109, 154-55, 163, 195
Milan, O., 54

INDEX

Milwaukee, 51, 54, 87, 118, 151, 172, 193
Mississippi Central R. R., 106, 169
Mississippi, closing of in 1861, 231
Mississippi river, indispensable to N. W., 226-32
Missouri compromise, 138-139
Mobile and Ohio R. R., 104, 169
Mohawk river valley, 2
Monroe, Mich., 81
Montgomery (Ala.) convention, 167
Montgomery and West Point R. R., 170
Montreal, 80, 113, 142-43, 146, 168, 169
Morpeth, Viscount, 67
Morrow, O., 180
Morton, O. P., 223, 227, 230
Muscle Shoals, 29, 111
Muskingum canal, 55, 121
Muskingum river, 8

Nashville, Tenn., 29, 143, 202
Nashville and Chattanooga R. R., 111, 170
(old) National road, 6, 84, 89, 94, 98, 114, 120, 209, 223
New Albany, Ind., 111, 145, 202
Newark, O., 55, 89, 93, 122, 157, 176, 178, 179, 200
New Buffalo, Mich., 81
New England, 31, 40, 74, 213
New Mexico organizing act, 100
New Orleans, Jackson and Great Northern R. R., 106, 169
New York Central R. R., 108-09, 112-13, 141, 143, 159, 163-64, 182, 184, 186-88, 205-06
New York and Erie R. R., 107-08, 112-13, 124, 141, 159, 163, 182, 184-85, 186-88, 205-06
New York harbor, 78-80
Nicaragua, 136
Niles, Senator, 131
Noble, Noah, 27
Northern New York R. R., 107, 112, 143
Northwestern Virginia R. R., 140, 179

Ogdensburg, N. Y., 113, 143
Ohio and Indiana R. R., 144, 174-77
Ohio and Mississippi R. R., 144, 186, 204, 219
Ohio and Pennsylvania R. R., 110, 120, 144, 173-77
Ohio canal, 14-17, 21, 35, 37, 39, 47, 55-56, 80-81, 88, 126, 155-57, 197, 212
Ohio river steamboats, 149, 150, 181, 200, 207, 208
Old Glade road, 184
Oregon question, 59-64, 66-75
Orient, trade, 132
Osborn, W. H., 218
Oswego canal, 112, 124

Pacific railroad, 130-39
Paducah, Ky., seizure of, 242
Pakenham, Richard, 60, 63, 65
panic of '57, 172, 184
Parkersburg, Va., 140, 144-46, 149-50, 161, 180, 198, 206-07, 219
Paris (Can.), 168
passes, 182, 184-85
Peel, Sir Robert, 64-68, 71-72
Pennsylvania and Erie canal, 80
Pennsylvania and Ohio canal, 80
Pennsylvania canal, 114
Pennsylvania R. R., 26, 112, 114, 120, 125, 140, 144, 149-50, 159, 160, 163-64, 173, 175, 177-82, 188, 198-201, 205-07
Pennsylvania state road, 5
Pennsylvania Works, 14, 17, 39, 140
Pennsylvania turnpike, 7, 9
Peoria, Oquawka and Burlington R. R., 172
Peru, Ind., 81
Petersburg and Lynchburg R. R., 170
Pettus, Gov., 231
Philadelphia and Wilmington R. R., 182
Pierce, Pres., 134-35
Pike, Albert, 136
Pillow, Gen., 238
Piqua, O., 88, 93, 122, 155
Pittsburgh, 5, 14-18, 20, 39, 52, 118, 120, 125, 140, 144-46, 149-50, 160, 163-64, 173-78, 180-81, 191, 198-201, 203, 206-08

Pittsburgh and Steubenville R. R., 177
Pittsburgh, Ft. Wayne and Chicago R. R., 145, 150, 160, 163, 174, 177-79, 185, 187-88, 197, 200, 206, 212
Plymouth, Ind., 178
Polk, J. K., 59-63, 65-68, 70-75, 78
pool, railroad, 189
Portage railroad, 14, 17, 18, 108, 140
Portland, Me., 142-43, 168
Portsmouth, O., 14-17, 88, 126, 157
Port Stanley, Ont., 143, 168
Port Stanley and London R. R., 143
Potomac company, 5
Prairie du Chien, Wis., 145
Prentiss, Col., 238, 240
preemption, 43, 103
prices, 39, 58, 128, 184, 165
Production in Northwest, 95, 204

Quebec, 142, 143, 169
Quincy, Ill., 145

racial stocks, 210, 223
Railroad consolidations, 172-82
Railroad conventions, 132, 164, 167, 183, 190
Railroaders' interest in Union, 216-222
railroad receiverships, 187
rate wars, 182-191
Rawlins, J. A., 219
rerouting of commerce in
    1825, 8, 16, 211, 213
    1835, 19-21
    1839, 35, 37
    1844, 55-56
    1849, 88-92
    1853, 112-14, 121-23
    1857, 153-57, 161-63
    1860, 204
Richmond and Danville R. R., 170
Rochester, 178
Rock Island, Ill., 145-46
Rock Island R. R., 152
Rock river, 120
runners, railroad, 185
Rusk, T. J., 134
Russell, Lord John, 64

St. Lawrence canals, 142

St. Lawrence valley, 2, 80, 225
St. Louis, 30, 52, 58, 86, 117, 126, 127, 131-32, 135, 137, 144-45, 148, 153, 160-62, 202-03, 205, 208, 219
St. Mary's (Can.), 168
St. Nicholas agreement, 185, 186
Salem and New Albany R. R., 110, 122, 145
Sandusky, O., 54, 81-82, 87-88, 190
Sandusky and Mansfield R. R., 82
Sandusky, Dayton and Cincinnati R. R., 88, 190
Sarnia, Ont., 168
Scioto river, 8
secession conventions, 231, 233, 235
sectional revalries and alliances, 10, 22, 24-26, 42, 49-50, 74, 98, 101, 135, 136
sectionalism in Old Northwest, 132, 135, 209-11, 225, 243
slavery, 102, 138, 209-10, 225, 244
slave trade in D. C., 100
Slidell, J., 229
Smith, Caleb B., 68
sources of exports, 1839, 34-35
    1844, 53-54
    1849, 86-87
    1853, 117-21
    1857, 148-51
    1860, 193-203
South Carolina R. R., 109, 136, 170
Southern Commercial Conventions, 137, 167, 215
Southern Pacific R. R., 178
Southwestern Bank, 28
Springfield, Ill., 163, 194, 203-4
Springfield, O., 88, 122, 190
Springfield, Mt. Vernon and Pittsburgh R. R., 175-77, 190
Steubenville, O., 175, 177-78, 180
Steubenville and Indiana R. R., 144, 173, 175-78, 180, 200, 207
stopping trade with South, 214-16, 226-45
Stratford, Ont., 142, 168
Sumter, Ft., 221, 236, 238, 246
Suspension Bridge, 142-43, 168
Swift, R. K., 236
Syracuse and Utica R. R., 41

INDEX

tariff, 44, 47, 66, 69, 71, 74
tariff-Oregon agreement, 71
taxes on railroads, 141
Tennessee Central R. R., 106
Terre Haute, Ind., 40, 82, 89, 95, 122
Terre Haute, Alton and St. Louis R. R., 174, 222
Terre Haute and Indianapolis R. R., 173, 221-22 174
Thomson, J. Edgar, 178
Tilghman, Col., 238
Tod, David, 221
Toledo, 40, 54, 56, 81, 87, 89, 118, 122, 126, 145-46, 151-52, 154-56, 161, 171, 193, 194, 196-98, 206
Toledo, Norwalk and Cleveland R. R., 109
Toledo and Wabash R. R., 154-55, 196
Toledo, Wabash and Western R. R., 145, 171
Toledo and Quincy R. R., 171
Tonawanda R. R., 41
Toronto, Can., 142-43
Turney, Sen., 73
Tuscumbia, Ala., 144
Tyler, A. O., steamboat, 231
Tyler, John, 42, 48-50

U. S. bank, 24, 28, 42
Utica and Schenectady R. R., 41

Vallandigham, C. L., 222, 228
Vicksburg, Miss., 134, 135, 231

Virginia and Tennessee R. R., 170

Wabash and Erie canal, 40, 56, 80, 88, 89, 111, 119, 122, 126-27, 154-55, 161, 163, 196, 212
Wabash valley, 20, 40, 117, 122, 155, 196, 201
Walker, Robert J., 64-65, 72
Washington, George, 5, 42
Webster, Daniel, 10, 22
Welland canal, 14-16, 18-21, 31, 34, 37, 46, 54, 80, 94, 112, 124, 159, 163, 205
Welland R. R., 168
Wellsville, O., 110
Western and Atlantic of Ga. R. R., 109, 111-12, 114, 121, 124, 170
Westward extension, 130, 139-40
Western Reserve, 9
Western R. R. of Mass., 184
Western Va., 219, 220
Wheeling, 6-7, 16, 108, 114, 118, 125, 140, 144-46, 149-50, 158, 161, 164, 179-81, 191, 199, 201, 204, 206, 207, 220
Whigs, 42-43, 58, 72, 73, 98
Whitewater canal, 32
Whitewater valley, 32
Terre Haute and Richmond R. R., 145,
Whitney, Asa, 130
Windsor, Ont., 142-43, 168, 169

Yancey, W. L., 234
Yates, Ricard, 223, 230, 236, 237

Zanesville, O., 55, 180